Advances in Discourse Studies

Advances in Discourse Studies brings together contributions from top scholars in the field, investigating the historical and theoretical relationships between new advances in discourse studies and pointing towards new directions for the future of the discipline. Covering areas such as conversation analysis, corpus-based discourse analysis and genre analysis, this book provides a unique survey of the most recent advances in methodology and approach to discourse analysis.

Featuring clear section introductions, discussion questions, classroom projects and recommended readings at the end of each section, as well as case studies illustrating each approach discussed, this will be an invaluable resource for students of interdisciplinary discourse analysis as well as to academics in a wider range of disciplines including linguistics, sociology, anthropology, psychology, communication studies and cultural studies.

Vijay K. Bhatia and **Rodney H. Jones** are Professors in the Department of English and Communication at the City University of Hong Kong. **John Flowerdew** is Professor at the School of Education, University of Leeds.

Advances in Discourse Studies

Edited by
Vijay K. Bhatia,
John Flowerdew and
Rodney H. Jones

Routledge
Taylor & Francis Group

LONDON AND NEW YORK

First published 2008
by Routledge
2 Park Square, Milton Park, Abingdon, Oxon OX14 4RN

Simultaneously published in the USA and Canada
by Routledge
270 Madison Ave, New York, NY 10016

*Routledge is an imprint of the Taylor & Francis Group, an informa
business*

Transferred to Digital Printing 2010

© 2008 Vijay K. Bhatia, John Flowerdew and Rodney H. Jones

Typeset in Sabon by
HWA Text and Data Management, Tunbridge Wells

British Library Cataloguing in Publication Data
A catalogue record for this book is available from the British Library

Library of Congress Cataloging-in-Publication Data
A catalog record for this book has been requested

ISBN 10: 0–415–39809–6 (hbk)
ISBN 10: 0–415–39810–X (pbk)

ISBN 13: 978–0–415–39809–1 (hbk)
ISBN 13: 978–0–415–39810–7 (pbk)

Contents

Contributors

Carol Berkenkotter, Professor, Department of Rhetoric, University of Minnesota, Minneapolis, MN, USA. Email: cberken@umn.edu

Vijay K. Bhatia, Professor, Department of English and Communication, City University of Hong Kong, China. Email: enbhatia@cityu.edu.hk

Douglas Biber, Regents' Professor of Applied Linguistics, Department of English, Northern Arizona University, Flagstaff, AZ, USA. Email: Douglas.biber@nau.edu

Lilie Chouliaraki, Professor and Chair of Media and Communication, Department of Media and Communication, London School of Economics and Politics. Email: L.Chouliaraki@lse.ac.uk

Traci Curl, RCKU Fellow, Department of Language and Linguistic Science, University of York, UK. Email: tsc3@york.ac.uk

Paul Drew, Professor, Department of Sociology, University of York, UK. Email: wpd1@york.ac.uk .

John Flowerdew, Professor of Applied Linguistics, University of Leeds, UK. Email: enjohnf@cityu.edu.hk

Lynne Flowerdew, Senior Lecturer, School of Education, University of Leeds, UK. Email: L.J.Flowerdew@education.leeds.ac.uk

Carey Jewitt, Reader in Education and Technology, University of London, UK. Email: c.jewitt@ioe.ac.uk

Ken Jones, Professor, Department of Education, Keele University, UK.

Rodney H. Jones, Associate Professor, Department of English and Communication, City University of Hong Kong, China. Email: enrodney@cityu.edu.hk

David Y.W. Lee, Assistant Professor, Department of English and Communication, City University of Hong Kong, China. Email: davidlee@cityu.edu.hk

Angel Lin, Associate Professor, Department of Curriculum and Instruction, Faculty of Education, Chinese University of Hong Kong, China. Email: AngelLin@cuhk.edu.hk

Maurice Nevile, Research Fellow Division of Communication and Education, University of Canberra, Australia. Email: Maurice.nevile@canberra.edu. au

Sigrid Norris, Associate Head of School (Research), Auckland University of Technology, New Zealand. Email: sigrid.norris@aut.ac.nz

Ron Scollon, Retired. Email: scollon@aptalaska.net

Graham Smart, Associate Professor. School of Linguistics and Applied Language Studies, Carleton University, Ottawa, Canada. Email: gsmart@ connect.carleton.ca

Acknowledgements

We would like to thank the Department of English and Communication of City University of Hong Kong for financial and administrative assistance in preparing this volume. In particular we would like to express our gratitude to Ms Kitty Leung, for her efficient and enthusiastic administrative support, and to Ms Annabel Knibb and Mr Richard Forest for helping to edit and proofread the manuscript.

1 Approaches to discourse analysis

Vijay K. Bhatia, John Flowerdew and Rodney H. Jones

In recent decades the social sciences have undergone a 'discursive turn' and become increasingly interested in the part played by language in the creation of the reality that surrounds us. This interest has been accompanied by the development of new theories and methods for the study of language use and its role in human society. Discourse analysis, though often seen as located within the discipline of linguistics, is in fact an interdisciplinary field of inquiry. With a history of less than 50 years it has acquired the status, stability, significance and integrity of a well-established discipline, extending the conventional boundaries of linguistics. Dating back to the 1960s, it has been defined as the analysis of linguistic behaviour, written and spoken, beyond the limits of individual sentences, focusing primarily on the meaning constructed and interpreted as language is used in particular social contexts.

This definition really contains two main ingredients: the idea that language can be analysed not just on the level of the phoneme/morpheme, the word, the clause or the sentence, but also on the level of the text, and the idea that language ought to be analysed not as an abstract set or rules, but as a tool for social action. Although early conceptualizations of discourse analysis were seen as an offshoot of linguistic analysis, focusing more on the 'language as text' side of the equation and drawing on the work of early text analysts like Propp (1958) and Jakobson (1937), in its present form it has moved to more of a focus on 'language in use', drawing on insights from sociology, psychology, semiotics, communication studies, rhetoric, as well as disciplines such as business and marketing, accountancy, organizational studies, law and information technology, to name only a few. In this regard, it has evolved as a fruitful way of understanding the use of language in a variety of institutional, academic, workplace and professional settings.

Another interesting aspect of the development of discourse analysis has been that it has attracted the attention not only of linguists and applied linguists, but also socio-political theorists, sociologists, anthropologists, computer experts, business and legal specialists, communication experts and organizational theorists. In this context, it is hardly surprising that discourse analysis has, in the last four decades developed into a variety of schools using different approaches, frameworks, procedures and methodologies and focusing on different kinds of semiotic data, with the aim of deriving insights for a variety of purposes.

The focus of most contemporary approaches to discourse on 'language in use' has its roots in a number of larger developments in the twentieth century in the fields of philosophy, anthropology, sociology and linguistics itself. The roots of this view of language are perhaps best traced to the work of Wittgenstein (1951/1972), who saw language as a series of 'games' through which people construct what he calls 'forms of life', particular ways of being in relation to others and their surroundings. Less than two decades later, with the publication of Austin's 1962 classic *How to Do Things with Words*, the notion that the study of language should involve more than just its structure but also the way it is used and the way social standards and practices shape and give rise to it became more prominent, at least in philosophical circles. Later, thinkers like Foucault and Derrida, though diverging considerably from the tradition of Austin, also made language, and in particular 'discourse', central to their understanding of social practice.

Just as the notion of language as social practice began to take hold among philosophers of language, social scientific disciplines particularly concerned with social practice began to recognize the centrality of language in much of what they were studying. Anthropologist Gregory Bateson and psychiatrist Jürgen Ruesch (Ruesch and Bateson 1951) argued that social and psychological phenomena cannot be separated from the 'matrix of communication' in which they occur. They were followed by a host of social and behavioural scientists, among them Goffman (1959) and Garfinkel (1967), who focused on the role of language in social behaviour and social formations. By the 1970s psychology, sociology, and anthropology had all taken a decidedly 'discursive turn', influenced not just by the structuralist linguistics of de Saussure, but also by a new breed of linguists who at around the same time were becoming more and more concerned with the relationship of language to social actions and to the socio-cultural worlds of those who use it.

In America this concern had given rise to the work in the early part of the twentieth century of Edward Sapir and Benjamin Whorf as well as others in the Boasian tradition of anthropological linguistics. In Europe this new concern for language in use was later exemplified by the work of Michael Halliday. Departing from structuralist and cognitive paradigms in grammar which saw language systems as autonomous and independent of language use, Halliday insisted that 'language is as it is because of its function in the social structure' (1973: 65) and called for the development of a 'sociological linguistics', a discipline which will allow us to see language on two levels, a macro-sociological level in which language 'serves to transmit the social structure, the values, the systems of knowledge, all the deepest and most pervasive patterns of the culture' (1973: 45), and a micro-sociological level in which meanings are seen as specific to particular contexts and situations. Halliday's systemic functional grammar (SFG) has had a profound influence on many contemporary schools of discourse analysis, including critical discourse analysis, mediated discourse analysis and multimodal discourse analysis. Although they were primarily developed at the level of the clause, the analytical tools of Halliday's grammar have been found to be well adapted to tracking participants, logical relations, processes, qualities, and evaluations of these by speakers and writers as they develop throughout a given text or across a group of texts (see e.g. Martin and Rose 2003).

The discourse analytical approaches that have grown out of these interdisciplinary developments are many, including register and genre analyses, critical discourse analysis, discursive psychology, conversation analysis, interactional sociolinguistics, the ethnography of communication, stylistics, mediated discourse analysis, corpus-based analysis, narrative analysis, multimodal discourse analysis, rhetorical-grammatical analysis, argumentation analysis, and many others, and no book on discourse could hope to cover all of them. Our intention in this volume is to explore seven major approaches to the study of discourse that we believe represent a range of directions which the intellectual traditions we described above have taken. Although all of them, to varying degrees, represent a concern for language use in the social world, they focus on widely varying aspects of its use and often define the social world in widely varying ways, from the immediate conversational context to the larger political, social or economic context. They are corpus-based approaches to discourse, genre analysis, conversation analysis, critical discourse analysis, multimodal discourse analysis, mediated discourse analysis and ethnographic approaches to discourse. Some of them, like genre analysis and conversation analysis, are decades old, while others, like mediated discourse analysis and multimodal discourse analysis, are more recent to the scene.

As the title of this book suggests, we are not as interested in describing the type of work that has been done using these various approaches as we are in showing how those working in these areas are charting new courses, which often involve borrowing from other fields and other schools of discourse analysis. In doing this we hope to understand not just what is unique about each of these approaches, but also where future possibilities for convergence and interdisciplinarity are opening up.

In order to do this, however, it is first necessary to understand the main questions upon which these approaches diverge and the different roads they have taken from common intellectual roots. As will become clear in our discussion, despite a common commitment to the study of texts and their use in social contexts, those working in the different approaches diverge on two of the most basic issues in this formulation: the question of what a text is, and the question of what counts as the social context in which that text is used. In a sense these differences can be seen as the result of the influence of multiple disciplines on the development of discourse analysis. Sociology and anthropology have encouraged analysts to view the use of language as a function of the context in which language is used, whereas linguistics has constrained discourse analysts to focus primarily on text, with context in the background. In recent years another factor has entered the equation, that is, the role of semiotic modes, other than written or spoken text, which has opened up the possibilities of looking at nonlinear extra-linguistic forms of communication such as pictures, diagrams, gestures, colours, differing fonts and their sizes, to name only a few. Finally, discourse analysts are faced with a variety of new media of communication including computer-mediated communication, SMS messaging and other new communication technologies.

In what follows, we would like to look briefly at where these different approaches 'have been' in terms of their historical and intellectual development in relation to the other approaches. We will also examine where these approaches stand on these fundamental questions of text and context, in preparation for, in the remainder of this volume, considering where they might be going and how their trajectories might converge.

Conversation analysis

Conversation analysis (CA) was developed in the late 1960s and early 1970s by Harvey Sacks, Emanuel Schegloff and Gail Jefferson (Sacks 1974; Sacks, Schegloff and Jefferson 1974; Schegloff and Sacks 1973). It has its roots in *ethnomethodology*, a branch of sociology developed by Harold Garfinkel (1967) which, like the 'ethnography of communication' of Gumperz and Hymes, chiefly concerns itself with the basic competences and interpretative processes members of a culture use to interact and interpret their experience. The central goal of conversational analysis, as Atkinson and Heritage (1984:1) emphasize, is 'the description and explication of the competences that ordinary speakers use and rely on in participating in intelligible, socially organized interaction'.

In contrast to earlier social scientific traditions, sociologists like Goffman (1981) and Garfinkel (1967) were adamant that people's lives should be studied only on their own terms without reference to theoretical preconceptions. Rather than starting with a theory and analysing people's behaviour *through* it, those in this tradition advocate intentionally setting aside theory to try to get at what's actually going on based on close analysis of people's (often mundane) speech and actions.

By analysing the properties of conversation, conversation analysts attempt to understand the patterns in social life. The assumption is that such patterns can be used to develop procedural rules governing talk-in-interaction. Echoing Austin and Steele, conversation analysts regard discourse as a kind of social action – we are always 'doing things with our words'. What is unique about their approach is their concern with the sequential organization of actions, and, in particular the mechanics of *turn-taking*. CA's guiding analytical principle, as Nevile reminds us in his chapter, is asking of each utterance in a conversation the question, 'Why that now?' Utterances are seen as 'paired actions' (Sacks, Schegloff and Jefferson 1974), always dependent on what has come before and what will come after. The most basic expression of this fundamental idea is the concept of the *adjacency pair*, a pair of utterances that are not just linguistically related but 'socially' related because they accomplish particular social actions. The ways utterances (and the actions they accomplish) are put together sequentially follow rules of *conditional relevance*, each utterance displaying a particular understanding of the previous utterance and creating the conditions for subsequent utterances.

In contrast with the ethnographer's data, which consists of interviews, field notes, lived experiences or narratives of participants, conversational analysts work on naturally occurring and closely transcribed conversational data. They regard observational data as prone to manipulation by researchers or the subjects themselves. As Atkinson and Heritage (1984) point out, observational data is often based on preconceived notions of what is probable or important. Although like ethnographers, conversation analysts also work on a selection of data, their data is conversational and not observational, consisting of very detailed transcriptions of natural talk.

The most dramatic difference between linguistic ethnographers and conversation analysis is on the issue of context. Whereas, for ethnographers, the wider social context is used to inform their understanding of why language is used the way it is, conversation analysts view context as constructed moment by moment through conversational moves, and argue that those aspects of context not conversationally attended to by participants should not be part of the analysis. That is not to say that conversation analysts do not concern themselves with larger issues of social identity and power (such as gender and institutional communication). Rather, they believe that the way to understand these issues is through a close analysis of the mechanics of interaction rather than with reference to larger social structures or ideologies.

Ethnographic approaches to discourse analysis

Although there are several ethnographic approaches to discourse analysis, most of them draw their inspirations from anthropology and social psychology and regard social context as the central aspect of communication. Present ethnographic approaches to discourse owe much to an American anthropological linguistic tradition that gave rise to the work of scholars like Gumperz and Hymes (1986), whose 'ethnography of communication' aims to provide a description of how members of a particular community are expected to perform linguistically in order to be considered 'competent' members. Communicative competence involves not just mastery of the linguistic system, but the ability to use language in conjunction with social practices and social identities in ways which others in the community will recognize to perform a myriad of social activities such as engaging in small talk, making transactions, joking, arguing, teasing, and warning. It is learnt within communities through participating in communication, anticipating others' responses, and incorporating generalities into our own repertoire of actions and meanings (Mead 1934).

Most traditions in ethnography from anthropology and linguistics aim to understand the social world in terms of the 'lived experience' of those who inhabit it. In this regard, they take what Pike (1967) calls an *emic* approach to language, seeking to discover patterns in language use based on the observation of natural social events of native participants. The participants themselves have learnt these patterns by participating in their communities and themselves observing by other members of the community. Despite this commitment to 'native' ways of understanding communication, ethnographic approaches to language invariably involve a process of selection based on the analyst's practical concerns and theoretical preoccupations. Data gathering typically involves documenting, describing and interpreting social practices through observation and analysis of a selection of socio-linguistic behaviours. This selection invariably takes place in the fieldwork, and often consists of what researchers finds interesting, and of course, depends on what the subjects allow them to observe. So there is a process of selection at both ends, by the observers and the ones being observed. In addition to these processes of selection, there is also another area of decision-making: when the observer prepares a record of their fieldwork, which consists of evidence for the identification, description and interpretation of social practices, they invariably make use of a specific theory or framework within which they select and interpret their observations. These observations are seen as the most important tool for ethnographic analysis of communication.

However, more recently several other instruments have also been added to the armoury of the ethnographer, which include structured or semi-structured interviews with participants in social interactions, focus group interviews, accounts of experienced participants, or what is often referred to as 'lived narratives of experience', to name a few. Using a combination of these tools, ethnographers interpret social behaviour of people in a specific society or culture to reach conclusions and make generalizations.

Smart (1998 and this volume) distinguishes several kinds of ethnographies, such as analytical, reflexive, naturalistic, institutional and interpretative. Following the Geertzian tradition of the *interpretation of cultures* (Geertz 1973), he uses 'interpretive ethnography' to 'explore a particular social group's discourse practices – as these are instantiated in writing, speaking, or other symbolic actions – in order to learn how members of the group view and operate within their mutually constructed conceptual world' (Smart).

From the point of view of a conventional understanding of discourse (textual) analysis, ethnographic analysis relies relatively less on actual analysis of linguistic data and more on text-external social and contextual factors. Ethnographers view purely linguistic analysis of data as less than satisfactory for understanding language as it is used in social and cultural contexts. At the same time, ethnographic approaches to discourse analysis have had an important influence on other approaches to discourse such as critical discourse analysis, genre analysis, mediated discourse analysis and multimodal discourse analysis, and they have also made important contributions to the fields of English for Specific Purposes (ESP) (Widdowson 1978; Swales 1981, 1990; Bhatia 1993) and what have come to be known as the 'new literacy studies' (Barton and Hamilton 1998; Gee 1996; Street 1984). Lynne Flowerdew (this volume) also makes a case for introducing an ethnographic element into corpus linguistics.

Corpus-based discourse analysis

Corpus-based analysis, which works with large amounts of machine-readable text, was initially used primarily in the fields of lexicography and grammar. It is only relatively recently that there have been extensive applications of corpus approaches to discourse analysis (Baker 2006). The earliest initiatives in corpus-based analysis of language use began with the creation of large (by the standards of those days) general corpora representing language use in a variety of contexts, both written as well as spoken, to draw insights from observations about how people use language, both in terms of lexico-grammar features and their functional variations. However, corpus development over the years has changed in several important ways. First the size of corpora has become much greater. The 'Bank of English' corpus contains about 450 million words, whereas the British National Corpus has about 100 million words. These large-scale general corpora are effective and reliable in providing insightful information about the preferred use of specific lexico-grammatical patterns in everyday language use. The most important aspect of this approach is that it makes it possible for linguists and discourse analysts to go beyond the analysis of sentences and short texts to the analysis of huge amounts of text. It is thereby possible to corroborate intuitions about individual instantiations concerning the functional value of particular language patterns by recourse to very large numbers of instances.

Work with large corpora has demonstrated that language follows to a large extent very regular patterns consisting of pre-constructed phrases. This is referred to as the 'idiom principle' by Sinclair (1991), in contrast to the 'open choice' principle, which refers to word-by-word 'slot and filler' combinations. According to Sinclair (1991) speakers primarily adhere to the idiom principle and only switch to the open choice principle when some constraint occurs which makes the idiom principle fail to function.

One implication of the idiom principle view of language is that these pre-constructed phrases may become the unit of analysis rather than individual words. In analysing such units it has become clear that certain words and phrases may take on particular 'semantic preferences' (typical areas of semantic meaning). Thus the word *glass* typically occurs with a lexical set of words to do with drinks, e.g. *sherry, lemonade, water, champagne, milk,* etc. (Baker 2006: 86). At the same time words and phrases may carry 'semantic prosodies' (typical areas of pragmatic meaning, or connotations). Thus, a word like *cause* typically collocates with negatively loaded words – e.g. *accident, concern, damage, death, trouble* – and thereby takes on a negative semantic prosody; *provide*, on the other hand, is typically used with positive collocates – e.g. *aid, care, food, opportunities, relief, support* – and thus takes on a positive semantic prosody (Stubbs 1996). It is only through isolating many examples of use derived from large amounts of text that observations such as these regarding semantic preference and prosody can be made.

More recently corpus-based analysis has also become useful in the study of language variations in specific academic and professional genres. These corpora are usually much smaller. Connor and Upton (1996) make a strong case for this kind of study of specialized corpora.

> While general corpora are important and provide a critical foundation for the study of language structure and use, they are less conducive for analysing language use in specific academic and professional situations. Consequently, there is now a strong and growing interest in compiling specialized corpora that focus on specific types of genres within specific contexts. Instead of being compiled for representativeness of language across a large number of communicative purposes, specialized corpora often focus on one particular genre ... or specific situation ... .
>
> (Connor and Upton 1996: 2)

One important advantage of working with smaller corpora is that corpus-specific semantic prosodies may be thrown up. For example, Flowerdew (1997) showed how, in a corpus of the discourse of the last British governor of Hong Kong, Chris Patten, words such as *economy, individual,* and *wealth,* all carried a positive semantic prosody.

One of the reasons for the popularity of corpus-based discourse analysis is the facility that it provides to handle and analyse large quantities of data with minimal effort. Discourse and register analyses in their early days were constrained by the fact that any manual processing and analysis of data was seen as an impossible task, but with the availability of computers and a variety of analytical software, these tasks have become not only less cumbersome, but the results have also become more reliable and convincing.

Biber (this volume), one of the well-known specialists in this field, proposes what he calls multidimensional studies of register variation, by identifying not simply the 'salient linguistic co-occurrence patterns in a language', but also by 'comparing spoken and written registers in the linguistic space defined by those co-occurrence patterns'. By doing so, it is possible, he claims, not simply to construct distinctive grammars of individual registers, but also co-variant lexico-grammatical patterns across registers.

Multimodal discourse analysis

Multimodal discourse analytical approaches regard text as just one of the many modes of communication available for social interaction. Although the three approaches we have seen so far vary significantly in terms of their focus on text and context, one factor that is still restrictive in all of them is the fact that they all take textual (linguistic) data to be the primary resource for social interactions. There is a widespread belief now that textual data is not necessarily the most important mode used for the construction and interpretations of social meaning. Kress and Van Leeuwen (1996: 34) rightly point out:

> The new realities of the semiotic landscape are ... primarily brought about by social and cultural factors: the intensification of linguistic and cultural diversity within the boundaries of nation-states, and by the weakening of these boundaries, due to multiculturalism, electronic media of communication, technologies of transport and global economic developments. Global flows of capital dissolve not only cultural and political boundaries but also semiotic boundaries.

Semiotic modes other than text can include gestures, posture, proxemics, visual images, document layout, music and architectural design, to name a few. Multimodality is especially important when one considers media such as film and TV, not to mention the increasing dynamics of electronic media. Idema (2003: 33) sums up the difference in traditional text- or language-based approaches to discourse analysis and the new multimodal approach to discourse analysis as follows:

> In general terms, the trend towards a multimodal appreciation of meaning making centres around two issues: first, the de-centring of language as favoured meaning making; and second, the re-visiting and blurring of the traditional boundaries between and roles allocated to language, image, page layout, document design, and so on .... This blurring of boundaries among the different semiotic dimensions of representation has been linked, on the one hand, to changes in our 'semiotic landscape', and, on the other hand, to analysts' realization that our human predisposition towards multimodal meaning making, and our own multi-semiotic development or ontogenesis, requires attention to more than one semiotic than just language-in-use.

Another interesting perspective on multimodal discourse analysis is that it not merely attempts to integrate all the possible semiotic modes of expressions, but can also integrate various other approaches to discourse analysis. Some working in multimodality have been influenced by conversational analysis, most notably Goodwin (1981). Others, like Kress and van Leeuwen (2001) and O'Toole (1994) borrow heavily from the systemic functional grammar of Halliday and the work of Australian 'social semioticians' like Kress and Hodge (1979) whom he inspired. Still others like Kendon (1990) owe a considerable debt to anthropologists like Birdwhistell (1970) and Scheflen (1974).

Finally, more recent approaches, like that of Norris (2004), owe a great deal to interactional sociolinguists like Tannen (1984) and mediated discourse analysts like Scollon (2001). The two chapters represented in this volume come from two of these broad traditions, Jewitt working in the tradition of social semiotics, and Norris claiming her debt to interactional sociolinguistics and mediated discourse analysis.

Genre analysis

In its earlier form, genre analysis was seen as an extension of linguistic analysis to study functional variation in the use of English in academic contexts. Swales' earliest work (1981) on research article introductions marked the beginning of the genre analytical model for a grounded description of academic research genres. The motivation was to use the findings for the teaching and learning of English for Specific Purposes. Unlike registers, which were identified on the basis of a specific configuration of three main contextual categories of field, mode and tenor of discourse, Swales identified genre on the basis of its communicative purpose. There are two other versions of genre analysis that emerged more or less the same time, one in Australia within systemic functional linguistic theory, and the other in the United States within the field of rhetoric. Although these three frameworks draw their inspirations from different sources, they seem to have considerable overlapping concerns and perspectives.

Genre analysis, whether defined in terms of *typification of rhetorical action*, as in Miller (1984), Bazerman (1994) and Berkenkotter and Huckin (1995), *regularities of staged, goal oriented social processes*, as in Martin *et al.* (1987) and Martin (1993), or *consistency of communicative purposes*, as in Swales (1990) and Bhatia (1993), can be viewed as the study of situated linguistic behaviour in institutionalized academic or professional settings. These are attempts to offer increasingly more complex ('thicker') descriptions of language use, incorporating, and often going beyond, the immediate context of situation, taking analyses beyond mere linguistic descriptions to offer explanation for specific uses of language in conventionalized and institutionalized settings. As we can see, the most important feature of this approach in all three manifestations of genre theory is the emphasis on conventions.

In more recent years, genre analysis has developed in the direction of a more comprehensive exploration of what Bhatia (2004) specifies as 'social space' to raise a number of other interesting issues, including some about the integrity of generic descriptions. He proposes a multi-perspective and multidimensional three-space model for the analysis of discourse as genre integrating social professional space, social space and textual space. One of the interesting aspects of this multi-perspective is the way it attempts to integrate a number of other approaches to discourse analysis into a single framework, some of which include ethnographic discourse analysis (Swales 1998), critical discourse analysis, corpus-based discourse analysis, and multimodal discourse analysis.

Critical discourse analysis

Critical discourse analysis (CDA) focuses on socio-political domination, which includes issues of social change, power abuse, ideological imposition, and social injustice by critically analysing language as social action. It is thus based on the assumption that the analysis of discourse provides insightful information on such social issues as they are largely constituted in language.

CDA regards discourse as an essential component of the constitution of society and culture and is viewed (along with material action) as a major form of social action. By studying discourse and society, CDA aims to challenge inequality, injustice, unfairness and lack of democracy in society by investigating social practices through a critical analysis of discourses and social actions. Van Dijk, one of the founders of CDA, typically characterizes its focus as the study of relationship between discourse, power, dominance and social inequality (van Dijk 1993, 1998).

In line with this view, Fairclough (1989: 20) views language as a form of social practice. He also regards CDA as exploring relationship between discourse and social actors. For him discourse has potential for the expression of particular ideologies and identities. This view of discourse is also in line with social psychological theories of discourse (cf. Potter and Wetherall 1987), which regard discourse as a primary vehicle for the construction of social and individual identities.

There are several approaches to critical discourse analysis. Fairclough (1995: 2) offers a multi-dimensional framework for studying discourse by mapping three separate forms of analysis onto one another: 'analysis of discourse, analysis of discourse practice (processes of text production, distribution and consumption) and analysis of discursive events as instances of sociocultural practice'. Van Dijk (1998) regards ideology as the basis for the representation of social groups and hence he finds a useful link between social structures and discourse structures. In general, van Dijk adopts a more socio-cognitive approach to analysis. Wodak (1996), on the other hand, uses CDA to study the issues of racism and anti-semitism by looking critically at the historical dimension of discourse.

CDA is not without its critics. Probably most notably Widdowson (2004 for the latest version) has criticized CDA for bias. The starting point for CDA, Widdowson claims, is a particular ideological commitment, which is then supported by the selection of texts that are suitable for presenting the desired analysis. There is a total lack of objectivity, according to Widdowson. There are a number of answers to this critique. Meyer (2001) provides some, namely that the analyst is necessarily subject to a certain bias, given that all human beings are socially positioned, that CDA is at least open about its commitment, and that, in the tradition of Kant, 'pure' cognition is unattainable. Meyer (2001) also provides a list of criteria for assessing the quality of CDA. This includes representiveness, reliability, validity, completeness, accessibility and triangulation (see also J. Flowerdew 1999).

Mediated discourse analysis

Mediated discourse analysis (MDA) shares the goals of CDA, but focuses on social action rather than on discourse. Like CDA, mediated discourse analysis takes the analysis, interpretation and explanation of social problems as its central concern; however, as Scollon (1998, 2001) points out, it does not regard that these social issues are constituted primarily in discourse. Instead it views discursive practice as just *one form of social practice*, not necessarily the main form of practice out of which society creates its institutions and power relations. Along with discourse, MDA argues, society and culture are constituted in the material products and a myriad of non-discursive practices.

Drawing heavily from Vygotskian psychology and sociocultural approaches to the mind (see, for example, Wertsch 1991), MDA aims to understand how discourse is used to take concrete social actions, and how, in those social actions social structures and ideologies are created and re-created. Like conversation analysis, it is concerned with the fundamental mechanics of human action and its sequential organization in 'chains of action'. At the same time, it also borrows from the other end of the disciplinary spectrum of discourse analysis, sharing with CDA and ethnographers of language a commitment to understanding the relationships between these concrete, situated social actions and social practice that reproduce larger patterns of social relations and ideology within the 'historical body' of the social actor. On the question of 'text or context', mediated discourse analysis claims neither, choosing to focus instead on where text and context come together in mediated actions.

The main concerns of mediated discourse analysis, as laid out by Jones and Norris (2005) are: first, mediated actions themselves, the concrete things we do when we interact in the world; second, mediational means, the 'cultural tools' (which may or may not be texts) with which we take actions, and which enable or constrain these actions; third, the 'practices' that develop through these actions as they become part of the 'historical body' of the social actor; fourth, the 'sites of engagement' in which multiple social practices converge, opening a window for a mediated action to occur

(Scollon 2001); and finally, the way 'agency' in social actions is distributed over individual social actors and cultural tools.

In terms of methodology, mediated discourse analysis uses resources from different frameworks, which include critical discourse analysis, ethnography and interactional sociolinguistics, and multimodal discourse analysis (Scollon 2001; Kress and Van Leeuwen 2001). According to Scollon (2001), MDA is itself a *nexus of practice* at which the perspectives of mediated action theory, anthropological linguistics and the ethnography of communication, conversational analysis and ethnomethodology, critical discourse analysis and the social practice theory of Bourdieu (1977) meet. He writes:

> ... mediated discourse as a theoretical framework mirrors the social world that it hopes to analyse... it has taken on an identity through the linkages overall that are made through concrete actions and projects over time ... we should not see this nexus of practice as a set of objectivized or structural relationships among different schools. On the contrary, these relationships exist only in and through concrete intersections of these practices in specific research projects.
>
> (Scollon 2001)

Interrelationships across discourse analytical approaches

At the beginning of the chapter we pointed out that these seven approaches were quite distinct and were the result of very different motivations and that they drew inspirations from different sources. However, as we moved along each one of these approaches, we discovered that in spite of these differences, some of these approaches were either influenced by others, or developed as reactions to some of them. Conversation analysis, for instance, was a reaction to an overwhelming concern with broad social structures and theory in then current approaches to sociology. Similarly, the multimodal approach to discourse analysis was a reaction to an equally overwhelming concern with text in other forms of discourse analysis such as conversation analysis and corpus-based discourse analysis. The corpus-based approach in itself was a reaction to a number of approaches that confined themselves to the detailed analysis of rather small sets of data. Genre analysis, in a similar manner, was a reaction to analyses of de-contextualized lexico-grammatical features of language, providing a way to make the analysis of texts more functional and grounded in professional contexts. Critical discourse analysis was an attempt to combine discourse analysis with social analysis, with implications for the understanding of socio-cultural practices. Finally, mediated discourse analysis was a reaction to what was seen as an overemphasis on the analysis of discourse without a sufficient understanding of the concrete social actions people use discourse to carry out.

If we look at these approaches more closely, we find that all of them can be plotted along two major dimensions of Text/Context and Semiotic Mode. These can be represented in the diagram shown in Figure 1.1.

If we look at these approaches as visually displayed in Figure 1.1, we find that all of these in some sense distinct approaches to discourse analysis differ from each other depending upon the extent to which they regard social context and/or semiotic forms that are used to construct discourses. Corpus-based analyses of discourse are almost entirely focused on textual materials (although see L. Flowerdew this volume), whereas multimodal analyses of discourse extend to include other semiotic modes. If we go to the extreme of social context, we find ethnographic approaches to discourse focusing almost entirely on social contexts, whereas conversation analysis shifts the focus to the other extreme, focusing almost entirely on textual data. The remaining three approaches to discourse analysis – genre analysis, critical discourse analysis and mediated discourse analysis – seem to be paying varying attention to both textual and other semiotic modes, on the one hand, and social context on the other. The other factor common to all these three is that they use varying combinations of frameworks and methodologies, giving a kind of multidimensional perspective on discourse. However, they

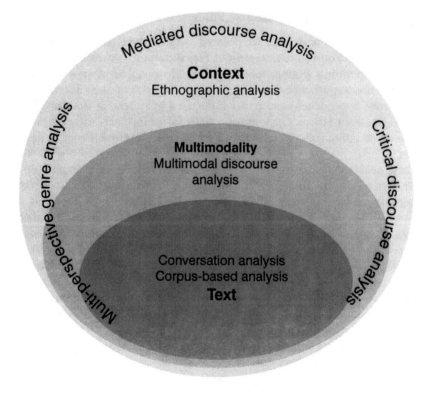

Figure 1.1   Approaches to discourse analysis: text, context and semiotic mode

differ essentially in terms of the objectives they serve and the applications to which they are suited. All of them pay some attention to texts and the social contexts in which they are grounded, and in turn provide interesting insights about the use of both language and social practices.

We have made a very brief attempt to introduce some of the main approaches to discourse analysis. There was neither an intention to offer detailed accounts of these approaches, nor to survey variations within these individual approaches. More detailed accounts of all these approaches will be offered in the chapters that follow, each one indicating how these approaches are developing from the basic theoretical roots traced here and are being exploited to analyse different forms of discourse in new ways. These chapters focus less on the historical development of these approaches and more on what lies ahead for them, and at the end of each section we provide our own suggestions for further work that might be done in these areas.

What should become clear in the chapters that follow is that these approaches are not developing in isolation, but rather in constant dialogue with one another, and it is in this conversation among approaches, we argue, that the real advances in discourse studies will be made. In one sense, although each individual approach provides a useful and credible view of the elephant, as we might say, none of them, on its own, can provide a full view of the elephant. This volume is an invitation to consider how these different approaches can be harnessed and integrated in order to have as comprehensive a view of the beast as is possible.

References

Atkinson, J.M. and Heritage, J. (eds) (1984) *Structures of Social Action: studies in conversation analysis*, Cambridge: Cambridge University Press.

Austin, J.L. (1962) *How to Do Things with Words: the William James Lectures delivered at Harvard University in 1955*, J.O. Urmson (ed.) Oxford: Clarendon Press.

Baker, P. (2006) *Using Corpora in Discourse Analysis*, London: Continuum.

Barton, D. and Hamilton, M. (1998) *Local Literacies: reading and writing in one community*, London: Routledge.

Bazerman, C. (1994) 'System of genres and the enhancement of social intentions', in Aviva Freedman and Peter Medway (eds) *Genre and New Rhetoric*, London: Taylor & Francis, 79–101.

Berkenkotter, Carol and Huckin, Thomas N. (1995) *Genre Knowledge I Disciplinary Communication: Cognition/Culture/Power*, Hillsdale, NJ: Lawrence.

Bhatia, Vijay K. (1993) *Analysing Genre: language use in professional settings*, London: Longman.

—— (2004) *Worlds of Written Discourse: a genre-based view*, London: Continuum.

Birdwhistell, R. (1970) *Kinesics in Context*, Philadelphia, PA: University of Pennsylvania Press.

Bourdieu, P. (1977) *An Outline of a Theory of Practice*, trans. R. Nice, Cambridge: Cambridge University Press.

Connor, U. and Upton, T.A. (1996) *Discourse in the Professions: perspectives from corpus linguistics*, Amsterdam: John Benjamins Publishing Company.

Fairclough, N. (1985) 'Critical and descriptive goals in discourse analysis', *Journal of Pragmatics*, 9: 739–63.

—— (1989) *Language and Power*, London: Longman.

—— (1995) *Critical Discourse Analysis: the critical study of language*, London: Longman.

Flowerdew, J. (1997) 'The discourse of colonial withdrawal: a case study in the creation of mythic discourse', *Discourse and Society*, 8(4): 493–517.

—— (1999) 'Description and interpretation in critical discourse analysis', *Journal of Pragmatics*, 31: 1089–99.

Garfinkel, H. (1967) *Studies in Ethnomethodology*, Englewood Cliffs, NJ: Prentice-Hall.

Gee, J.P. (1996) *Social Linguistics and Literacies: ideology in discourses*, London: Taylor & Francis.

Geertz, Clifford, (1973) *The Interpretation of Culture*, New York: Basic Books.

Goffman, E. (1959) *The Presentation of Self in Everyday Life*, Garden City, NY: Doubleday.

—— (1981) *Forms of Talk*, Oxford: Basil Blackwell.

Goodwin, Charles (1981) *Conversational Organization: interaction between speakers and hearers*, New York: Academic Press.

Gumperz, J.J. and Hymes, D. (1986) *Directions in Sociolinguistics: the ethnography of communication*, Oxford: Blackwell.

Halliday, M.A.K. (1973) *Explorations in the Functions of Language*, London: Edward Arnold.

Idema, Rick (2003) 'Multimodality, resemiotization: extending the analysis of discourse as multi-semiotic practice', *Visual Communication*, 2 (1): 29–57.

Jakobson, R. (1937) *Lectures on Sound and Meaning*, Cambridge, MA: MIT Press.

Jones, R. and Norris, S. (2005) *Discourse in Action: introducing mediated discourse analysis*, London: Routledge.

Kendon, A. (1990) *Conducting Interaction: patterns of behaviour in focused encounters*, Cambridge: Cambridge University Press.

Kress, G. and Hodge, R. (1979). *Language as Ideology*, London: Routledge.

Kress, G. and Van Leeuwen, T. (1996) *Reading Images: the grammar of visual design*, London: Routledge.

Kress, G. and Van Leeuwen, T. (eds) (2001) *Multimodality*, London: Sage.

Martin, J.R. (1993) 'A contextual theory of language' in B. Cope and M. Kalantzis (eds) *The Powers of Literacy: a genre approach to teaching writing*, Pittsburgh, PA: University of Pittsburgh Press, pp. 116–36.

Martin, J.R., Christie, F. and Rothery, J. (1987) 'Social processes in education: a reply to Sawyer and Watson (and others)', in I. Reid (ed.) *The Place of Genre in Learning: current debates*, Geelong: Deakin University Press, pp. 46–57.

Martin, J.R. and Rose, D. (2003) *Working with Discourse: meaning beyond the clause*, London: Continuum.

Mead, G.H. (1934) *Mind, Self and Society from the Standpoint of a Social Behaviorist*, Chicago, IL: University of Chicago Press.

Meyer, M. (2001) 'Between theory, method and politics: positioning of the approaches to CDA', in Wodak, R. and Meyer, M. *Methods of Critical Discourse Analysis*, London: Sage, pp. 14–31.

Miller, C.R. (1984) 'Genre as social action', *Quarterly Journal of Speech*, 70: 157–78.

Norris, Sigrid, (2004) *Analysing Multimodal Interaction: a methodological framework*, London: Routledge.

O'Toole, M. (1994) *The Language of Displayed Art*, Madison, NJ: FDU Press.

Pike, K.L. (1967) *Language in Relation to a Unified Theory of the Structure of Human Behaviour*, The Hague: Mouton and Co.

Potter, J. and Wetherall, M. (1987) *Discourse and Social Psychology Beyond Attitudes and Behaviour*, London: Sage.

Propp, V. (1958) *Morphology of the Folktale*, Austin, TX: Texas University Press.

Ruesch, J. and Bateson, G. (1951) *Communication: the social matrix of psychiatry*, New York: W.W. Norton and Company, Inc.

Sacks, H. (1974) 'An analysis of the course of a joke's telling in conversation', in J. Sherzer and R. Bauman (eds) *Explorations in the Ethnography of Speaking*, London: Cambridge University Press.

Sacks, H., Schegloff, E.A. and Jefferson, G. (1974) 'A simplest systematic for the organization of turn taking in conversation', *Language*, 50: 696–735.

Scheflen, A.E. (1974) *How Behavior Means*, New York: Anchor Books.

Schegloff, E.A. and Sacks, H. (1973) 'Opening up closings', *Semiotica*, 8: 289–327

Scollon, R. (1998) *Mediated Discourse as Social Interaction: a study of news discourse*, London: Longman.

—— (2001) *Mediated Discourse: the nexus of practice*, London: Routledge.

Sinclair, J. (1991) *Corpus, Concordance, Collocation*, Oxford: Oxford University Press.

Smart, G. (1998) 'Mapping conceptual worlds: using interpretive ethnography to explore knowledge-making in a professional community', *The Journal of Business Communication*, 35(1): 111–27.

Street, Brian V. (1984) *Literacy in Theory and Practice*, Cambridge: Cambridge University Press.

Stubbs, M. (1996) *Text and Corpus Analysis*, Oxford: Blackwell.

Swales, J.M. (1981) *Aspects of Article Introductions*, Aston ESP Research Report No. 1, Birmingham: Language Studies Unit, University of Aston.

—— (1990) *Genre Analysis: English in academic and research settings*, Cambridge: Cambridge University Press.

—— (1998) *Other Floors, Other Voices: a textography of a small university building*, Rhetoric, Knowledge and Society Series, London: Lawrence Erlbaum Associates.

Tannen, D. (1984) *Conversational Style: analysing talk among friends*, Oxford: Oxford University Press, 2005.

Van Dijk, T. (1993) 'Principles of critical discourse analysis', *Discourse and Society*, 4: 249–83.

—— (1998) *Ideology*, London: Sage.

Wertsch, J.V. (1991) *Voices of the Mind: a sociocultural approach to mediated action*, Cambridge, MA: Harvard University Press.

Widdowson, H.G. (1978) *Teaching Language and Communication*, Oxford: Oxford University Press.

—— (2004) *Text, Context, Pretext: critical issues in discourse analysis*, Oxford: Blackwell.

Wittgenstein, L. (1972) *Philosophical Investigations*, trans. G.E.M. Anscombe, Oxford: Basil Blackwell and Mott.

Wodak, R. (1996) *Disorders of Discourse*, London: Longman.

Part I

Conversation analysis

In recent years, conversation analysts have developed the fundamental principles of Sacks and Schegloff in various ways, often involving overlaps with and borrowing from other fields of linguistics and discourse analysis. There has been a considered movement, for example, from an almost exclusive focus on the lexico-semantic features of talk to an interest in the role of prosodic features (Couper-Kuhlen and Selting 1996), grammatical features (Ochs *et al.* 1996), and non-verbal communication (such as gesture, pausing and gaze) (Goodwin 2000; Heath 1986) in conversation. There have also been considerable efforts to find ways of applying conversation analysis (CA) principles that were developed from data in English to other languages such as Japanese (Tanaka 1999) and Finnish (Sorjonen 2001), discovering how different language systems provide different resources for the organization of talk.

Categorization analysis, which was, in fact, one of Sacks's earliest preoccupations (Sacks 1972) is also becoming a more prominent feature of CA in studies that show how social categories are used in interaction and the conversational machinery of claiming, imputing, affirming or challenging social identity (Hester and Eglin 1997). Another important recent development has been the movement towards using CA to understand people's behaviour in various workplace settings (Drew and Heritage 1992; Heath 1997; Nevile this volume) and in the study of computer mediated communication and human-computer interaction (HCI) (see, for example, Luff *et al.* 1990; Norman and Thomas 1991).

At the same time, the approach to analysis and the theoretical principles of CA have been extremely important in the development of other approaches to discourse. They have had, for example, a profound influence on the development of interactional sociolinguistics as practised by people like Tannen (1989), and have also been adopted by discursive psychologist like Potter and Weatherall (1987), who study how mental states are constituted in discourse. Mediated discourse analysis, as well, owes a debt to CA for providing a framework for understanding the workings of the 'interaction order' and the sequential organization of mediated actions. Finally, CA has been beginning a relationship with corpus-based discourse analysis, with many conversation analysts working with rather large collections of texts like telephone calls (Drew and Curl this volume) and pilot talk (Nevile this volume) and looking for patterns over a range of texts. Corpora (and, increasingly, computer based tools) help analysts to identify common forms of conversational organization and then to 'distributionalize' (Sacks 1974) these phenomena or forms, determining the positions or sequential circumstances in which they are most likely to occur.

The two chapters in this section represent two of these new directions in which CA is advancing, namely the movement towards taking into account the grammatical forms utterances in conversation take and the application of CA to workplace practices. In their chapter, Drew and Curl not only expand CA's methodological scope by describing how the syntax of turn construction plays a systematic part in determining the actions which are accomplished in turns, but also significantly expand CA's preoccupation with the sequential organization of conversational actions by considering 'initial actions', asking where they come from and what forms they are most likely to take. Through their examination of phone conversations, they are able to show how the syntactic forms utterances take are associated with characteristic and appropriate 'places' in interaction and typically used to deal with particular interactional circumstances or contingencies.

Nevile's chapter is an example of the application of CA's methodology to workplace interactions. In particular he focuses on the effect of sequence and timing on organizing interactions in collaborative work, showing how the temporal organization of turn taking is relative to demands and goals of particular work settings, in his case, the flight deck of a commercial airliner. He also argues convincingly that deviations from the normal flow and timing of talk can act as a warning signal that workplace activities may not be progressing as they should.

Useful further reading on conversation analysis can be found in Drew (2005), Ford *et al.* (2002), Ochs *et al.* (1996), Wooffitt (2005), ten Have (1999) and Schegloff (forthcoming).

References

Billing, M. (1997) 'Whose terms? Whose ordinariness? Rhetoric and ideology in conversation analysis', *Discourse and Society*, 10: 543–58.

Couper-Kuhlen, E. and Selting, M. (eds) (1996) *Prosody in Conversation*, Cambridge: Cambridge University Press.

Drew, P. (2005) 'Conversation analysis', in K. Fitch and R. Sanders (eds) *Handbook of Language and Social Interaction*, Mahwah, NJ: Lawrence Erlbaum, pp. 71–102.

Drew, P. and Heritage, J. (1992) *Talk at Work: interaction in institutional settings*, Cambridge: Cambridge University Press.

Goodwin, C. (2000) 'Action and embodiment within situated human interaction', *Journal of Pragmatics*, 32: 1489–522.

Ford, C., Fox, B.A. and Thompson, S.A. (eds) (2002) *The Language of Turn and Sequence*, Oxford: Oxford University Press.

Heath, C.C. (1986) *Body Movement and Speech in Medical Interaction*, Cambridge: Cambridge University Press.

—— (1997) 'Analysing work activities in face to face interaction using video', in D. Silverman (ed.) *Qualitative Methods*, London: Sage.

Hester, S. and Eglin, P. (eds) (1997) *Culture in Action: studies in membership categorisation analysis*, Washington, DC: University Press of America.

Luff, P., Gilbert, G.N. and Frohlich, D.M. (eds) (1990) *Computers and Conversation*, London: Academic Press.

Norman, M.A. and Thomas, P.J. (1991) 'Informing HCI design through conversation analysis', *International Journal of Man–Machine Studies*, 35: 235–50.

Ochs, E., Schegloff, E.A. and Thompson, S.A. (eds) (1996) *Interaction and Grammar*, Cambridge: Cambridge University Press.

Potter, J. and Wetherell, M. (1987) *Discourse and Social Psychology: beyond attitudes and behaviour*, London: Sage.

Sacks, H. (1972) 'An initial investigation of the usability of conversational data for doing sociology', in D.N. Sudnow (ed.) *Studies in Social Interaction*, New York: Free Press, pp. 31–74.

—— (1974) 'An analysis of the course of a joke's telling in conversation', in R. Bauman and J. Sherzer (eds) *Explorations in the Ethnography of Speaking*, Cambridge: Cambridge University Press, pp. 337–53.

Schegloff, E.A. (forthcoming) *Sequence Organization in Interaction: a primer in conversation analysis I*, Cambridge: Cambridge University Press.

Sorjonen, M.-L. (2001) *Responding in Conversation: a study of response particles in Finnish*, Amsterdam: John Benjamins.

Tanaka, H. (1999) *Turn-taking in Japanese Conversation: a study in grammar and interaction*, Amsterdam: John Benjamins.

Tannen, D. (1989) *Talking Voices*, Cambridge: Cambridge University Press.

ten Have, P. (1999) *Doing Conversation Analysis: a practical guide*, Thousand Oaks, CA: Sage.

Wooffitt, R. (2005) *Conversation Analysis and Discourse Analysis: a comparative and critical introduction*, London: Sage.

2 Conversation analysis

Overview and new directions

Paul Drew and Traci Curl

The background and programme of conversation analysis

Conversation analysis (CA) is founded on a sociological conceptualization of the basically social nature of language use in human interaction. However as the work in CA has developed, it has come to be a truly multi-disciplinary field; and in this account of recent developments and the directions in which we see CA heading, we will highlight particularly the implications which CA's methods and findings are having for core areas in linguistics – focusing especially on the syntax of social actions in talk. But to begin with, we will briefly review the background to CA's programme.

CA is a field of study concerned with the norms, practices and competences underlying the organization of social interaction. Notwithstanding its name, it is concerned with all forms of spoken interaction including not only everyday conversations between friends and acquaintances, but also interactions in medical, educational, mass media and socio-legal contexts, relatively 'monologic' interactions such as lecturing or speech-making, and technologically complex interactions such as web-based multiparty communication. Regardless of the interaction being studied, CA starts from the perspective that (*contra* both Chomsky and Parsons) the details of conduct in interaction are highly organized and orderly and, indeed, that the specificities of meaning and understanding in interaction would be impossible without this orderliness.

The central sociological insight of CA is that it is through conversation that we conduct the ordinary, and perhaps extraordinary, affairs of our lives. When people talk with one another, they are not merely communicating thoughts, information or knowledge. Our relationships with one another, and our sense of who we are to one another, are generated, manifest, maintained and managed in and through our conversations, whether face-to-face or on the telephone. People construct, establish, reproduce and negotiate their identities, roles and relationships in conversational interaction. In our interactions with others, we don't just talk; conversation is not, to adapt Wittgenstein's phrase, 'language idling'. We are *doing* things, such as inviting someone over, asking them to do a favour or a service, blaming or criticizing them, greeting them or trying to get on first name terms with them, disagreeing or arguing with them, advising or warning them, apologizing for something one did or said, complaining about one's treatment, telling about troubles, sympathizing, offering to help and the like. These and other such activities are some of the primary forms of social action. They are as real, concrete, consequential and as fundamental as any other form of conduct. So when we study conversation, we are investigating the actions and activities through which social life is conducted. It is therefore primarily an approach to social action (Schegloff 1996).

Methodologically, CA seeks to uncover the practices, patterns and generally the methods through which participants perform and interpret social action. CA emerged from two intellectual streams in sociology. The first derives most proximately from the work of Goffman (e.g. 1983a), who argues that social interaction constitutes a distinct institutional order comprised of normative rights and obligations that regulate interaction, and that function in broad independence from the social, psychological and motivational characteristics of persons. The second is Garfinkel's ethnomethodology (Garfinkel 1967; see also Heritage 1984a), which stresses the contingent and socially constructed nature both of action and the understanding of action, and the role of shared methods in the production, recognition and shared understanding of joint activities. CA's fusion of these two perspectives (through the work of Sacks; see especially Sacks 1992 and Schegloff's 1992 account of Sacks's analytic programme) resulted in an appreciation of the ways in which the Goffmanian interaction order structures the production, recognition and analysis of action as it unfolds in real time through the use of shared methods or practices. This process (and its analysis) is possible because participants reflexively display their analyses of one another's conduct in each successive contribution to interaction.

At the most basic level CA seeks to discover patterns in social interaction in order to find evidence of *practices* of conduct, in the systematic design of turns at talk. To be identified as a practice, particular elements of conduct must be recurrent, specifically situated, and attract responses that discriminate them from related or similar practices. A central feature of this procedure is that the analysis of the practices used to perform a social action (e.g. using a figurative expression to close down a topic, prefacing an answer to a question with *oh*, or identifying a co-interactant by name in the course of a turn) can be validated through the examination of others' responses.

In pursuit of the goal of identifying basic interactional and communicative competencies, CA focuses on *sequences* of actions. In performing some current action, participants generally project (empirically) and require (normatively) the production of a 'next' or range of possible 'next' actions to be done by another participant. Moreover, in constructing a turn at talk, they normally address themselves to immediately preceding talk, and design their contributions in ways that exploit this basic positioning. In the production of next actions, participants display an understanding of a prior action and do so at a multiplicity of levels – for example, by an 'acceptance' a speaker can show an understanding that the prior turn was possibly complete, that it was addressed to them, that it was an action of a particular type (e.g. an invitation) and so on. Within this framework, the grasp of a 'next' action that a current projects, the production of that next action, and its interpretation by the previous speaker – are the products of a common set of socially shared practices. CA analyses are thus simultaneously analyses of action, context management and intersubjectivity – because all three of these features are simultaneously, if tacitly, the objects of the participants' actions.

Based on this framework, CA has developed as an empirical discipline focused on a range of domains of interactional conduct, including turn-taking (the allocation of opportunities to speak among participants), the organization of conversational sequences, the internal structuring of turns at talk and the formation of actions, the organization of repair (dealing with difficulties in speaking, hearing and understanding talk), story-telling and narrative, phonetic and prosodic aspects of talk, body behaviour and so on. These organizations form the technical bedrock on which people build their social lives, and construct their sense of sociality with one another.

Interaction of any kind is made possible through participants sharing certain communicative competencies. These consist partly of knowledge about the language, of the ways that elements of language (including lexis, grammar and syntax, intonation, prosody and so forth) are organized, combined and deployed. But they include, most crucially, knowledge also of the structures, patterns, norms and expectations concerning the social organization of (verbal) action in sequences of interaction. Such 'knowledge' is not generally something of which we are aware at any conscious level. It is, however, salient to participants in interaction in their establishing a mutual understanding of what they are saying and doing in the talk. Thus the coherence of talk, and the mutual understandings which underlie it, rest on a 'common set of methods or procedures' (Heritage 1984a: 241); and these in turn are the constituents of our basic communicative competencies. So when we study conversation, we are attempting to discover what are the essential and quite fundamental shared competencies that make all coherent social action – including communication – possible between members of a culture. These competencies or sense-making practices (Pomerantz and Mandelbaum 2005) consist of the practices and devices that are the focus of CA research. That is, the aim of research in CA is to discover and explicate the practices through which participants produce and understand conduct in interaction. These practices are uncovered, in large part, through identifying patterns in talk.

In these respects CA lies at the intersection between sociology and other cognate disciplines, especially linguistics and social psychology. Certainly research in CA has paralleled developments within sociolinguistics, pragmatics, discourse analysis and so forth towards a naturalistic, observation-based science of actual verbal behaviour, which uses recordings of naturally occurring interactions as the basic form of data (Heritage 1984a). All levels of linguistic production (e.g. syntax, phonetics) can be related to the actions (such as greetings, invitations, requests) or activities (instructing, cross-examining, performing a medical examination and diagnosing, etc.) in which people are engaged when interacting with one another. In this way conversational organizations underlie social action (Atkinson and Heritage 1984); hence CA offers a methodology, based on analysing sequences in which actions are produced and embedded, for investigating how we accomplish social actions.

In summary, CA investigates the organizations of and interconnections between four underlying characteristics of talk-in-interaction (see e.g. Drew 2005), which are:

- turn-taking
- turn design or construction
- sequence and sequence organization
- action.

Grammar and interaction

It is worth highlighting two points in the account we have given so far of CA's programme. First, we noted that CA has focused largely (though not exclusively) on *sequence*, and especially on responses, and how responses both display understandings of prior actions and themselves create contingencies for subsequent actions – thereby helping to shape the unfolding sequence (sequential patterns). Second, we stressed that all levels of linguistic production are involved in turn design – the construction of a turn-at-talk from a range of elements or components, including word selection, syntactic and grammatical features, phonetic and prosodic aspects, as well as (in face-to-face interaction) gaze, posture, bodily orientation and the like. Until recently CA research focused largely on word selection (lexis); with some rare exceptions, the ways in which different linguistic resources were integrated into turn design, and the role played by other levels of linguistic production in the management of action, were not much investigated. For instance, Couper-Kuhlen and Selting (1996: 11) pointed out that prosody had been largely neglected in the empirical study of spoken interaction: despite its being no less important than other (linguistic) turn design components, research had tended to focus on lexico-syntactic features, due perhaps to the legacy of the influence of literacy on studying language use. They further argued that:

> ... prosody can be seen as one of the orderly 'details' of interaction, a resource which interlocutors rely on to accomplish social action and as a means of steering inferential processes. Prosodic features... can be reconstructed as *members' devices* [authors' emphasis], designed for the organization and management of talk in social interaction. They can be shown to function as part of the signalling system which – together

with syntax, lexico-semantics, kinesics, and other contextualizing cues
– is used to construct and interpret turn constructional units and turns-
at-talk.

(Couper-Kuhlen and Selting 1996: 25)

Although we mentioned that research has tended to focus on lexico-syntactic
features of talk-in-interaction, it would be more accurate to say that CA
has not much investigated grammar in general, or syntax in particular, at
all formally or systematically. Until recently, our approach to grammar has
been rather *ad hoc*, drawing on observations about grammatical or syntactic
features as and when they seemed salient, but without taking grammar/syntax
as the principal object of systematic inquiry. We should just note that the
emphasis in CA research on lexis should be taken to include all those kinds
of verbal objects, including *oh* (Heritage 1984b and 2002a), *mm* (Gardner
1997), particles (Sorjonen 2001) and laughter (Jefferson 1979; Haakana
2001; Glenn 2003), the use and semantics of which have generally been
beyond traditional theories of language; one of the strengths of CA has been
that it encompasses all those seemingly trivial, flawed, 'meaningless' and
incidental details of speech, most of which cannot be handled or explained
through traditional linguistic theories. At any rate, only recently has CA's
methodology, based on sequential analysis, been deployed to investigate at
all formally the ways in which grammar and syntax are *practices* for talk-in-
interaction. A certain awakening of how grammar and interaction intersect
came with the publication (like its companion volume by Couper-Kuhlen
and Selting on prosody, also in 1996) of a collection focusing on the ways
in which the grammar and syntax of various languages are employed to
perform various different practices in conversation (Ochs *et al.* 1996). Since
then, a small number of studies have begun to explore how the syntax of
turn construction plays a systematic part in determining both the actions
which are accomplished in turns, and the precise affordances (including
inferential character) of those designs/actions (examples are Heritage 2002b
and Tanaka 1999). It is this direction of research in CA that we want to
highlight and illustrate in the remainder of this chapter.

  CA's focus on patterns of unfolding sequences of interaction, most
notably perhaps in the accounts of various kinds of adjacency pairs and the
preference organization associated with the sequencing and formation of
alternative responses to 'initial' actions such as invitations, requests and
the like (e.g. Drew 1984; for perhaps the best account of adjacency pairs,
see Sacks's lectures 1–5, Spring 1972, in Sacks 1992, vol. 2), has resulted
in our having given less attention to the 'initial' actions themselves, how
they are formed, and, in short, how such sequences are generated in the
first place. Recent work in CA, including our own research, has begun to
investigate precisely the question of how 'initial' actions come to be formed,
syntactically, as they are (e.g. Heinemann 2006; Curl *et al.* forthcoming).
That is, we are beginning to ask, for instance, how speakers come to select

from among a number of alternative syntactic forms that might be available, a particular form with which to initiate or perform a certain action. We are putting 'initial' in inverted commas in order to highlight the fact that while studies in CA have tended to treat actions such as assessments, invitations, complaints, etc. as 'first' actions (e.g. first pair parts in adjacency pairs), in reality they also emerge from ongoing interaction; they do not come from nowhere – they arise out of whatever particular interactional circumstances and contingencies that obtain up to that point. Goffman summarizes this matter in his usual pithy manner, thus:

> Most important of all, the sense in which current utterance is conditioned by immediately prior turn's talk – when, indeed, there is such talk – does not speak to the many elements of the same current utterance that are not in any way determined by prior turn (or prior utterance in the same turn), yet are nonetheless determined in ways that satisfy Felicity's Condition. In any case, an account of second utterances in terms of their contingency on a first leaves unexplained how there could be any firsts; after all, from where could they draw their design? Conversation could never begin. Or, once begun, would be one utterance away from the end. Tails would know how to wag, but there would be no dogs.
>
> (Goffman 1983b: 50)

To illustrate this, consider the ways in which we make offers to others, particularly when offering some kind of assistance. Reviewing a large corpus (somewhat over 20 hours) of telephone calls recorded in homes both in the US and UK, of conversations between family, relatives, friends, colleagues and sometimes to service organizations of one kind or another (shops, banks, doctors, etc.), we found that offers were made predominantly using one of three syntactic forms: these three forms are illustrated in the following brief excerpts.

Example 1 (Holt:2:3:1)

```
 1   Les:   .hh And he now has: u-a:: um (1.1) I don't think eez called
 2          it consultancy (0.2) They find positions for people: in the
 3          printing'n paper (0.4) indus [try:,
 4   Mar:                               [Oh I see: [:.
 5   Les:                                          [ hh An:d if: your
 6          husband would li:ke their addre[ss.
 7   Mar:                                  [Y e : [: s,
 8   Les:                                         [ <As they're
 9          specialists,
10   Mar:   Ye::s?
11          (.)
12   Les:   Uhm: my husband w'd gladly give it to him.
```

Example 2   (NB:IV:10:19)

```
1   Lot:    =W'l listen (.) e-uh: dih you want me uh come dow'n getchu
2           to [morrow er] a n y th]ing?
3   Emm:       [n:N o : :] dea:r.]
4   Emm:    No [: I'm]fine]
5   Lot:       [to the] sto::]re 'r anythi:ng?
```

Example 3   (NB:IV:4:4)

```
1   Emm:    W'l anyway tha:t's a'dea:l so I don'know what to do about
2           Ba:rbara .hhhhh (0.2) c'z you see she w'z: depe [nding on:
3   (L):                                                  [(°Yeh°)
4   Emm:    him taking 'er in tuh the L.A. deeple s:- depot Sundee so
5           ['e siz]
6   Lot:    [I:'ll] take 'er in: Sundee,
```

In the first example, Lesley is offering to put Mary's husband, who is evidently in the printing trade but currently unemployed, in touch with an employment agency specializing in that field. She does so using the conditional form, *if* (your husband would like ...), (*then*) (my husband will ...) (the contingent clause is not in fact initiated with *then*; as is most commonly the case, it is left implicit). Lottie constructs her offer in Example 2, to collect her sister, Emma, to take her shopping, in an interrogative syntactic form as a *do you want* construction. By contrast, Lottie's offer in the third example, from a different telephone call, is syntactically declarative, *I'll do ... .* We see, then, that in each case, the offer is made through the selection of a particular syntactic form: syntax is as much part of turn design as is the choice of words, or prosodic features and so on. These three syntactic forms – conditionals, *Do you want* interrogatives and declaratives (and related formats) – were the most commonly occurring in our data corpus.

   In order to investigate the interactional contingencies that may be associated with a given form, which can often be pretty close to the interactional 'functions' of a form or practice, we can do what Sacks termed 'distributionalize' a phenomenon/form (Sacks 1974). That is, we look to see where in talk that practice or form tends to occur, or in what sequential circumstances or positions that form is found/systematically used (see, for example, Drew and Holt 1998 for an account of investigating the systematic distribution of an object, there of figurative expressions in conversation). When we examined the distribution of the occurrence of these three syntactic forms for offering, it appeared that the first, conditionals, occurred at the beginnings of telephone calls, when an offer was the first topic after the call openings; by contrast, *Do you want ... ?* interrogatives occurred in call closings; whilst declarative forms occurred in what might loosely be considered the 'middles' of calls, i.e. not close to the beginning or ends of calls.

This emerging pattern turned out to be somewhat true, but misleading. We began to find cases that did not fit this pattern of occurrence. For instance, in the following example Lesley makes an offer using the conditional format, although this is not during or even near the beginning of the call.

Example 4   (Holt:X(C):1:1:3:5)

```
 1   Les:   The other thin:g (.) was (.) uhm .t.h we've had an
 2          invoice: fr'm Scott's .hh (.) Now if they deliver it
 3          (0.5) to you: UH (0.7) we- (.) we wanted t'pay the
 4   Les:   carriage w'l they haven't invoiced us f'r any
 5          carriage.
 6   Phi:   .hwhh (.) We:l [l
 7   Les:                  [So-
 8          (0.2)
 9   Phi:   [they
10   Les:   [if they come t'you an' invoice you f'carriage say
11          that it's we that're paying oka:y?
```

Lesley makes this offer, to pay for some plants that she has asked to be delivered to Philip ('if they come t'you an' invoice you f'carriage say that it's we that're paying oka:y?', lines 10–11; though notice that Lesley began something like this offer in lines 2–3, 'if they deliver it (0.5) to you: …'), using the conditional form – the form which was emerging was that used in call beginnings. However, she makes this offer 2 minutes 40 seconds into the call, and therefore at some distance from the beginning. Space prevents us showing other instances where forms were, as in Example 4, used 'inappropriately', according to our emerging hypothesis; suffice it to say that we found a few, not many, instances of declarative forms used in call closings, and *Do you want … ?* interrogatives in 'middles'. There was an association, a correlation perhaps, between these three syntactic forms and the three different positions in telephone conversations; but the association did not hold for all.

It turned out that underlying the distributional pattern which we had begun to suspect was another – a pattern which was itself associated with beginnings, 'middles' and endings of calls, but one which – rather like an intervening variable – was not the determining factor in speakers' selections of the appropriate syntactic form. A clue to this is to be found in Example 4, and particularly Lesley's initiating this topic, and her offer, with 'The other thin:g (.) was..' (line 1). Her preface *The other thing* is a way to indicate that this is part of her agenda, one of the reasons for calling. Right at the beginning of the call, Lesley offers her condolences to Philip on the death of his mother the day before; that topic, the funeral arrangements, etc., quite naturally take precedence. But now in Example 4 it turns out, and Philip discovers, that Lesley has called specifically to make this offer. It is that – that this is the reason for Lesley's call – which informs the selection of the conditional construction with which to make the offer. Of course, the opening of a conversation, whether on the telephone or face to face, is where, generally, a speaker introduces the reason for initiating the interaction. But there can be circumstances, such as this in Example 4 (i.e. that the death of Philip's mother is more important, and takes precedence) in which a reason for calling comes to be delayed.

We'll see, then, that the conditional offer in Example 1 is the reason why Lesley has phoned Mary.

Example 5   (Holt:2:3)

```
1    Mar:   One three five?
2           (.)
3    Les:   Oh hello, it's um: Leslie Field he:re,
4    Mar:   Oh ⌃ hello:,
5    Les:   Hello, .tch.h I hope you don't mind me getting in touch
6           but uh- we met your husband little while ago at a Liberal
7           meeting.
8           (0.3)
9    Mar:   Ye: [s?
10   Les:       [.hh And he wz: (0.3) i-he told us something of what'd
11          happen:ed,
12          (0.5)
13   Les:   to him .hh An:' I wondered haa- (0.2) i-he said he m::ight
14          have another position in vie:[w,
15   Mar:                                [Mmhm,
16   Les:   .hh (.) Uhm (0.3) .tch Well I don't know how that went, .h
17          uh (.) It's just thet I wondered if he hasn:'t (0.3) uh
18          we have friends in: Bristol
19   Mar:   Ye:s?
20   Les:   who:-(.) uh: thet u-had the same experience.
21   Mar:   Oh↑:_:.
22   Les:   And they uhm: .t (0.2) .hh He worked f'r a printing an:'
23          paper (0.9) uh firm[u-
24   Mar:   Ye:s,
25   Les:   uh[:- which ih puh- uh: part'v the Paige Group.
26   Mar:     [Yeh,
27          (.)
28   Les:   .hh And he now has: u-a:: um (1.1) I don't think eez called
29          it consultancy (0.2) They find positions for people: in the
30          printing'n paper (0.4) indus[try:,
31   Mar:                               [Oh I see: [:.
32   Les:                                          [ hh An:d if: your
33          husband would li:ke their addre[ss.
```

34	Mar:	[Y e : [: s,
35	Les:	[<As they're specialists,
36	(.)	
37	Les:	Uhm: my husband w'd gladly give it to him.

Again, Lesley's preface 'I hope you don't mind me getting in touch' (line 5) explicitly indicates this (the upcoming offer, which here as in all such cases is preceded by some account of the circumstances of making the offer) is the reason she has called.

Compare this with Example 3 above, in which Lottie offers to take Emma's daughter (Barbara) and her family to catch the Greyhound bus at the LA depot.

Example 3   (NB:IV:4:4)

```
1   Emm:  W'l anyway tha:t's a'dea:l so I don'know what to do about
2         Ba:rbara .hhhhh (0.2) c'z you see she w'z: depe [nding on:
3   (L):                                              [(°Yeh°)
4   Emm:  him taking 'er in tuh the L.A. deeple s:- depot Sundee so
5         ['e siz]
6   Lot:  [I:'ll] take 'er in: Sundee,
```

Lottie's offer is made spontaneously, in response to Emma's expression of a problem 'I don'know what to do about Ba:rbara' (lines 1–2), regarding Barbara getting to the bus depot (lines 2–4). This illustrates the distribution of offers made in declarative forms; they occur in the sequential position of responses to the other's explicit account of a problem, and are thus spontaneous offers generated interactionally by the other's expression of a problem or difficulty (and not reasons for calling).

The other syntactic form, *Do you want ... ?* interrogatives, also appear to be interactionally generated, but not by some immediately preceding or explicit expression of trouble, as for the declarative forms, but by some need which the speaker educes the other might have. Here is a case in point; Chloe and Claire are members of a group of women who meet regularly in one another's homes to play bridge; evidently Chloe is hosting the next game, and at the point where their conversation is ending (lines 8–12) Claire offers to bring more chairs for the event.

Example 6   (SBL:2:2:3:28)

```
1   Chl:  We:ll it was [fu:n Clai [re,
2   Cla:              [hhh     [Yea:: [:h,]
3   Chl:                            [° M]m°
4   Chl:  [(an')
5   Cla:  [I enjoyed every minute o [f it,
6   Chl:                          [Yah.
```

```
 7            (0.4)
 8    Cla:    Okay well then u-wi'll see: you: Sa'urde[e.
 9    Chl:                                    [Saturdee night.
10    Cla:    Seven thirty?
11            (.)
12    Chl:    Ya[h.
13    Cla: +  [hhhh D'you want me to bring the: chai:[rs?
14    Chl:                                           [hahh
15    Chl:    Plea::: (.) NO: (0.2) °Yah,°
16            (0.3)
17    Chl:    I:'ve got to get chairs. Bring 'em one more time.
```

Plainly Chloe does not indicate that she has any difficulty as regards seating, or that she needs chairs. Chloe is educing (inferring, or bringing out something which was latent) from just a little earlier in their conversation (4 minutes before), in which they resolved the matter of Claire not having score tallies by Chloe agreeing to make and bring them.

Example 7 (SBL:2:2:25)

```
 1    Chl:    hhh Now waita minute Claire don't we need tallies?
 2            (1.8)
 3    Chl:    °( ),°
 4            (0.5)
 5    Cla:    YEH w'l why dun' [I j's   ] make ]up ] Why c-]
 6    Chl:                    [W'dju ] bring ]the] tallie  ][s?
 7    Cla:                                             [Why can'l d's
 8            make those thin:gs up I made bef:o::re. Dz it haftuh be so
 9            ni:[ce?
10    Chl:    [e-Heavens n [o make 'em up.[h
11    Cla:    [.hhhh       [Oka:y.
```

Example 7 is taken from earlier in the call in which Example 6 occurs. From this, and evidently from previous experience – see Chloe's 'I:'ve got to get chairs. Bring 'em one more time.' in line 17, Example 6 – Claire infers something else (chairs) which Chloe might need (and apparently does so correctly). So offers done syntactically as *Do you want...?* interrogatives are made in response to a difficulty or need which is found to be *implicit* (never explicit) in something said earlier in the talk (never in the immediately prior turn(s)).

Thus each of the three different syntactic forms for offering have their characteristic and appropriate 'places' or uses; each of the forms is used to handle or deal with different interactional circumstances or contingencies. It is evident that speakers orient to the appropriateness of a given form when making an offer, in cases where they begin using a certain 'inappropriate' form (e.g. *Do you want* … *?* in response to an explicit expression of trouble) but do not complete it, and then self-repair their talk so as to select the correct/appropriate construction.

The connections we've explored and illustrated briefly here, between syntactic form and interactional circumstances or contingencies, is a relatively new direction for CA research – one which promises to open up significant aspects of the interface between CA and core linguistic areas, and promises also significant findings regarding the role played by features of linguistic design, here syntax, in participating meaningfully and coherently in talk-in-interaction. This is by no means the only new direction taken by CA research; others include the application of CA's methodology to our understanding of workplace or institutional interactions, especially medical consultations (Heritage and Maynard 2006). But the direction we have outlined here is one that promises fresh insights into the linguistic design of social action in talk – by focusing not so much on responses to actions, and the subsequent unfolding sequences, which have hitherto been the main line of CA enquiry (as we noted before, for instance in the research on adjacency pairs), but instead on how those initial forms emerge in the first place, and how they are constructed linguistically. This complements, and might contribute to, the work on 'emergent grammar' (e.g. Hopper 1998).

References

Atkinson, J.M. and Heritage, J. (eds) (1984) *Structures of Social Action: studies in conversation analysis*, Cambridge: Cambridge University Press.

Couper-Kuhlen, E. (1996) 'The prosody of repetition: on quoting and mimicry', in E. Couper-Kuhlen and M. Selting (eds) *Prosody in Conversation*, Cambridge: Cambridge University Press, pp. 366–405.

Couper-Kuhlen, E. and Selting, M. (eds) (1996) *Prosody in Conversation*, Cambridge: Cambridge University Press.

Curl, T.S. (2006) 'Offers of assistance: constraints on syntactic design', *Journal of Pragmatics*, 38: 1257–80.

Curl, T., Drew, P. and Ogden, R. (forthcoming) *Linguistic Resources for Social Action*, Cambridge: Cambridge University Press.

Drew, P. (1984) 'Speakers' "reportings" in invitation sequences', in J.M. Atkinson and J. Heritage (eds) *Structures of Social Action: studies in conversation analysis*, Cambridge: Cambridge University Press, pp. 129–51.

—— (2005) 'Conversation analysis', in K. Fitch and R. Sanders (eds) *Handbook of Language and Social Interaction*, Mahwah, NJ: Lawrence Erlbaum, pp. 71–102.

Drew, P. and Heritage, J. (1992) *Talk at Work: interaction in institutional settings*, Cambridge: Cambridge University Press.

Drew, P. and Holt, E. (1998) 'Figures of speech: figurative expressions and the management of topic transition in conversation', *Language in Society*, 27: 495–523.

Gardner, R. (1997) 'The conversational object *Mm*: a weak and variable acknowledging token', *Research on Language and Social Interaction*, 30: 131–56.

Garfinkel, H. (1967) *Studies in Ethnomethodology*, Englewood Cliffs, NJ: Prentice Hall.

Glenn, P. (2003) *Laughter in Interaction*, Cambridge: Cambridge University Press.

Goffman, E. (1983a) 'The interaction order', *American Sociological Review*, 48: 1–17.

—— (1983b) 'Felicity's condition', *American Journal of Sociology*, 89: 1–53.

Haakana, M. (2001) 'Laughter as a patient's resource: dealing with delicate aspects of medical interaction', *Text*, 21: 187–219.

Heinemann, T. (2006) ' "Will you or can't you?" Displaying entitlement in interrogative requests', *Journal of Pragmatics*, 38: 1081–104.

Heritage, J. (1984a) *Garfinkel and Ethnomethodology*, Cambridge: Polity Press.

—— (1984b) 'A change-of-state token and aspects of its sequential placement', in J.M. Atkinson and J. Heritage (eds) (1984) *Structures of Social Action: studies in conversation analysis*, Cambridge: Cambridge University Press, pp. 299–345.

—— (2002a) 'Oh-prefaced responses to assessments: a method of modifying agreement/disagreement', in C.E. Ford, B. Fox and S. Thompson (eds) *The Language of Turn and Sequence*, Oxford: Oxford University Press. pp. 196–234.

—— (2002b) 'The limits of questioning: negative interrogatives and hostile question content', *Journal of Pragmatics*, 34: 1427–46.

Heritage, J. and Maynard, D. (eds) (2006) *Communication in Medical Care: interaction between physicians and patients*, Cambridge: Cambridge University Press.

Hopper, P.J. (1998) 'Emergent grammar', in M. Tomasello (ed.) *The New Psychology of Language: cognitive and functional approaches to language structure*, Mahwah, NJ: Lawrence Erlbaum, pp. 155–75.

Jefferson, G. (1979) 'A technique for inviting laughter, and its subsequent acceptance/declination', in G. Psathas (ed.) *Everyday Language: studies in ethnomethodology*, New York: Irvington, pp. 79–96.

Ochs, E., Schegloff, E.A. and Thompson, S. (1996) *Interaction and Grammar*, Cambridge: Cambridge University Press.

Pomerantz, A. and Mandelbaum, J. (2005) 'Conversation analytic approaches to the relevance and uses of relationship categories in interaction', in K. Fitch and R. Sanders (eds) *Handbook of Language and Social Interaction*, Mahwah, NJ: Lawrence Erlbaum, pp. 149–70.

Sacks, H. (1974) 'An analysis of the course of a joke's telling in conversation', in R. Bauman and J. Sherzer (eds) *Explorations in the Ethnography of Speaking*, Cambridge: Cambridge University Press, pp. 337–53.

—— (1992) *Lectures on Conversation*, 2 volumes, G. Jefferson (ed.) Oxford: Blackwell.

Schegloff, E.A. (1992) 'Introduction', in H. Sacks (1992) *Lectures on Conversation Volume 1*, G. Jefferson (ed.), Oxford: Blackwell, pp. ix–lxii.

—— (1996) 'Confirming allusions: toward an empirical account of action', *American Journal of Sociology*, 104(1): 161–216.

—— (2007) *Sequence Organization in Interaction: a primer in conversation analysis I*, Cambridge: Cambridge University Press.

Sorjonen, M.-J. (2001) *Responding in Conversation: a study of response particles in Finnish*, Amsterdam: John Benjamins.

Tanaka, H. (1999) *Turn-Taking in Japanese Conversation: a study in grammar and interaction*, Amsterdam: John Benjamins.

ten Have, P. (1999). *Doing Conversation Analysis: a practical guide*, Thousand Oaks, CA: Sage.

3 Being out of order

Overlapping talk as evidence of trouble in airline pilots' work

Maurice Nevile

Introduction

Research in conversation analysis (CA) uses recordings of naturally occurring interaction to uncover the language, practices and processes of reasoning by which people accomplish social actions and create the intelligible and recognizable orderliness of everyday life (see Sacks 1992; Hutchby and Wooffitt 1998; ten Have 1999; Wooffitt 2005). As Drew and Curl (this volume) explain, CA shows how patterns in talk reveal how participants produce and understand conduct in interaction, in real time. Drew and Curl (this volume) point to the range of aspects of interaction on which CA focuses, such as turn-taking, the organization of conversational sequences, the structure of turns at talk, the actions that participants undertake, repair (dealing with difficulties in interaction), as well as prosodic and embodied details of interaction. In this chapter I contribute to an expanding direction for research in CA, *interaction in institutions and workplaces* (Drew and Heritage 1992; McHoul and Rapley 2001; Arminen 2005), and focus on an area where CA is well suited to advance discourse analysis: *how talk for work is organized in time*. Participants at work can time their relative turns at talk, moment-to-moment, in ways that realize the interests, demands, goals and constraints of the setting, and so to accomplish work acceptably. I will examine transcriptions from recordings of naturally occurring interaction from one specific collaborative work setting: the airline cockpit.

Generally, I am interested here in the significance of timing in the sequential organization of turns in interaction as evidence for how airline pilots create and understand the progress of their work. Specifically, I examine moments when two pilots talk simultaneously, what CA describes as *overlapping talk*. I will suggest that in the airline cockpit such moments can signify *trouble* in the flow of talk for work. Pilots talking in overlap are talking *out of order*, because overlapping talk is a departure from the typical temporal and sequential order of cockpit talk. Pilots almost always allow one another's talk to emerge complete and in the clear, and so talk only one at a time (Nevile 2007b). Overlapping talk is therefore evidence in talk's very timing of something non-routine, maybe even problematic, in pilots' work together, or for the flight's progress. I conclude by pointing to the future potential value of such CA-based research for developing work practice.[1]

Conversation analysis and temporal order in interaction

An interest in temporal order is a fundamental feature of CA. Analysts have shown the importance to participants themselves of just how and when this or that happens in interaction, to know moment-to-moment just what it is that they are doing and what is going on, what Arminen (2005: x) refers to as the 'time-bound fabric of social actions'. CA is fundamentally concerned with how participants organize matters of *when* and *what next*, and this is reflected in CA's guiding analytic principle: *why that now?* Some CA studies of work, and related research in ethnomethodology, have focused directly on the impact of time for organizing interaction for collaborative work (e.g., Lynch *et al.* 1983; Ochs and Jacoby 1997; Button and Sharrock 1998; Goodwin 1994, 2002).[2] These studies examine how participants collaborate to time their conduct appropriately to accomplish setting-specific work goals, including how participants produce and coordinate their talk and non-talk activities (e.g. gestures, gaze, etc.), use objects and resources, act relative to physical features of the local environment, and respond to evolving circumstances. This chapter furthers a line of research examining how pilots accomplish timeliness and order for talk for work (Nevile 2004a, 2004b, 2005a, 2005b, 2006). I will focus on moments of overlapping talk as evidence of occasions when that timeliness and order is vulnerable (see also Nevile 2007a; Nevile and Walker 2005).

Overlapping talk

The model of turn-taking for ordinary conversation at the heart of CA accounts for the fact that, while usually one party talks at a time, moments of overlapping talk do commonly occur (Sacks *et al.* 1974). More often than not, however, such moments can be accounted for (e.g. as interruption), and participants have various resources for dealing with them (see Schegloff 2000 for a substantial overview of research on overlap, and also Schegloff 2002; Jefferson 2004; and Lerner 2004). In pilots' talk, on the other hand, overlapping talk is unusual, occurring (at most) less than a handful of times per flight (Nevile 2007b; see data in Nevile 2004a). At first this might seem unsurprising, because the content, allocation and order of pilots' turns at talk are scripted for them in advance, and pilots are instructed in training not to speak simultaneously. However, pilots do not always talk according to the script (Nevile 2001, 2004a, 2005a), and to speak one party at a time is something pilots must manage and accomplish in interaction, *in situ* in real time (Nevile 2007b).

Research in CA has shown that a very common type of overlapping talk occurs when one participant starts talking *just as* the other speaker comes to a recognizably possible end of their turn. A recipient *projects* the end of the speaker's turn and starts up as next speaker just a little early (see Schegloff 2000), for example to increase the chances of emerging as next speaker, or to gain something by demonstrating and acting early on an understanding of the turn's trajectory. Airline pilots, however, seem not to do this, even though their talk is highly predictable and projectable. Pilots follow official procedural wordings that act as a script specifying who is to say what, and when. Instead, overlapping talk mostly does not occur because pilots are *oriented* to precisely time new talk to start at the *actual* end of another's turn, when current talk is *actually* ended (Nevile 2007b). An absence of overlapping talk reflects pilots' orientation to the *strictly sequential nature of their work*. Pilots treat turns at talk as they treat the tasks they perform to fly their aircraft, as acceptably occurring such that a next one is begun *only when a prior one is complete*. A new turn, like a new task, becomes relevant only when another has actually been completed. So, what might be happening on those occasions when pilots *do* find themselves talking simultaneously, in overlap?

The data

The transcriptions here are made from audio and video recordings of pilots at work on actual routine passenger flights. Some transcriptions are from recordings I made by arrangement with two Australian airlines. In total I made 18 flights that varied in length from around 40 minutes to over two hours.[3] Other transcriptions are from commercially produced cockpit videos of German airlines. Segments here are therefore taken from different airlines, flights and crews. The transcriptions include technical language, and so for clarity and space I explain only the particular point of interest, and occasionally omit lines of talk not relevant to that point (e.g. overheard radio talk). To preserve anonymity of individual airlines I have changed some wording and use the generic flight descriptor 'Airline One Two Three'. Where necessary I have provided translations from German to English. The transcription system, simplified from the notation originally developed by Gail Jefferson (see e.g. ten Have 1999) is given in full at the end of this chapter.

Being out of order

I will consider segments when talk is treated as expected, relevantly next, but *delayed*, and when one or both pilots treat circumstances as *uncertain* and needing resolution. In either case, overlapping talk is a departure from the orderly flow of talk and action and is evidence of trouble in the pilots' progress through the tasks required to conduct the flight.

Delay

The first two segments show overlapping talk occurring when one pilot treats another's talk as *delayed*, when a pilot does not respond with next talk that could be expected according to formal procedures for the sequential ordering for tasks. Delayed talk signals trouble because it can block the pilots' progress to the next talk and so through the sequence of tasks for the flight (Nevile 2007a). The pilot last to speak treats the delayed talk as accountable by starting up again as speaker to offer a new version of the prior talk, or to initiate the next task regardless. The moment of overlapping talk occurs when the other pilot almost simultaneously produces the expected but delayed talk.

In this first example the pilots finalize preparations for takeoff.[4] The Captain (C) calls ('it's your go', line 3) for the First Officer (FO) to say information for conducting the takeoff, as the Pilot-Flying (PF) in control of the aircraft on this flight (lines 5–6). The First Officer concludes with 'no changes to the brief', (line 6), making relevant an acknowledging response from the Captain. However, this acknowledgement from the Captain is not immediately forthcoming. There are 1.9 seconds of silence before the First Officer pursues the Captain's acknowledgment (Pomerantz 1984) by remodelling his concluding wording with 'as discussed'. The First Officer finds himself talking in overlap as the Captain almost simultaneously begins the delayed acknowledgement.

```
 1          (2.0)
 2   C:            ( ) give us seven four we'll cross ah: one hundred on a heading bug
 3                 (0.9) both to ADF (0.5) a:nd it's your go.
 4          (2.5)
 5   FO:           okay: go-around nine thousand ASEL (0.3) right comma:nd (0.5) and
 6                 ah (0.8) no changes to the brief,
 7          (1.9)
 8   FO:    →      a[s discussed].
 9   C:     →       [that's::]: understood.
10          (4.3)
11   C:            a:nd the checks when you're ready hhh- =
12   FO:           = checks,
13          (1.2)
```

In the second segment a Captain releases the 'flight control lock' ('lock's coming off', line 6), making it now possible for him to call for the First Officer to resume a suspended checklist. That would be a next relevant task once the lock comes off. After ten seconds pass the First Officer treats that call as delayed. He begins to talk for the next item of the checklist ('fli-', line 8), which is the flight control lock, *without* being called by the Captain to do

so. However, the Captain almost simultaneously makes the expected call for
resuming the checklist (line 9), and so the pilots talk briefly in overlap.

```
1           (7.2)
2    C:                  (I) might just turn around eh?
3           (0.4)
4    FO:                 ye:p (.) sounds good.
5           (13.9)
6    C:                  o:kay: lock's coming off,
7           (10.1)
8    FO:    →            fl [i-
9    C:     →               [and the rest of the check.
10   FO:                 flight controls,
11          (0.3)
12   C:                  checked,
13   FO:                 checked and takeoff clearance,
14          (0.5)
15   C:                  not required here:
16          (0.3)
17   FO:                 okay (.) check's complete.
18          (0.5)
```

Here there is only brief overlapping talk because the First Officer cuts off
his talk immediately after the Captain starts up. The First Officer only
resumes once the Captain completes. Despite starting up first, the First
Officer concedes speakership to the Captain, and so orients to the Captain
as the legitimate next speaker who, according to procedure, should first call
for the checklist to be resumed. That call makes it acceptable for the First
Officer to then say the 'challenge' for the next checklist item 'flight controls'
(line 10).

   In these first two segments overlap occurred, breaking the typically orderly
flow of non-overlapping cockpit talk. One pilot treated another's talk as
expected but delayed, and so making trouble for the progression of talk and
action through the sequence of flight tasks. Overlapping talk resulted when
the expected talk and remedy talk were initiated almost simultaneously.

Uncertainty

The next three segments concern a critical cockpit task, receiving clearance
(permission) from Air Traffic Control (ATC), and in each case overlapping talk
occurs when one or both pilots treat an aspect of the clearance as *uncertain*.
In the first two examples the trouble concerns receipt of the clearance, and
in the last example the trouble concerns the content of the clearance.

   The general procedure is that clearance for some action is given, over
the radio, to the pilot responsible for radio duties and acting as the flight's

spokesperson – usually the Pilot-Not-Flying (PNF). Any radio talk to and from controllers is *potentially* hearable to both pilots, but pilots follow procedures to talk for establishing a shared crew awareness of a clearance (see Nevile 2004a for examples of this). Clearance is required for many aspects and stages of a flight, and to act without clearance can be an extremely serious and professionally (even legally) sanctionable lapse, especially because it could lead to flight-threatening situations.

In the first two segments, the overlapping talk is associated with a moment when a Pilot-Flying, the pilot actually in control of the aircraft and who does *not* speak to the controller, asks the other pilot if clearance has been received.

Here a German crew prepare their aircraft for landing. The PNF calls the air traffic controller to announce their position ('established', line 2). The controller's reply is too faint to be transcribed but the PNF heard it because he 'reads back' that the flight is 'cleared to land …' (line 5). Importantly, note that this radio exchange does not become the subject of talk between the two pilots. Instead, 20.5 seconds pass before talk for a new task, then a further 18.8 seconds before the PNF tells the PF '>we have been< cleared to land.' (line 11). It would seem the pilots then establish a shared awareness of the clearance (lines 12–14). However, overlapping talk occurs later as the PNF concludes talk for a different task, the landing checklist, the third task *since* the talk of the clearance (lowering landing gear, extending wing flaps, landing checklist). As the PNF says 'completed', the PF asks in overlap, 'and we've been cleared to land?' (line 24).

1	PNF:	*Muenchen contro:l gruss Gott Airline (.) One Two °Three Four°*
2		*established.* °
3	(1.6)	
4	ATC:	{INAUDIBLE NON-TRANSCRIBABLE REPLY – TOO FAINT}
5	PNF:	*cleared to land zero eight left Airline One Two °Three Four.°*
6	(20.5)	
7	PF:	flaps two.
8	(0.8)	
9	PNF:	flaps two.
10	(18.8)	
11	PNF:	>we have been< cleared to land.=
12	PF:	=cleared to land?=
13	PNF:	=ja. {'yes'}
14	PF:	okay::.
15	(2.7)	
16	PF:	gear down.
17	(0.5)	
18	PNF:	gear down.
		{SOUND OF LANDING GEAR BEING LOWERED}
		{SOME TALK OMITTED, CONCERNING EXTENDING THE WING FLAPS}

```
19          (4.4)
20  PF:        landi:ng (0.2) checklist.=
21  PNF:       =landi:ng (.) all green.
22  PF:        landing all green.
23  PNF:       landing checklist complet[ed::. ]
24  PF:    →                            [and we've] been cleared to land?
25  PNF:       jawohl. {'yes certainly'}
26          (24.0)
```

The PF asks if the flight has landing clearance, even though this matter was covered earlier. It is evidence the PF is still uncertain, but why might he be so? Perhaps the controller's faint (non-transcribable) talk (line 4), and the PNF's delay in formally announcing the clearance (line 11), made the clearance less salient for the PF. The PF did not himself speak to the controller. Also, the earlier sequence of talk to establish crew awareness of the clearance was itself atypical. An unremarkable PF reply would have been an acknowledgement by repeating key wording, with flat or falling intonation, as in 'cleared to land.'. However, the PF's reply is produced with marked rising intonation, as a checking question. We can see that the PNF treats it as a question because he replies 'ja.', to which the PF responds 'okay::.'. This four-turn sequence is overly elaborate relative to routine untroublesome cockpit talk (see Nevile 2004a). It can therefore be evidence that acting on an awareness of the landing clearance is proving possibly problematic for the PF. So we see overlapping talk occurring, talk out of order, when a matter is treated as uncertain and troublesome for conducting tasks for the flight.

In the next segment, also concerning the landing phase of flight, talk to establish shared awareness of a clearance is not delayed, in fact it does not occur. The controller tells the Captain the flight is cleared for 'a visual approach' (line 2), but the Captain does not initiate crew talk about this, nor include the 'visual' clearance in his readback to the controller (which is possibly hearable to the First Officer) (line 5). Instead, after talking to the controller, the Captain prompts the First Officer to discuss speeds to be used (line 7) (the First Officer is the Pilot-Flying on this flight). Much later the First Officer treats the clearance as uncertain, by asking, 'we're cleared for a visual approach?' (line 13). Overlapping talk occurs when the Captain replies.

```
1  ATC:        >Airline One Two Three< ah (.) two miles east centreline and closing,
2              reduce to final approach speed er (1.4) cleared a visual approach
3              caution: wake turbulence, (.) contact tower on final.
4          (1.5)
5  C:          reduce to (.) final approach, tower on final, (.) Airline One Two Three.
6          (0.9)
7  C:          o::kay:: speeds,
8  FO:         okay I might (0.3) decrease: ah: (0.7) to:: one hundred and eight,
```

```
 9          (0.3)
10   FO:           for the approach,
11          (1.8)
                   {FURTHER TALK CONCERNING SPEEDS, OVER APPROXIMATELY 40 SECONDS}
12          (1.1)
13   FO:           we're cleared for a visual approach?=
14   C:            =ye:s [we're] cleared.
15   FO:    →            [okay]
16   FO:           and (gi::ve) (.) spinner (.) standby (spinner out) thanks.
17          (1.8)
```

The overlap occurs when the Captain extends his answer beyond a simple 'yes' by adding 'we're cleared' (line 14). The First Officer starts up after 'yes', a possible point of completion for the Captain's response, and so his 'okay' (line 15) occurs in overlap with the Captain's talk. So, treating a matter as uncertain is again associated with a moment of overlapping talk, a break in the typical ordered flow of cockpit talk.

This last segment is from a German airline flight and includes three instances of overlapping talk. It is a complicated segment but it is particularly revealing of what can go on behind the closed cockpit door. The crew treat as uncertain the taxiway route to take as they prepare to taxi to the runway for takeoff. The controller responsible for aircraft ground movements tells the First Officer his aircraft is to use taxiway 'delta three' (line 4). The pilots do not discuss this part of the taxi clearance. Some seconds later, the Captain asks the First Officer about the taxiway (line 8). The Captain identifies 'delta two', which is *incorrect* (it is *not* the taxiway specified by the controller), but the First Officer *incorrectly agrees* (line 9). The crew could now make a very serious error by using the wrong taxiway. However, a couple of seconds later the Captain asks the First Officer to confirm with the controller (line 12). The Captain treats the matter as still uncertain. The First Officer makes the call (lines 15–19, 23) and both pilots acknowledge the controller's reply with 'okay' (lines 21–2). I will focus first on the overlap occurring later at line 27.

```
 1   FO:           and ground Airline (0.3) one two three request taxi.
 2          (1.5)
 3   ATC:          Airline: one two three (0.2) taxi: (.) cross the bridge (0.5) right
 4                 turn (.) charlie one (0.4) delta three (0.2) to hold behind bay two.
 5          (1.5)
 6   FO:           cross the bridge (.) charlie one delta three:: (0.5) fo:r (0.2) runway
 7                 one three Airline >one two three<.
                   {SOME UNRELATED TURNS OMITTED}
 8   C:            via delta two hat er uns gegeben ne? {'he gave us via Delta two yeah?'}
                   {OVERHEARD RADIO TALK TO/FROM OTHER AIRCRAFT OMITTED}
 9   FO:           via charlie one and delta two ja. {'via charlie one and delta two yes'}
```

```
10              (1.2)
                {OVERHEARD RADIO TALK TO/FROM OTHER AIRCRAFT OMITTED}
11              (0.8)
12    C:        confirm Sie bitte noch[mal {'please confirm it again'}
13    FO:                           [ja   {'yes'}
14              (1.5)
15    FO:       a[nd ah: (0.2) ground] Airline one two three confirm via delta two
16    C:    →    [confirm via delta two.]
17              (3.2)
18    ATC:      Airline one two three (0.3) right turn charlie one delta three
19              (0.3) to hold behind bay three.⁵
20              (0.3)
21    C:        okay.
22    FO:       okay:.
23    FO:       charlie one delta three Airline (0.2) one two three.
24    C:        flaps twenty.
25              (1.2)
26    FO:       fla[ps twenty.
27    C:    →    [aber er hatte ( ) zu delta two gesagt ( )= {'but he had said to delta two'}
28    FO:       =ja:. {'yes'}
```

Long after the taxiway choice is apparently resolved, overlapping talk occurs when the Captain raises the matter again during a later sequence of talk for a new and unrelated task. The Captain has called for the wing flaps to be set (line 24), but *as* the First Officer responds with the required talk for that task (line 26) the Captain begins to talk, initiating and continuing to talk in overlap (line 27). Significantly, the Captain starts up early in the First Officer's turn, well before a point where the First Officer might be heard as completing his turn. This kind of overlap, where one party starts up early in another's current turn, in formal procedural talk for a task, is very unusual in routine airline cockpit data. In many hours of recordings for routine flights I have noted only a few such occurrences, though I found more than one instance of such overlap in the cockpit voice recording for an air accident involving a cargo flight (Nevile and Walker 2005).

While the correct taxiway has now been established, the Captain's talk concerns the origin of the crew's incorrect understanding. At issue here is the responsibility of the error, locating the source of the trouble. He claims the controller had originally told them taxiway 'delta two', and has now told them a different taxiway. This is incorrect. The overlap here is particularly remarkable because it suggests the Captain is now not attending to the First Officer's new on-task talk, confirming the flaps set at twenty. The Captain's talk addresses a matter not immediately relevant for flying the aircraft now, and not the current focus of the First Officer's talk.

I will comment briefly on a second earlier instance of overlap in this segment. The Captain initiates and continues overlapping talk by addressing talk to the First Officer *while* the First Officer is calling the Air Traffic Controller (lines 15–16). The First Officer is carrying out the Captain's request of him to confirm the correct taxiway (line 12). Such overlap is also rarely seen in routine data (Nevile 2004a). The Captain's talk can increase the demands on the First Officer because he is now being spoken to while he is talking to someone else. Evidence of this is that during the overlap the First Officer's turn stalls with 'ah:' and then a (0.2) second silence (line 15).

These last three segments show overlapping talk occurring when pilots treated some matter as uncertain and needing resolution. This occurred when talk for procedures to develop awareness of a controller's clearance was somehow impaired: talk to/from controller was faint, or was not 'read back' to the controller, or was understood incorrectly. In all three segments, pilot–pilot talk about the clearance was delayed or non-existent. In such circumstances the pilot actually in control of the aircraft, whose work is directly impacted by a clearance, treated the clearance as uncertain and needing resolution. Overlapping talk arose when that pilot sought to resolve the uncertainty.

Conclusion

In this chapter I have drawn upon the guiding analytic principle of conversation analysis (CA) – *why that now?* – to examine moments of overlapping (simultaneous) talk in a setting for collaborative work: the airline cockpit. This focus was motivated by an earlier finding that such moments are unusual in cockpit interaction (Nevile 2007b). As they perform tasks, pilots precisely time new turns such that just one pilot talks at a time. Pilots orient to the strictly sequential nature of their work by allowing one another's talk to emerge as complete, even in a setting where talk is highly projectable and so particularly vulnerable to overlap at the end of turns. Pilots create a recognizably ordered flow of talk in time with no overlap.

So, what might be going on when this flow is broken, when two pilots *do* talk at the same time, and one pilot's talk does not emerge complete? Why might pilots occasionally talk *out of order*? Transcriptions from naturally occurring interaction, of pilots talking for work on actual passenger flights, showed that moments of overlapping talk can be evidence of *trouble in the routine and unremarkable temporal order of actions for work*. The examples here were not mere mistiming, but were associated with non-routine or even problematic moments for pilots' progress through flight tasks. Overlapping talk was a break in the typically ordered, non-overlapping flow of talk for tasks. Moments of trouble occurred when talk was treated as *expected but delayed*, or when one or both pilots treated some matter as *uncertain*.

I considered two areas where CA research is well placed to advance discourse analysis: interaction at and for work; and specifically, the significance of how *talk is organized in time* for accomplishing collaborative work. As an approach to the discourse of institutions and workplaces, CA's particular strength lies in its detailed transcriptions and focus on the practices by which participants themselves, moment-to-moment, create and understand what it is they are doing, and what is going on. CA can explore how institutions are 'talked into being' (Heritage 1984: 290) through patterns of talk in interaction. CA can shed light on the significance of how talk at work emerges in time, not just for the moment, for one exchange or sequence of turns, but as part of an extended temporal and sequential order to perform actions and so realize the wider goals and constraints of the specific setting.

Studies in conversation analysis and ethnomethodology can show how non-typical or deviant instances of a phenomenon can reveal aspects of taken-for-granted locally created order (Heritage 1984: 291–2; Lynch *et al.* 1983: 223), and can be examined for why that order was threatened or not realized on some specific occasion. In the airline cockpit, moments of overlapping talk were notable as deviations from the typical flow of turns in the cockpit, from how cockpit talk typically emerges in real time as a recognizable, acceptable and constitutive feature of interaction for pilots' work. Trouble in the temporal flow of pilots' talk was associated with trouble in the flow of pilots' understanding and action for performing tasks.

CA's analytic principles and methods for analysing the real-time details of interaction therefore make it valuable for identifying the taken-for-granted *in situ* competencies for performing work (Peräkylä and Vehviläinen 2003). Attention to turn-taking and sequence organization make CA especially able to examine competent timing. In many work settings, like the airline cockpit, a critical feature of competent conduct is to talk and act at just the right time, relative to task progress, others' contributions, and evolving circumstances (Nevile 2004b, 2007b). CA can uncover what participants themselves treat as competent timing, as evidenced in their own conduct, and also how such competencies are learned in the course of work. For example, in the complex sequential organization of talk and non-talk activities for surgical team work, we can see how the precise timing of questions (Mondada in press) or gestures (Koschmann *et al.* 2007) is consequential for instruction and learning, and specifically for how the less-expert learn to see and understand features of the body and medical procedures in relevant and situation-bound ways. Or, in the airline cockpit, a captain might *and*-preface a turn to prompt a junior ranked and usually less experienced first officer to initiate an action that is now due, and so make available and knowable the appropriate timing of an action within an extended and predetermined sequence of actions for tasks to complete a flight (Nevile 2007a).

Lastly, CA investigations of temporality for talk at work can potentially inform professional practice and offer a new perspective on intractable issues for particular work settings. For example, in commercial aviation and related research in aviation human factors psychology, and in air accident investigation, there is growing interest in better understanding pilots' communication and behaviour, because 'human factors' are a contributing factor in most airline accidents (Faith 1998; and see Nevile 2004a). When analyzing recorded voice data for accidents, often a great deal rests on investigators' interpretations of what a pilot said, or what was meant by what was said, or how talk was understood, or how the mood in the cockpit or the pilots' working relationship could best be described. Research in CA and ethnomethodology may enlighten such interpretations. In particular, it can address recent calls in aviation circles to examine how moments of uncertainty, confusion, distraction, and human error emerge and are managed, to 'reconstruct the unfolding mindset [of the people involved] in parallel and tight connection with how the world was evolving around these people at the time' (Dekker 2001: 39).

Overlapping talk, at least in the form of simultaneous radio transmissions, was a contributing factor in the greatest air disaster in history, the 1977 runway collision of two Boeing 747 aircraft at the Canary Islands (Faith 1998: 175–8). In my own transcription and analysis of a half-hour cockpit voice recording (CVR) for an Australian air accident, I found around 20 instances of overlapping talk (Nevile and Walker 2005). The official investigation, a few years earlier, had pointed to problems in the pilots' communication, and that the pilots were not working in harmony. I suggested that frequent overlapping talk possibly contributed to the creation of an interactional context for the pilots' error that contributed to the accident.

In the airline cockpit, overlapping talk might be an interaction and human factors equivalent of automated technological warnings. It can signal possible evidence of trouble, not in the functioning of aircraft systems or the flight's progress, but in the functioning and progress of pilots' conduct together. We saw here that overlapping talk might make maximally salient to pilots a moment of delay or uncertainty, two potential threats to pilots' work, *as* such a moment. As they continually monitor that all's well, pilots could attend not only to flashing alert lights, alarm tones, and voiced alerts, but also to overlapping talk as a deviation from the routine sequential flow and timing of their talk together.

Transcription notation

C	Captain (pilot of senior rank, with ultimate command/responsibility of a flight)
FO	First Officer (pilot of junior rank relative to Captain)
PF	Pilot-Flying (pilot in control of the flight)
PNF	Pilot-Not-Flying (pilot assisting the PF)
ATC	Air Traffic Control
[ ]	Overlapping talk, occurring simultaneously with other talk
=	No hearable break or gap between turns (latched turns)
→	Indicates the line of interest
Airline One	Talk over the radio (e.g. to/from air traffic control)
<u>set</u>	Talk that is louder than surrounding talk
°three°	Talk that is quieter than surrounding talk

<set>	Talk that is slower than surrounding talk
>set<	Talk that is faster than surrounding talk
se:::t	Lengthening of a sound. The longer the sound the more colons
.	Falling pitch
,	Flat or slightly rising intonation, talk which sounds incomplete
?	Rising pitch
hh-	Outbreath
fli-	Talk which is cut off abruptly
(3.4), (0.3)	Silence measured in seconds and tenths of seconds
(.)	Silence of less than a fifth of a second i.e. less than (0.2)
(checked)	Doubt about transcription of talk
( )	Talk which could not be transcribed
{OMITTED}	Explanatory comment
{'yes'}	English translation

Notes

1 This research was supported by a research fellowship at the University of Canberra, Australia. I thank Johanna Rendle-Short for helpful comments on early notes from which I developed the ideas here.
2 See also research outside the CA and ethnomethodology tradition, for example papers by Lemke and Scollon in Norris and Jones (2005).
3 I thank the two Australian airlines that allowed me to film their crews, and especially the captains and crews who welcomed me aboard. The airlines' involvement was limited to assistance for collecting recorded data, and so I am entirely responsible for all transcriptions, analyses, and interpretations.
4 Nevile (2007b) gives an earlier discussion of this example.
5 The bay number (is it two or three?) is discussed by the pilots later.

References

Arminen, I. (2005) *Institutional Interaction: studies of talk at work*, Aldershot: Ashgate.

Button, G. and Sharrock, W. (1998) 'The organizational accountability of technological work', *Social Studies of Science*, 28(1): 73–102.

Dekker, S.W.A. (2001) 'The disembodiment of data in the analysis of human factors accidents', *Human Factors and Aerospace Safety*, 1: 39–57.

Drew, P. and Heritage, J. (eds) (1992) *Talk at Work: interaction in institutional settings*, Cambridge: Cambridge University Press.

Faith, N. (1998) *Black Box: the final investigations*, 2nd edn, London: Boxtree.

Goodwin, C. (1994) 'Professional vision', *American Anthropologist*, 96(3): 606–33.

—— (2002) 'Time in action', *Current Anthropology*, 43, Supplement, S19–35.

Heath, C. and Luff, P. (2000) *Technology in Action*, Cambridge: Cambridge University Press.

Heritage, J. (1984) *Garfinkel and Ethnomethodology*, Cambridge: Polity Press.

Hutchby, I. and Wooffitt, R. (1998) *Conversation Analysis: principles, practices and applications*, Cambridge: Polity Press.

Jefferson, G. (2004) 'A sketch of some orderly aspects of overlap in natural conversation', in G. Lerner (ed.) *Conversation Analysis: studies from the first generation*, Amsterdam and Philadelphia, PA: John Benjamins.

Koschmann, T., LeBaron, C., Goodwin, C., Zemel, A. and Dunnington, G. (2007) 'Formulating the triangle of doom', *Gesture*, 7(1): 97–118.

Lerner, G.H. (2004) 'Collaborative turn sequences', in G. Lerner (ed.) *Conversation Analysis: studies from the first generation*, Amsterdam and Philadelphia, PA: John Benjamins.

Lynch, M., Livingston, E. and Garfinkel, H. (1983) 'Temporal order in laboratory work', in J. Coulter (ed.) *Ethnomethodological Sociology*, Brookfield, VT: Edward Elgar.

McHoul, A. and Rapley, M. (eds) (2001) *How to Analyse Talk in Institutional Settings: a casebook of methods*, London: Continuum International.

Mondada, L. (in press) 'La compétence comme dimension située et contingente, localement évaluée par les participants', *Bulletin VALS-ASLA*, 84, Winter 2006–2007.

Nevile, M. (2001) 'Understanding who's who in the airline cockpit: pilots' pronominal choices and cockpit roles', in A. McHoul and M. Rapley (eds) *How to Analyse Talk in Institutional Settings: a casebook of methods*, London and New York: Continuum.

—— (2004a) *Beyond the Black Box: talk-in-interaction in the airline cockpit*, Aldershot: Ashgate.

—— (2004b) 'Integrity in the airline cockpit: embodying claims about progress for the conduct of an approach briefing', *Research on Language and Social Interaction*, 37(4): 447–80.

—— (2005a) '"Checklist complete." Or is it? Closing a task in the airline cockpit', *Australian Review of Applied Linguistics*, 28(2): 60–76.

—— (2005b) 'You always have to land: accomplishing the sequential organization of actions to land an airliner', in S. Norris and R. Jones (eds) *Discourse in Action: introducing mediated discourse analysis*, London: Routledge.

—— (2006) 'Making sequentiality salient: *and*-prefacing in the talk of airline pilots', *Discourse Studies*, 8(2): 279–302.

—— (2007a) 'Action in time: ensuring timeliness for collaborative work in the airline cockpit', *Language in Society*, 36(2): 233–57.

—— (2007b) 'Talking without overlap in the airline cockpit: precision timing at work', *Text & Talk*, 27(2): 225–49.

Nevile, M. and Walker, M.B. (2005) 'A context for error: using conversation analysis to represent and analyse recorded voice data', *Human Factors and Aerospace Safety*, 5(2): 109–35.

Norris, S. and Jones, R. (eds) (2005) *Discourse in Action: introducing mediated discourse analysis*, London: Routledge.

Ochs, E. and Jacoby, S. (1997) 'Down to the wire: the cultural clock of physicists and the discourse of consensus', *Language in Society*, 26: 479–505.

Peräkylä, A. and Vehviläinen, S. (2003) 'Conversation analysis and the professional stocks of interactional knowledge', *Discourse and Society*, 14(6): 727–50.

Pomerantz, A. (1984) 'Pursuing a response', in J.M. Atkinson and J. Heritage (eds), *Structures of Social Action: studies in conversation analysis*, Cambridge: Cambridge University Press.

Sacks, H. (1992) *Lectures on Conversation*, 2 vols, ed. Gail Jefferson, Oxford: Basil Blackwell.

Sacks, H., Schegloff, E.A. and Jefferson, G. (1974) 'A simplest systematics for the organization of turn-taking for conversation', *Language*, 50: 696–735.

Schegloff, E.A. (2000) 'Overlapping talk and the organization of turn-taking for conversation', *Language in Society*, 29: 1–63.

—— (2002) 'Accounts of conduct in interaction: interruption, overlap, and turn-taking', in J.H. Turner (ed.), *Handbook of Sociological Theory*, New York: Kluwer Academic/Plenum Publishers.

ten Have, P. (1999) *Doing Conversation Analysis: a practical guide*, London: Sage.

Wooffitt, R. (2005) *Conversation Analysis and Discourse Analysis: a comparative and critical introduction*, London: Sage.

Suggestions for further work

1 Gather a small corpus of conversations around a particular kind of task in an institutional or workplace setting. Identify places in the corpus in which the task seemed to be progressing successfully and times when problems arose and analyse them in terms of their timing and sequential organization. Explore the extent to which deviations from the formal organization of conversation can predict problems in task accomplishment.

2 Choose a particular kind of conversational action (making a request or an apology, for example) and track the different grammatical forms it takes through a range of conversations. Explore how syntactic forms may be related to particular parts or stages in conversations and with particular conversational circumstances and contingencies.

3 Drew and Curl define conversation analysis as an approach to social action and identify its central concern as discovering 'evidence of *practice* in conduct'. Two other approaches represented in this book – critical discourse analysis and mediated discourse analysis – also concern themselves with social action and social practice. What are the differences between the way conversation analysis defines and approaches 'action' and 'practice' and the ways these concepts are treated in other perspectives?

4 Conversation analysis has been accused of not paying sufficient attention to the workings of power in interaction. Think of how the methods illustrated by Nevile and Drew and Curl can inform our understanding of the power relations between speakers in different settings and the implications of such questions for the development of conversation analysis, especially in workplace or institutional settings that you might be interested in.

5 Drew and Curl demonstrate how conversation analysis can be enriched by attention to such issues as grammar and syntax. What other ways can the study of grammar inform conversation analysis? Which other areas in linguistics can be fruitfully blended with conversation analysis, and which cannot?

Part II

Ethnographic-based discourse analysis

In sharp contrast to the fine-grained analysis of the moment-by-moment mechanics of social interaction advocated by conversation analysts are more ethnographic approaches to studying verbal communication in context. In such approaches conversations are just part of a wide range of data, which include as well observations, interviews with participants and subjective impressions of the researcher. It is important to remember, however, as Lin points out in her chapter in this part, that, although conversation analysis and ethnography use very different tools and hold sharply varying perspectives on the nature of discourse, the aims of these two approaches are essentially the same: to uncover the shared norms or cultural conventions governing *who* can say *what, when* in particular communicative situations. Whereas conversation analysts go about this through a detailed analysis of a restricted range of data, ethnographers seek to understand these issues through a 'thick description' of the cultural and conceptual world in which their subjects live (Geertz 1973).

Although they owe their greatest debt to American anthropological linguistics (see, for example, Hymes 1974) and its commitment to 'understanding of the crucial role played by language (and other semiotic resources) in the constitution of society and its cultural representations' (Duranti 2001: 5), ethnographic approaches to discourse also owe much to other approaches to discourse including genre studies (Bazerman 1994; Bhatia 1993), activity theory (Engeström and Middleton 1996), critical discourse analysis (Fairclough 1992), socio-cultural approaches to learning (Lave and Wenger 1991; Rogoff 1990), and the archaeology of knowledge (Foucault 1972).

The rather broad perspective ethnography takes in its project to explore lives of participants as they live them has, in fact, led to a kind of theoretical eclecticism, resulting in, as Smart points out in his chapter, a wide variety of approaches, each specific to particular researchers and their individual repertoire of theories. Ethnography has also significantly influenced other approaches to discourse, in particular Wodak's brand of critical discourse analysis, which has involved critical ethnographic studies in such areas as anti-Semitism, racism, nationalism and unemployment (see, for example,

Reisigl and Wodak 2000), work on linguistic ideologies by researchers like Schieffelin (see, for example, Schieffelin *et al.* 1998), as well as studies on gender and discourse such as those conduced by Ochs (see, for example, Ochs 1991). It has also played a large role in the development of more recent approaches to discourse, notably mediated discourse analysis and multimodal discourse analysis.

Ethnographic approaches to discourse have proven especially fruitful in explorations of the 'construction of knowledge' in schools and workplaces (see, for example, Cross 2001; Engeström and Middleton 1996), as both the chapters in this volume illustrate. In his chapter, Smart demonstrates how ethnographic approaches can be applied to the study of discourse use in a large financial organization (the Bank of Canada) as well to tertiary educational settings to understand the ways students make transitions from the discursive practices expected of them at university to those expected of them in the world of work. In his discussion Smart also underlines a number of important issues central to ethnographic approaches to discourse, perhaps most important being the need for ethnographers to strike a balance between theoretical concepts – those which they bring with them to the field – and empirically grounded concepts – those which grow out of the lived experience of participants. Both conversation analysts and ethnographers are engaged in a search for *patterns*, but, whereas conversation analysts look for 'objective' patterns within actual talk, ethnographers attempt to discover what Smart calls 'patterns of intersubjectivity' in their social engagement with participants.

Lin's chapter illustrates how an ethnographic approach to discourse can be combined with activity theory to understand the contextual motivations behind particular questioning strategies in classrooms. Her chapter also presents a challenge to approaches that claim to uncover local ways of 'sense making' through the micro-analysis of talk. The 'local rationality' of many classroom practices, she argues, cannot be truly understood without reference to the larger activity systems and institutional cultures in which they are situated, and attempts to change such practices and introduce and sustain new models of pedagogy will require broader institutional and systemic changes.

Useful further reading on ethnographic approaches to discourse can be found in Agar (1986), Heath (1980), Philipsen (1992) and Saville-Troike (1982).

References

Agar, M. (1986) *Speaking of Ethnography*, Thousand Oaks, CA: Sage.

Bazerman, C. (1994) 'Systems of genres and the enactment of social intentions', in A. Freedman and P. Medway (eds) *Genre and the New Rhetoric*, London: Taylor & Francis, pp. 79–101.

Bhatia, V. (1993) *Analysing Genre*, London and New York: Longman.

Cross, G.A. (2001) *Forming the Collective Mind: a contextual exploration of large-scale collaborative writing in industry*, Cresskill, NJ: Hampton Press.

Duranti, A. (2001) 'Linguistic anthropology: history, ideas, and issues', in A. Duranti (ed.) *Linguistic Anthropology: a reader*, Malden, MA: Blackwell.

Engeström, Y. and Middleton, D. (eds) (1996) *Cognition and Communication at Work*, Cambridge: Cambridge University Press.

Fairclough, N. (1992) *Discourse and Social Change*, Cambridge: Polity Press.

Foucault, M. (1972) *The Archeology of Knowledge and the Discourse on Language*, New York: Pantheon Books.

Geertz, C. (1973) *The Interpretation of Cultures*, New York: Basic.

Heath, S.B. (1980) *Ways with Words: language, life and work in communities and classrooms*, Cambridge: Cambridge University Press.

Hymes, D. (1974) *Foundations in Sociolinguistics: an ethnographic approach*, Philadelphia, PA: University of Pennsylvania Press.

Lave, J. and Wenger, E. (1991) *Situated Learning: legitimate peripheral participation*, Cambridge: Cambridge University Press.

Ochs, E. (1991) 'Indexing gender: language as an interactive phenomenon', in A. Duranti and C. Goodwin (eds) *Rethinking Context*, Cambridge, Cambridge University Press, pp. 335–58.

Philipsen, G. (1992) *Speaking Culturally: explorations in social communication*, Albany, NY: State University of New York Press.

Reisigl, M. and Wodak, R. (2000) *Discourse and Discrimination: rhetorics of racism and anti-semitism*, London and New York: Routledge.

Rogoff, B. (1990) *Apprenticeship in Thinking: cognitive development in social context*, Cambridge: Cambridge University Press.

Saville-Troike, M. (1982) *The Ethnography of Communication: an introduction*, New York: Basil Blackwell, Inc.

Schieffelin, B.B., Woolard, K.A. and Kroskrity, P.V. (eds) (1998) *Language Ideologies: practice and theory*, Oxford: Oxford University Press.

4 Ethnographic-based discourse analysis

Uses, issues and prospects

Graham Smart

This chapter considers the potential of ethnographic-based discourse analysis for studying learning and knowledge-making in school and workplace settings. The chapter describes the uses of the methodology, discusses five related issues, looks at two of the author's own ethnographic studies for illustrative purposes, and reflects on future prospects for ethnographic-based discourse analysis.

Uses for research

I want to begin by differentiating between two terms: 'method' and 'methodology'. While these terms are used interchangeably by some researchers, others, myself included, find it useful to distinguish between them. According to this distinction, a method is a set of procedures for collecting and analysing research data. A methodology, on the other hand, is broader: a methodology is a method *plus* an underlying set of ideas about the nature of reality and knowledge. With this distinction in mind, then, how can the methodology of ethnographic-based discourse analysis best be described? I will approach this question by invoking as a touchstone the 'interpretive ethnography' originated by the anthropologist Geertz in the 1970s and developed over the decades since by researchers such as Adler and Adler (1988), Agar (1986), Hammersley and Atkinson (1995), Denzin (1997) and Van Maanen (1988). For Geertz (1973: 24), the goal of interpretive ethnography is 'to aid us in gaining access to the conceptual world in which our subjects live'.

Interpretive ethnography in the Geertzian tradition is used to explore a particular social group's discourse practices – as these are instantiated in writing, speaking, or other symbolic actions – in order to learn how members of the group view and operate within their mutually constructed conceptual world. The goal of such research is to gain a quasi-insider's understanding of how group members interact and communicate with one another, what they believe and value, how they define and solve problems, how they create and apply knowledge, and how they accomplish learning and work. Ethnographers use a variety of methods for gathering data, including participant observation, interviews, text analysis, surveys and focus groups. As data are gathered and analysed, the researcher works to produce a 'thick description' of the local conceptual world that is discursively created and maintained by the group under study.

Ethnographic-based discourse analysis is particularly appropriate for exploring learning and knowledge-making in school and workplace settings. Indeed, Geertz (1983: 156) specifically advocates the efficacy of interpretive ethnography for studying knowledge-building in the local spheres of academic and professional activity that comprise 'modern thought'. For Geertz (1983: 153), this research, in viewing cognition as largely social in nature – a 'matter of trafficking in the symbolic forms available within a particular community' – would focus on 'systems of symbols' (1983: 182) as 'modes of thought, idiom to be interpreted' (1983: 120). With its focus on a social group's discourse practices – on its situated use of language and other symbol systems – interpretive ethnography provides a unique approach to discourse analysis, one that allows researchers to explore and describe in detail the social contexts within which texts are produced, read, and used in activities of learning and knowledge-making. Notable works that do this are Latour and Woolgar's *Laboratory Life: the construction of social facts* (1979), Heath's *Ways with Words: language, life and work in communities and classrooms* (1980), Prior's *Writing/Disciplinarity: a sociohistoric account of literate activity in the academy* (1998), and Swales's *Other Floors, Other Voices: a textography of a small university building* (1998).

Methodological issues

I now want to consider five issues associated with ethnographic-based discourse analysis – some seen in the methodological literature and others that have come up for me as I have read ethnographic accounts by other researchers. The first issue is one of definition: what kind of research 'qualifies' as ethnography, and what does not? Here I would like to make several further distinctions. One sometimes sees the terms 'ethnography', 'qualitative research', 'naturalistic research' and 'field research' used as synonyms. I would argue for the benefit of maintaining a clear distinction between ethnography, on the one hand, and the broader terms qualitative research, naturalistic research and field research on the other. Ethnography, at least as conceived in the Geertzian tradition, is a more specific term than the others, with ethnography seen as one particular kind of qualitative or naturalistic or field research.

I would also advocate for differentiating between the terms 'ethnography' and 'case study'. While these two terms are also sometimes used interchangeably, I think it useful to distinguish between a case study, which focuses on a small number of informants in their everyday rounds of life or on a single significant event, and an ethnography, which looks at the local culture of a social group, viewed as a collective, and produces a holistic account of the shared conceptual world that is discursively constructed and maintained by the group.

A further distinction pertains to ethnography and textual analysis. Some researchers have used the term 'textual ethnography' to refer to historical studies that analyse a body of written texts produced over a period of time in the past by a particular social group. While such texts can clearly constitute a very rich kind of data and lead to important findings, I would suggest that it muddies the waters to refer to a historical study limited to written texts as an ethnography.

Another matter related to defining ethnography is the length of time a researcher needs to spend in a given site in order to produce an ethnographic account. Although it is difficult to provide a specific standard here, if we keep in mind that the goal of ethnography is to study the discourse of a social group broadly and deeply enough to eventually acquire a quasi-insider's understanding of the group's life-world, this is clearly not the work of a day or a week or a month. I have a cautionary anecdote here. A few years ago, a well-known scholar, someone whose work I respect very much, asked me whether I thought that a study based on a single morning's visit to a business organization, in which one of her research assistants had interviewed several employees and gathered some documents, could be described as an ethnography. I told her that, definitely, I would have to say not. This is an extreme example, I think, of what Rist (1980) has called 'hit and run forays' into the field or 'blitzkrieg ethnography'. Inevitably, ethnographic-based discourse analysis demands a considerable commitment of time. But more on this theme later.

A second issue that I wish to raise concerns the meaning of the term 'thick description' as originated by Geertz. While the notion has been taken by some methodologists and researchers to mean simply a highly detailed account of a culture (quite understandably, given the face meaning of the phrase), a close look at Geertz's work and methodological logic reveals something much more specific. For Geertz (1973: 14), a thick description of the culture of a social group comprises an account of that group's 'interworked systems of construable signs', its 'structures of meaning ... and systems of symbols' (1973: 182) and its 'mutually reinforcing network of social understandings' (1983: 156). In other words, a thick description is an account of the discursive system used by the members of a social group to construct a particular shared version of reality, a unique conceptual world.

A third issue to address here relates to the relationship between ethnography and theory. I want to approach this by considering the relationship between ethnography and theory at different points in the research process. Some commentators have suggested that a researcher should begin the study of a given social group unencumbered by any particular theories, in order to see more directly and clearly what is going on within the group. Other commentators have claimed that a researcher cannot hope to produce theory as the outcome of an ethnographic project since the findings are site-specific and therefore entirely ungeneralizable.

Regarding the first concern, whether it is permissible for a researcher to begin an ethnographic study with certain theoretical notions already in mind, I would argue that not only is this permissible, it is both advisable and pretty much inevitable. As researchers, we all have theoretical constructs with which we are familiar from previous work, and we naturally tend to bring these theoretical constructs with us into the field. To support this view, I refer once again to Geertz. As we have seen, for Geertz (1973: 14) the goal of interpretive ethnography is to produce a 'thick description' of a social group's 'interworked systems of construable signs', its 'structures of meaning ... and systems of symbols' (1973: 182). And according to Geertz, the way a researcher develops such an account is to bring together two types of concepts, what Geertz calls 'experience-near' concepts and 'experience-distant' concepts. He distinguishes between these types of concepts in this way:

> An experience-near concept is, roughly, one in which someone – a patient, a subject, in our case an informant – might himself naturally and effortlessly use to define what he or his fellows see, feel, think, imagine and so on, and which he would readily understand when similarly applied by others. An experience-distant concept is one which specialists of one sort or another – an analyst, an experimenter, an ethnographer – employ to forward their scientific, philosophical, or practical aims.
>
> (Geertz 1983: 57)

According to Geertz, the ethnographer's job is to take the informants' own indigenous, locally produced concepts and 'place them in illuminating connection' with the 'concepts theorists have fashioned to capture the general features of social life' in order to produce 'an interpretation of the way a people lives which is neither imprisoned within their mental horizons, ... nor systematically deaf to the distinctive tonalities of their existence' (1983: 57). The result of this merging of the researcher's disciplinary theories with the informants' own locally produced theories about the way their world works is a 'thick description' of the community's meaning-making activity – of its 'symbolic action' (1973: 27) – a description that 'hovers over' the informants' 'experience-near' constructs of reality (1973: 25). This brings us to the other question of whether ethnographers can contribute to theory-building in their disciplines. Can the thick description of a particular social group's discourse and conceptual world be used to generalize about social life beyond the specific case? I believe the answer to this question is a qualified 'yes', a claim I return to in discussing my study of economists at the Bank of Canada.

The fourth issue of concern here is whether, and if so how, an ethnographic researcher can maintain a balanced, critical perspective vis-à-vis the conceptual reality created and inhabited by the informants in his or her study. As we have seen, ethnography-based discourse analysis, in offering a way of investigating the discourse practices employed by a social group in constructing its particular life-world, provides an effective way of examining intellectual collaboration within an academic or professional community. Having said this, however, we need to acknowledge the caveat that a researcher studying the discourse practices of his or her informants must attempt to maintain a balance of *engagement with* and *detachment from* the informant's conceptual reality. The researcher must be able to explore and describe this reality without over-identifying with it and forgetting that it is a cultural construction.

To address this particular issue, we need first to consider the ethnographic researcher's engagement with the group under study. Geertz (1983: 58) claims that the researcher must 'swim in the stream of the subjects' experience' in order to gain access to their conceptual world. To accomplish this, the researcher needs to interact with members of the group over an extended period of time, usually focusing on a particular cluster of informants. In part, what the researcher is seeking are converging perspectives – commonalities across the informants' utterances (in whatever discursive form these might take) – that point to significant areas of intersubjectivity: domains of shared focus, perception and understanding. Ultimately, the researcher's aim is to connect observed areas of intersubjectivity into a larger pattern, to map out the features of the group's shared conceptual world.

Given this aim, a researcher intent on studying the life-world of a social group in a school or workplace setting must attempt to map out its locally constructed reality, or world-view, through ongoing social engagement with the informants. However, this brings with it the danger that in working intensively over an extended period of time to develop an understanding of the group's world-view, the researcher may come to identify with this world-view too closely, unable to see beyond it as is necessary if the researcher is to situate it within the broader currents of social life. To head off this danger, the researcher must find a way of balancing engagement with the group under study with a degree of detachment. In this vein, Latour and Woolgar (1986: 278) point to the importance of 'maintaining analytic distance upon explanations of activity prevalent within the culture being observed'. Similarly, Hammersley and Atkinson (1995: 102) counsel researchers to avoid 'total commitment', 'surrender' or 'becoming' – so that some part of the researcher's attention and awareness is held back, some degree of critical distance retained. The dilemma for the researcher, of course, is how to preserve adequate critical distance from the world-view of the social group under study as he or she works intensively to develop an account of the group's culture. I will consider this question again shortly when discussing my Bank of Canada study.

The final issue I want to raise is whether, and under what conditions, ethnographic-based discourse analysis is compatible with other methodologies?

Can ethnographic-based discourse analysis be combined with another approach within a single research project? This is a leading question, admittedly, and my answer to it is 'yes' – ethnographic-based discourse analysis can indeed be effectively combined with another approach within a research project, under certain conditions. Once again, I will take up this issue later in the chapter in describing a study that a co-researcher and I have been conducting.

Two ethnographic studies

To illustrate the uses of ethnographic-based discourse analysis and to provide a context for further considering several of the methodological issues mentioned above, I will describe two of my own ethnographic studies. The first is a recently completed research project at the Bank of Canada, in Ottawa, which examined the technology-supported discourse practices of the Bank's economists. The second is a multiple-site 'participatory action research' study in which a co-researcher and I collaborated with 24 student-interns from a university professional writing programme to investigate how writing functioned within the interns' worksites and to observe what the interns experienced as they moved from classroom to professional setting.

The Bank of Canada study – a single-researcher, single-site ethnography

In my study at the Bank of Canada, the country's central bank, I explored the work-world and intellectual collaboration of the organization's approximately 275 economists (Smart 2006). Drawing on qualitative data gathered over more than two decades, the study explores two aspects of the economists' discourse practices. First, it looks at how the economists employ a set of written and oral genres, used together with the technology of computer-run economic models, to collaborate in creating specialized knowledge about current and future developments in the Canadian economy and in applying this knowledge in directing national monetary policy. Second, the study investigates the economists' use of another set of technology-supported discourse genres to orchestrate the Bank's external communications with government, the media, the business sector, financial markets, labour and academia – communications that for a central bank are essential to maintaining public legitimacy as the national monetary-policy authority.

The Bank of Canada study, an interpretive ethnography in the Geertzian mould, presents a thick description of the discursive system employed by the Bank's economists to construct a conceptual world featuring a shared understanding of economic reality. The study exemplifies the distinction between an ethnography of a social group and a case study of one or several informants or of a single event. The account produced through the study draws on interviews with 32 Bank economists at different levels in the organizational hierarchy to depict the culture of their professional community.

On the question of how much time a researcher needs to spend in a site in order to produce an authentic ethnography, my study at the Bank of Canada covered 23 years – 14 years as an in-house writing consultant and trainer in which I continuously gathered and analysed data, and nine years of sporadic but fruitful research after I left the organization (this time-span is obviously exceptional). Based on this experience and that of other ethnographers, I would suggest that a researcher employing the Geertzian approach to ethnographic-based discourse analysis needs to spend months, and ideally a year or more, regularly observing in a site in order to produce a thick description of a social group's life-world. Admittedly, this is a rather imprecise standard and is intended to be suggestive rather than prescriptive.

On the issue of the relationship between ethnography and theory, and the question of whether a researcher can begin a study with certain theories already in mind as conceptual tools, I have mentioned that I think the answer is 'yes'. In my case, I came to the study of the Bank's economists already working under the influence of the theoretical concepts of epistemic rhetoric, genre and inscription, and then went to the theoretical well along the way to draw on concepts of modelling, activity, distributed cognition, situated learning, intertextuality, multimodality, organizational change and the social production of information to help me interpret my data. An implication of this, of course, is that an ethnographic account is inevitably distinctive in nature – specific to a particular researcher and his or her individual repertoire of theories.

A related question is whether the accounts constructed by ethnographers can contribute to theory-building in their disciplines. Can a thick description, the ethnographic account of a particular community's discursively constructed life-world, be assumed to hold for other social groups in other settings? Clearly, we need to be cautious here: a researcher cannot legitimately move from producing an account of a single professional organization, for example, to claiming that the 'grounded' theory (Glaser and Strauss 1967) derived from this account will necessarily apply to other organizations. But I would contend that my account of the Bank *can* serve as a heuristic for researchers wishing to examine the discourse practices and intellectual collaboration of other professional groups. In this vein, Eisner (2001: 141) argues persuasively for the wider heuristic use of theory produced by qualitative studies of specific local sites:

> [Theory] distills particulars in ways that foster generalizability. Although theory loses some local color when particulars are left behind, theory makes distinctions and packages thematic relationships so that they will travel well; when we distill, we come away from a research site with ideas that can sensitize us to situations and events like the ones from which the

theory was derived ... The generalizations derived from qualitative case studies are essentially heuristic devices intended to sharpen perception so that our patterns of seeking and seeing are more acute.

Indeed I would go somewhat further than Eisner does. Unless the Bank of Canada is completely unique, which is unlikely given the similar role and culture of central banks around the world and the Bank's continual interactions with other national and international organizations, I would suggest that some aspects of the ethnographic account produced from my study very likely do apply to other professional organizations. One reason for this is that in many ways the account accords with ethnographic research by other scholars on the discourse practices of professionals in a variety of other organizational sites. For example, Winsor (US engineers), Schryer (Canadian veterinarians), Harper (staff at the International Monetary Fund) and Van Nostrand (government and industry actors in the US defence procurement system) have all produced ethnographic accounts of professional discourse that resonate with certain findings of my study. I think it reasonable to assume, therefore, that aspects of my account are likely to be applicable to other professional organizations, perhaps in a descending scale of probability:

– Bank of Canada
– other central banks
– other economic policy organizations
– other public-policy organizations
– other professional organizations.

At the same time, however, the question of how applicable specific findings from my study of the discourse practices and intellectual collaboration of the Bank's economists are to any other particular professional organization could only be determined by on-site research in that organization.

The student-intern study – a collaborative multiple-site ethnography

My co-researcher Nicole Brown and I conducted a study of student-interns from an undergraduate professional writing programme in a large university in the US Midwest (Smart and Brown 2002, 2006). I refer to this study primarily to demonstrate how ethnographic-based discourse analysis can be combined with another research methodology within a single project. The caveat here is that the two methodologies need to share similar assumptions about the nature of reality and knowledge.

The study included data gathered from 40 student-interns over a four-year period. During the final two years of the project, Nicole and I combined ethnographic-based discourse analysis and 'participatory action research' to collaborate with 24 student-interns as fellow researchers. The interns worked in a variety of professional organizations, including high-tech companies, newspapers, a magazine, a university press, a media and public relations firm, an auto manufacturing plant and a number of non-profit organizations. The interns typically spent 10 hours a week in their host organizations over a 15-week period, and also participated in a weekly two-hour internship class team-taught by Nicole and me. In their worksites, the interns produced various written genres, including print- and web-based user documentation, computer-based training materials, newspaper and magazine articles, texts for museum displays, newsletters, employee handbooks, grant proposals, websites and scripts for TV and radio. In our study, Nicole and I collaborated with the interns to investigate how writing functioned in their respective worksites and what the interns experienced as they transitioned from classroom to professional setting.

During the weekly internship class, we coached the student-interns in methods of collecting and analysing data from their worksites. In their professional writing courses, the interns were trained to do research, so this process was not unfamiliar to them. What was new, however, was playing the role of self-reflexive ethnographer investigating how writing functions in a particular social environment while examining one's own experiences as a social actor. We rehearsed the interns in the role of participant-observer and in the practices of recording field-notes and conducting interviews. We also coached the interns in using theories of activity, genre and situated learning to analyse the data collected. An important aim of the internship class – and this reflected the 'participatory action research' aspect of the project – was to engage the interns in constructing knowledge about the social and professional realities of their respective worksites and in applying this knowledge in ways that were beneficial to them.

In the student-intern study, we were able to integrate ethnographic-based discourse analysis with participatory action research in a way that enriched the research and contributed to its outcomes. An important factor here is that the two methodologies share similar social-constructionist assumptions about the nature of reality and knowledge. Both methodologies perceive human life and knowledge-building as occurring within a changing social world constructed through discourse. And in both cases, the research participants are encouraged to think and talk about their own perceptions, understandings and social roles.

Prospects for ethnographic-based discourse analysis

In considering the future prospects for ethnographic-based discourse analysis as a methodology for studying learning and knowledge-making in academic and workplace settings, I feel a certain ambivalence. On the one hand, I would like to see ethnographic-based discourse analysis evolve and adapt so that it can be paired with methodologies such as participatory action research and the other exciting kinds of interdiscursive, multi-modal, nexus-exploring approaches described elsewhere in this volume. On the other hand, though, I would hope to see certain features of ethnographic-based discourse analysis as conceived in the Geertzian tradition of interpretive ethnography retained in such combining of methodologies. And indeed, perhaps these hopes are reconcilable.

To suggest some of the possibilities for ethnographic-based discourse analysis, I will conclude by referring to a study that I have on the drawing board at the moment – an investigation of environmental discourse. This will be a multiple-site ethnographic inquiry that will proceed on two levels. I plan to explore the broad discursive field within which various social groups – such as environmental activists, business corporations, scientists, politicians, think-tanks and faith communities – use language and other symbolic forms to represent the phenomenon of climate change, to generate related knowledge and to make arguments in attempting to influence public opinion and government policy. At the same time, I want to examine the transitional experiences of graduates from the Environmental Studies programme in my university as they move into writing-intensive professional positions in some of the social groups mentioned above.

At this point, I see this research drawing on three strands of theory – activity-based genre theory, critical literacy and situated learning – as well as, methodologically, on discourse-analytic approaches developed by researchers in environmental politics such as Dryzek (2005) and Hajer (1995). After some preliminary textual analysis of discourses produced by the groups mentioned above (much of it accessible from the World Wide Web), I intend to conduct case studies with individuals working in certain of the social groups mentioned above as well as case studies with several Environmental Studies graduates. The next step will be to carry out a multiple-site ethnographic study in several organizations involved in the Canadian public-policy process as it relates to climate change.

Acknowledgements

I would like to thank Desmond Allison, Natasha Artemeva, Richard Darville and Jaffer Sheyholislami for their helpful comments on an earlier version of this chapter.

References

Adler, P. and Adler, P. (1987) *Membership Roles in Field Research*, Newbury Park, CA: Sage.

Agar, M. (1986) *Speaking of Ethnography*, Thousand Oaks, CA: Sage.

Denzin, N. (1997) *Interpretive Ethnography: ethnographic practices for the 21st century*, Thousand Oaks, CA: Sage.

Dryzek, J. (2005) *The Politics of the Earth: environmental discourses*, 2nd edn, New York: Oxford University Press.

Eisner, E. (2001) 'Concerns and aspirations for qualitative research in the new millennium', *Qualitative Research*, 1: 135–45.

Geertz, C. (1973) *The Interpretation of Cultures*, New York: Basic.

—— (1983) *Local Knowledge*, New York: Basic.

Glaser, B. and Strauss, A. (1967) *The Discovery of Grounded Theory: strategies for qualitative research*, New York: Aldine.

Hajer, M. (1995) *The Politics of Environmental Discourse: ecological modernization and the policy process*, Oxford: Oxford University Press.

Hammersley, M. and Atkinson, P. (1995) *Ethnography: principles in practice*, London: Routledge.

Harper, R. (1998) *Inside the IMF: an ethnography of documents, technology and organizational action*, London: Academic Press.

Heath, S.B. (1980) *Ways with Words: language, life and work in communities and classrooms*, Cambridge: Cambridge University Press.

Latour, B. and Woolgar, S. (1979) *Laboratory Life: the construction of social facts*, 2nd edn, Beverly Hills, CA: Sage.

Prior, P. (1998) *Writing/Disciplinarity: a sociohistoric account of literate activity in the academy*, Mahwah, NJ: Lawrence Erlbaum.

Rist, R. (1980) 'Blitzkrieg ethnography: on the transformation of a method into a movement', *Educational Researcher*, 9: 8–10.

Schryer, C. (1993) 'Records as genre', *Written Communication*, 10: 200–34.

Smart, G. (2006) *Writing the Economy: activity, genre and technology in the world of banking*, London: Equinox.

Smart, G. and Brown, N. (2002) 'Learning transfer or transformation of learning? Student interns reinventing expert writing practices in the workplace', *Technostyle*, 18: 117–41.

—— (2006) 'Developing a "discursive gaze": participatory action research with student interns encountering new genres in the activity of the workplace', in N. Artemeva and A. Freedman (eds) *Rhetorical Genre Studies and Beyond*, Winnipeg: Inkshed Publications.

Swales, J. (1998) *Other Floors, Other Voices: a textography of a small university building*, Mahwah, NJ: Lawrence Erlbaum.

Van Maanen, J. (1988) *Tales of the Field: on writing ethnography*, Chicago, IL: University of Chicago Press.

Van Nostrand, A.D. (1997) *Fundable Knowledge: the marketing of defense technology*, Mahwah, NJ: Lawrence Erlbaum.

Winsor, D. (1996) *Writing Like an Engineer: a rhetorical education*, Mahwah, NJ: Lawrence Erlbaum.

—— (2003) *Writing Power: communication in an engineering center*, Albany, NY: State University of New York Press.

5 Using ethnography in the analysis of pedagogical practice

Perspectives from activity theory

Angel Lin

Classroom research and the search for effective pedagogies: early studies

The linguistic and discursive turn in classroom and pedagogical research can be said to have arrived in the mid-1970s to the 1980s when educational researchers started to focus on analysing the fine details of interactions in the classroom. Instead of following the experimental research paradigm, this line of research generally follows the interpretive research paradigm (see Lin 1998 for a delineation of the different research paradigms influencing classroom research) and draws on tools from interactional sociolinguistics and discourse analysis.

Sinclair and Coulthard's seminal work on classroom discourse analysis (1975) remains today the classical study that has laid down the basic discourse analytical framework and units which subsequent classroom researchers have frequently referred to and built upon. One of the most significant contributions of Sinclair and Coulthard's work is the explicit, systematic, detailed description of one type of recurrent sequence of utterances in the classroom: the Initiation–Response–Feedback/Follow-up (IRF) exchange sequence, which is ubiquitous in classrooms.

In this chapter I would like to problematize this paradigm of discourse analysis as it is applied to classroom practice and to show how a more ethnographic approach to discourse can accommodate both a fine-grained analysis of interaction as exemplified by approaches like conversation analysis and a broader view of social practice and ideology. Fine-grained procedural analysis of discourse and ethnographic approaches, I will argue, are not as at odds with each other as they are often portrayed, but rather can be effectively integrated to transcend the limitations of the IRF model for classroom discourse we have inherited from Sinclair and Coulthard.

In the next section I will look at key studies focusing on the functions and the debates on educational consequences related to the use of the IRF sequence in the classroom. Then in the following section I will look at what insights can be drawn from such approaches as conversation analysis and activity theory to have a situated understanding of the use of the IRF sequences in the classroom, drawing on a classroom example from Hong Kong. Finally, I will discuss why pedagogical change needs to be initiated both in the classroom and in the larger context beyond the classroom, and look at some directions for future work that links the micro processes of classroom interactions and pedagogical practices to analysis of the larger layers of contexts in which these classroom processes and pedagogical practices are embedded.

Recent research on the 'triadic dialogue' in the classroom

Nassaji and Wells (2000) provide a good summary of the research literature and debates on the IRF triadic dialogue that is ubiquitous in many classrooms. The teacher, in his or her twin role as the 'primary knower' and the 'manager' or 'facilitator' in the classroom (Nassaji and Wells 2000) in general retains the right to 'have the last word'. For instance, in the example of an IRF exchange below, the teacher has the last word on the student's contribution by evaluating it as correct:

> T: Which way did the Wolf go to Red Riding Hood's Granny's cottage?
> S: He took a short cut through the forest.
> T: That's right.

> (2000: 377)

Nassaji and Wells (2000) argue that this triadic dialogue has a built-in mechanism that enables the teacher, as the primary knower in the classroom, to fulfil the valuable functions of confirming students' knowledge to be correct or not, evaluating the quality of information contributed by the student(s), making repairs if necessary (e.g. when the information contributed is incomplete or erroneous), assigning speaking rights in an orderly way (e.g. to ensure that the discussion proceeds in an orderly way), and checking students' understanding (i.e. the 'monitoring' function). When the teacher makes good use of the third slot in this triadic sequence, e.g. by asking a follow-up question that requires students to elaborate/expand, exemplify, justify or repair their contributions, the triadic dialogue is serving a good pedagogical function.

By using a wide range of options in the feedback/follow-up slot of the IRF sequence, Nassaji and Wells (2000) argue that the triadic dialogue can be put to good use by teachers after all. The pedagogical effect of the triadic dialogue thus hinges on how the teacher uses it, especially in the feedback/follow-up slot. If teachers use more of the 'negotiatory' type of questions (that require 'substantive responses') rather than the 'known information' type of questions, and if teachers can choose not to foreclose the discussion by giving an answer themselves but to invite other students to contribute, Nassaji and Wells (2000) argue that the triadic dialogue can lead to fruitful co-construction of useful knowledge through participatory discussion, which is moderated by the teacher in the roles of primary knower, manager/ facilitator, monitor and initiator.

Tsui's recent studies (2004a, 2004b) on how classroom interactions impact on the space of learning offer even more interesting findings on the pedagogical effects of different uses of the triadic dialogue (while Tsui does not directly focus on the IRF sequence, her data analysis does speak to the differential effects of different uses of the IRF sequence by the teacher). Tsui (2004b) convincingly argues that if teachers are sensitive to students' contributions in expanding and enriching the semantic dimensions or different aspects of the object of learning and are able to build on that in their feedback to students' responses, then the space of learning is expanded. However, if the teacher is not sensitive in building on students' responses but follows strictly their own teaching agenda, then the space of learning is narrowed (Tsui 2004a).

The status and functions of the triadic dialogue thus seem rather settled in the recent research literature. Armed with recent research findings teacher educators should be able to inform teachers about how they can make good use of the triadic dialogue, and about different ways to maximize its benefits and minimize its negative effects. Education reform and pedagogical change should then proceed with teacher training and reflective workshops to draw teachers' attention to the different (positive and negative) ways of using the triadic dialogue. In fact, this kind of recommendation is not new in the research literature. Bereiter and his colleagues (Bereiter 1986; Bereiter and Scardamalia 1987) proposed pedagogical change along similar lines almost two decades ago. In the next section we shall first briefly revisit the old debate on the IRF sequence (started by Carl Bereiter and James Heap in the mid-1980s) and then bring in an analysis of some new data from two Hong Kong classrooms to show how research on the triadic dialogue and on pedagogical analysis can benefit from insights from activity theory and conversation analysis within an ethnographic framework.

Situated understanding of the use of the triadic dialogue: perspectives from conversation analysis, ethnography and activity theory

As mentioned in the first section above, early classroom studies were largely driven by the desire to find out the best teaching methods while using a more or less experimental research design. After the linguistic/discursive turn in classroom studies, the overarching desire to use classroom studies to find out about (e.g. to describe) the best practices (effective pedagogies) and differentiate them from ineffective practices was still pervasive. Broadly speaking we can classify classroom studies into two main types. The first type of study generally has the overarching aim to describe effective pedagogical practices and to differentiate them from ineffective ones, usually by reference to some educational principles or norms; e.g. expanding or narrowing the space of learning (see, for example, Tsui 2004a, 2004b), or providing students with opportunities to practise higher-order vs. lower-order thinking and reading skills (Bereiter 1986; Bereiter and Scardamalia 1987).

On the other hand, the second type of study generally has the aim to describe classroom interactions and practices to uncover the 'good sense' or local rationality of these practices. Its aim, however, is not an apologetic one (i.e. to defend existing practices) but to find out first and foremost how classroom participants are doing what they are doing, with the implied aim to uncover why they are doing it. The first type of study has usually been (but not exclusively) engaged in by researchers with a background in educational psychology (e.g. Bereiter 1986; Bereiter and Scardamalia 1987) whereas the second type of study is usually engaged in by interactional sociolinguists, school ethnographers or conversation analysts with an interest in analysing interactions in educational settings (e.g. Mehan 1979; Heap 1985). Traditionally these two types of studies seldom interact but in the rare case when they do, the differences in their overarching research paradigms are brought into sharp relief.

For instance, the intellectual exchange between Heap (1985, 1986) and Bereiter (1986) helps to bring out key differences in their research concerns. Bereiter (1986) launched a serious critique of the IRF triadic sequence, arguing that this way of running the lesson deprives students of opportunities to practise higher-order cognitive skills (e.g. in reading lessons). Heap (1986), in response, argued for the cultural function of the IRF discourse format, which allows for the teacher to socialize students into the cultural models of a community by providing culturally appropriate feedback and by shaping students' contribution towards co-constructing acceptable cultural knowledge and values. Heap's classroom research (see Heap 1985, 1990, 1991) provides a good source of examples of how conversation analysis (CA) can be applied in the detailed description and analysis of classroom and pedagogical practices. Below I shall outline how the 'point' of a lesson (Heap 1985) can be uncovered through such a procedural analysis.

Uncovering the 'point' of a lesson

The 'point' of a lesson refers to what the lesson ultimately does for the teachers and the students (or the purpose of the lesson), not as self-reported by the teacher or students themselves but as manifested in what they actually do in the lesson, and in the sets of *recurrent procedures* (or symbolic/discursive tools) that they use to accomplish the 'point' (or purpose) of the lesson. One must bear in mind that the point of the lesson is not usually explicit (or completely available) to teachers and students consciously – so they may not be able to tell you directly if confronted by such a question – they might tell you something else which they think they are doing: e.g. teaching and learning reading skills. But what counts as 'reading skills' is not always completely transparent to them; the analyst has to look at what teachers and students actually do (and what recurrent procedures they employ) in the classroom to find out or 'uncover' what actually (implicitly) counts as 'teaching and learning reading skills' for them.

Below are some typical organizational/structural features of classroom lessons:

1   Classroom lessons constitute one example of recurrent 'speech events' (e.g. debates, public speeches) in sociolinguistic terms with often implicit, unspoken, but shared norms or conventions governing *who* (i.e. participants in different roles) can speak *what* at *what times*. For instance, participants in a formal debate cannot all speak at the same time. They occupy different roles (e.g. team members, team chair, and they are divided into two opposing teams, members of which take alternate turns to speak, etc.). So, according to their roles members have different speaking rights and there are conventions governing their turn-taking practices. Likewise, we need to see classroom participants as occupying different roles and each role has different (and differential) speaking rights; e.g. the teacher can assign speaking rights to students; s/he can occupy most speaking turns; s/he is the one who 'chairs' or 'directs' the lesson – i.e. s/he sets the agenda, sets the tasks, assigns time for tasks, assigns different students to do different things and answer different questions. The teacher role gives the teacher a lopsided domination over the agenda of the lesson and over *who* can speak/do *what when* all through the lesson.

2   The teacher occupying the position/role of the 'chair' of the lesson also bears the burden of driving the lesson forward, moving along the pre-set agenda of the lesson. Usually teachers see themselves as 'covering' this unit, 'teaching this passage', 'doing this exercise with the students', 'going through this worksheet (e.g. doing answer-checking) with students', 'helping students to complete this task, to get all the answers correct', 'enabling students to do their worksheets at home', and so on. Usually, in a teacher's mind, a lesson is organized into a sequence of tasks/texts/worksheets to 'cover' or 'go through' with students.

3   Usually when asked about the objectives of the lesson, teachers will say this is a reading lesson, a grammar lesson or a writing lesson. In this sense, to teachers, the nature of a lesson is given by its major task – students are to do reading, writing, and grammar tasks, and so on. While students practise these language skills globally, both the topics and the contexts for language use are set by teachers or the assigned textbook/worksheets. Students are usually induced or dragged into engaging in these 'language uses' willingly or unwillingly by the teacher.

4   The teacher usually employs two basic 'tools' to drive a lesson forward, or to move students along a pre-set agenda: One tool is the Initiation-Response-Feedback (IRF) 'discourse format' (Heap 1985). A discourse

format is a sequence of utterances each of which has a specific function, and the sequence recurs in a predictable pattern or format. The other tool that the teacher often employs is the worksheet or the textbook. Below we shall focus on the functions of these two basic tools in the teacher's repertoire to get a lesson moving towards her/his pre-set teaching goals or to get students moving along a pre-set lesson agenda. Examples from a Chinese language classroom in Hong Kong will be used.

I shall draw on the methods of ethnography and the analytical concepts of activity theory to account for why the IRF triadic format is used in the lesson in ways that might lead to educationally undesirable consequences and yet is still used by the teachers in lessons like this with 'a good sense' (i.e. serving local rationality) in the activity system in which the lessons, teachers and students are all situated.

The researcher conducted class observation of a Chinese language lesson in a low-banding (i.e. low academic-standard) co-educational secondary school in Hong Kong as part of a larger literacy research project in February 2006. No audio or videotaping was made (at the request of the teachers concerned) but the researcher made detailed observational notes during the class observations. The teachers conducted their lessons as usual and the purpose of the research was to compare English and Chinese language lessons.

In this Chinese language lesson (at form 2 or grade 8) a listening exercise was conducted, focusing on problems threatening the survival of Chinese white dolphins and solutions to these problems, with students required to list these problems and solutions. In the answer-checking phase, the teacher writes on the blackboard a table with two columns, one with the heading 'Problems', and the other with the heading 'Solutions'. She then elicits answers from the students, asks follow-up questions to get more elaborate answers and then re-shapes/re-phrases students' answers into acceptable answers, which she finally writes down in the table.

Most of the time the teacher's work seems to be that of rephrasing students' fragmented, Cantonese answers into more elaborate answers phrased in Standard Written Chinese and then writes them down on the blackboard for students to copy into their listening exercise books. This process becomes a bit repetitive and tedious towards the end of the lesson and one student is heard to shout out, 'Miss, you can just copy the model answers from your book onto the blackboard!' The student's meaning seems to be: 'Don't bother to go through the asking and answering question procedures; just give us the model answers from the teacher's book!' The teacher ignores this remark and goes on with the answer-checking sequences using the IRF triadic format until all questions have been gone through.

The 'point' of this lesson thus seems to be the establishment of a corpus of certified true answers (cf. Heap 1985, 1986) to the listening comprehension questions on the text. The ways these answers are organized (e.g. conceptual organizer; see Figure 5.1) and the linguistic format (e.g. Standard Written Chinese) in which these answers are formulated follow the teacher-directed answers (also pre-set in the text-book) and there is no encouragement of students to venture outside these organizers; e.g. encouraging students to come up with alternative conceptual organizers.

Likewise, the teacher has been doing the bulk of the conceptual (e.g. providing the organizer for extracting information from the listening text) and linguistic rephrasing work for the students (e.g. rephrasing students' Cantonese answers into acceptable SWC answers).

The synoptic analysis of the Chinese lesson above shows that the IRF format has been used by the respective teachers to co-construct a corpus of certified correct (or model) answers to a more or less pre-set list of questions (within a pre-given conceptual/organizing framework) on texts. The IRF format serves at least two functions for the teachers:

1   The teacher uses it to move the lesson forward, to organize discussion topics tightly around the format and content of the pre-set list of questions. We can call this *the converging function*; i.e. the teacher maintains tight control over digressions (or attempts to minimize them) from the conceptual framework and format of the examination questions.

2   The teacher uses it to do a lot of re-phrasing/re-coding (e.g. from colloquial Cantonese to Standard Written Chinese), to re-shape students' answers into a form that can fit into the pre-given conceptual/analytical framework for organizing ideas about or content of the text. The IRF format allows the teacher to take material from the students and work it into acceptable answers to exam type questions – i.e. to certify it as correct with reference to model answers. We can call this *the certifying function*. Most of this higher-order linguistic re-coding and conceptual re-organization work is done by the teachers in the feedback slot of the IRF format.

Figure 5.1 gives a summary of my analysis of the 'point' of this lesson.

The converging and certifying functions together serve the overall 'point' (or aim) of the lesson: to co-construct with students a corpus of certified correct answers to examination questions on texts. Some students can see through this 'point'. For instance, in the Chinese listening lesson analysed above, a student towards the end of the lesson shouts out to the teacher, asking her just to copy her model answers from her teacher's book onto the blackboard.

If we adopt the criteria of progressive educators (e.g. Bereiter 1986; Bereiter and Scardamalia 1987) to measure the performance of this teacher, we would doubtless find her falling short of our expectations: she does not allow students to discuss the text critically, to venture out of the pre-given questions and conceptual framework on the text, and worse still, she does

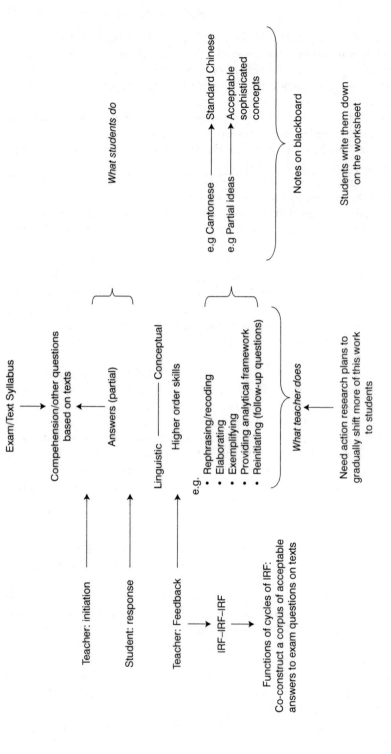

Figure 5.1 The 'point' of the lesson

all or most of the higher-order thinking and linguistic work for the students. The standard recommendation at the end of this piece of classroom research should then be that of providing the teacher with more training in the use of alternative discourse formats (e.g. 'reciprocal questioning': see Brown and Palincsar 1989), or in using the IRF format in more creative ways to expand the space of learning (e.g. Nassaji and Wells 2000; Tsui 2004a, 2004b). While this recommendation is indeed needed, we also need to use ethnography to look at the overall 'activity system' (the layers of ethnographic contexts) in which the teachers, students and their classroom practices are situated, to understand why teachers are doing what they are doing, beyond the common observation that they might not know better; i.e. they merely do not know how to have alternative practices.

Contextualized analysis of pedagogical practices

Many conversation analysts might object to the use of any ethnography in combination with the procedural analysis of classroom interactions and pedagogical practice. However, if we adopt perspectives from activity theory (AT) we can see that principles from CA and ethnography can both be drawn upon in the AT framework in our research on discourse and practice in pedagogical settings. Below I shall first outline some key perspectives offered by AT.

Activity theory has its historical and philosophical origins in writings from Kant and Hegel to Vygotsky, Leont'ev and Luria. From the perspective of AT, society is seen as a system of multi-layered networks of interconnected activity systems. These socially shared, collective activity systems serve as units of analysis by the researcher (vs. traditional unit of analysis: the individual teacher's teaching style or the individual lesson). AT thus provides us with useful tools for conducting an ethnographic, contextualized analysis of pedagogical practices and discourse, avoiding the pitfalls of leaving out the contexts of pedagogical practices and discourse in our analysis. According to AT, an activity system has the following characteristics (based on Engeström 1993):

Characteristics of activity systems:

- Activity systems are longitudinal, socio-historical-cultural formations, constituted and evolving over time by people and institutions.
- Activity systems are self-reproducing/perpetuating until internal contradictions/tensions grow to a point to trigger change/transformation of the system.
- Multivoicedness, creating internal contradictions and debates, is an essential feature in an activity system – driving change/transformation.
- Activity systems are socially distributed/shared and collective.
- Activity systems are mediated by cultural tools/artefacts (both symbolic tools such as signs/language and discourse formats, and physical tools such as teaching equipment and worksheets, textbook exercises, etc.).

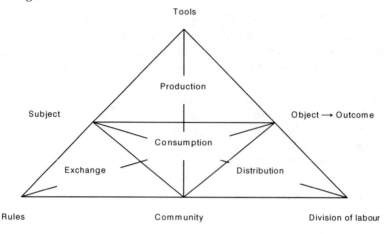

Figure 5.2   The basic structure of human activity (adapted from Engeström, 1993: 68)

- Activity systems are motivated by goals; AT studies processes of goal-formation in an activity system.

Figure 5.2 gives a diagrammatic representation of the key elements and their relations in an activity system (or ethnographic context).

How can AT help us contextualize our lesson analysis? At this point it is important for us to understand AT not as an ultimate piece of truth about human activities, but as a heuristic tool, a working model that we might draw upon to add to our repertoire of analytical tools to conduct a more holistic, contextualized, ethnographic analysis of pedagogical practices. Below I shall attempt to apply AT tools to analyse the Chinese lesson we discussed above.

Heuristic tools from AT for contextualized analysis of pedagogical practices:

- Subject: classroom participants: teacher (T) and students (Ss).
- Object: worksheet/textbook exercise (modelled on examination question formats and organizing frameworks) on the listening and reading texts.
- Production: the co-construction (by T and Ss) of a corpus of answers (to the worksheet questions/tasks) certified to be correct by T (in the feedback slot of the IRF discourse format).
- Mediating tools: the IRF discourse format used in the answer-checking lesson stage.
- Outcome: completed worksheets/completed exercises with 'model' answers.
- Community: the school teachers, students, school administration who share this system of school practices, participating in forming specific ways of recognizing/counting school work (teaching and learning work)

as being accomplished; e.g. how many worksheets/textbook exercises are covered; how many students score high grades in both internal and public exams.

- Rules/norms: the rules/norms of the school community governing how school work is (recognized) to be done and evaluated (e.g. assessment patterns, institutionally defined ways of displaying knowledge or learning).
- Division of labour: teacher and different students participate together (e.g. through contributing to speaking turns in the IRF discourse sequence) in co-constructing a certified corpus of 'correct' answers to the worksheet questions/textbook tasks.
- Consumption:
  - Teacher uses the correctly completed worksheets/textbook exercises as an indicator/proof of accomplishment of his/her teaching work → accountable to self and school authorities.
  - Students use the correctly completed worksheets/textbook exercises as an indicator/proof of accomplishment of his/her learning work → in exchange for scores/grades.

In summary, then, the teacher seems to use the IRF discourse format and the textbook worksheet (modelled on examination formats) for at least three important functions: to motivate students to pay attention (because they will help students to get good scores in examinations), to organize and structure the lesson, and to provide a quick, easy indicator of whether students have learnt what the teacher has taught in the lesson; i.e. using the worksheet as *a motivator*, as *an organizer* and as *a test* or *displayer* of 'knowledge/ skills learnt'. The process of this activity is mediated by the tools of the IRF discourse format and the worksheet.

It can thus be seen that while CA and other forms of discourse analysis are strong in uncovering and analysing the symbolic tools in the AT framework, other ethnographic methods are needed to uncover and analyse other important components encompassed in the activity system; e.g. the norms/rules of the community, the ways of exchange of the products (e.g. how completed answer sheets can be exchanged for grades by students, how covered textbook exercises count as recognized tokens of tasks accomplished in the school-determined schemes of work for teachers, and so on). Procedural models like CA and that of Sinclair and Coulthard can only help us analyse one portion of the activity system in which education participants are situated, and ethnography has an important role to play in our research as it is needed to uncover and analyse other important components of the activity system.

Initiating and sustaining change in pedagogical practices: what are the considerations?

How can we initiate change (and sustain it if we ever succeed in initiating it) in pedagogical practices? The more contextualized perspective on classroom discourse I am suggesting here makes it obvious that giving teachers training in alternative pedagogical practices (e.g. using reciprocal questioning instead of the IRF discourse format, or learning creative ways of using the IRF) is necessary but not sufficient. That is because if we want the change to be sustained in the activity system in which both teachers and students are situated, there should be corresponding change in the key elements of the activity system, thus providing incentives for initiating and sustaining the change in pedagogical practices. Again, ethnography is needed to find out about possibilities for change in the other aspects of the activity system.

Any activity system has internal contradictions and tensions. In my ethnographic observations of classrooms I can see that there are some students (although in the minority) who voice their discontent with such kind of pedagogical practices. Students' discontent can provide a good starting point and stimulus for teachers to reflect critically on their own practices. Is this the best way to teach students about the text? Am I just focusing too much on exam preparation, neglecting the development of critical literacy/reading skills?

If enough teachers and school administrators start to reflect critically on what they are doing and what some students are trying to say to them, they might be able to start changing their school norms, cultures and practices. Perhaps we can develop alternative ways of helping students to prepare for examinations while at the same time allowing opportunities for critical discussion and use of texts. Perhaps, as a community, we can propose to the government's assessment authorities to change their ways of assessment, their formats and frameworks of setting questions on texts; e.g. to set more open-ended kinds of questions that encourage alternative, open-ended answers and diverse conceptual frameworks. With CA alone, these answers are hard to come by, and it becomes clear that a whole repertoire of CA and ethnographic research methods needs to be deployed for our purposes.

Coda: discourse research, ethnographic research and praxis within and beyond the classroom

It can be seen from the discussion above that our research on pedagogical practices and classroom discourse analysis will inevitably take us beyond the classroom and beyond mere micro analysis of talk so that we can understand classroom processes in terms of the contexts of larger activity systems (uncovered by ethnographic methods). These classroom practices serve good functions (or have 'local rationality': see Heap 1990), but the 'good sense' of the practices often cannot be understood without reference to the larger activity systems and institutional cultures in which they are situated. To change these practices into more progressive pedagogical practices such as those recommended by progressive educators, we need to study the larger activity systems and ethnographic contexts and think of ways of changing key elements in the activity systems that will provide new incentives, new cultures and norms that will sustain the new pedagogical practices. Any recommendation to change the classroom practice must also give due consideration to the inter-relatedness of different elements and forces within the larger activity system which shapes or motivates the specific pedagogical practice in question. Our classroom discourse research will thus lead us to consider the sociocultural and socio-political situatedness of the pedagogical practices that we study, and this is why we are not only discourse analysts (in the narrow sense) but also ethnographers, as well as sociocultural and socio-political participants. For instance, our research will lead us to advocacy work: e.g. advocating for change in public exam formats and practices. It will lead us towards research, critical ethnography as well as advocacy for critical literacy and public pedagogy (see Carrington and Luke 1997). Traditional ways of conceptualizing and conducting classroom discourse research as merely looking at micro classroom processes will therefore need to take a critical ethnographic and sociocultural turn (e.g. Hall and Verplaetse 2000; Hall 2001; Lin 1999), if classroom discourse research is to have a more far-reaching impact on initiating and sustaining educational and pedagogical change in the schooling system. More multi-methodological perspectives in future research are needed.

References

Bereiter, C. (1986) 'The reading comprehension lesson: a commentary on Heap's ethnomethodological analysis', *Curriculum Inquiry*, 16(1): 65–72.

Bereiter, C. and M. Scardamalia (1987) 'An attainable version of high literacy: approaches to teaching higher-order skills in reading and writing', *Curriculum Inquiry*, 17(1): 9–30.

Brown, A.L. and Palincsar, A.S. (1989) 'Guided, cooperative learning and individual knowledge acquisition', in L. Resnick (ed.) *Knowing, Learning, and Instruction: essays in honor of Robert Glaser*, Mahwah, NJ: Lawrence Erlbaum, pp. 393–451.

Carrington, V. and Luke, A. (1997) 'Literacy and Bourdieu's sociological theory: a reframing', *Language and Education*, 11(2): 96–112.

Engeström, Y. (1993) 'Developmental studies of work as a testbench of activity theory: the case of primary care medical practice', in S. Chaiklin and J. Lave (eds) *Understanding Practice: perspectives on activity and context*, Cambridge: Cambridge University Press.

Hall, J.K. (2001) *Methods for Teaching Foreign Languages: creating a community of learners in the classroom*, Upper Saddle River, NJ: Prentice Hall.

Hall, J.K. and Verplaetse, L.S. (eds) (2000) *Second and Foreign Language Learning through Classroom Interaction*, Mahwah, NJ: Lawrence Erlbaum.

Heap, J.L. (1985) 'Discourse in the production of classroom knowledge: reading lessons', *Curriculum Inquiry*, 15(3): 245–79.

—— (1986) 'Cultural logic and schema theory: a reply to Bereiter', *Curriculum Inquiry*, 16(1): 73–86.

—— (1990) 'Applied ethnomethodology: looking for the local rationality of reading activities', *Human Studies*, 13: 39–72.

—— (1991) 'Ethnomethodology, cultural phenomenology, and literacy activities', *Curriculum Inquiry*, 21 (1): 109–17.

Lin, A.M.Y. (1998) 'Understanding the issue of medium of instruction in Hong Kong schools: what research approaches do we need?', *Asia Pacific Journal of Language in Education*, 1(1): 85–98.

—— (1999) 'Doing-English-lessons in the reproduction or transformation of social worlds?', *TESOL Quarterly*, 33(3): 393–412.

Mehan, H. (1979) *Learning Lessons: social organization in the classroom*, Cambridge, MA: Harvard University Press.

Nassaji, H. and Wells, G. (2000) 'What's the use of "triadic dialogue"?: an investigation of teacher–student interaction', *Applied Linguistics*, 21(3): 376–406.

Sinclair, J.M. and Coulthard, R.M. (1975) *Towards an Analysis of Discourse*, London: Oxford University Press.

Tsui, A.B.M. (2004a) 'The semantic enrichment of the space of learning', in F. Marton and A. Tsui, with P. Chik, P.Y. Ko, M.L. Lo, I. Mok, F.P. Ng, M.F. Pang, W.Y. Pong and U. Runnesson, *Classroom Discourse and the Space of Learning*, Mahwah, NJ: Lawrence Erlbaum, pp. 139–64.

—— (2004b) 'The shared space of learning', in F. Marton and A. Tsui, with P. Chik, P.Y. Ko, M.L. Lo, I. Mok, F.P. Ng, M.F. Pang, W.Y. Pong and U. Runnesson, *Classroom Discourse and the Space of Learning*, Mahwah, NJ: Lawrence Erlbaum, pp. 165–86.

Suggestions for further work

1   Smart suggests that one of the chief challenges of the ethnographer is to balance the use of 'experience-near' concepts – those 'natural' to the participants – and 'experience-distant' concepts – those fashioned by the researcher. What are some of the difficulties of integrating these two kinds of concepts, and what, if any, are the benefits of engaging this tension?
2   Choose a workplace or institutional setting and design a study in which attention to the context in which texts are produced and received can inform our understanding of the construction of local knowledge and 'sense-making'. What kinds of data would be appropriate for such a study and how could it be best obtained?
3   Since they often involve more direct contact with producers and consumers of discourse than other approaches to discourse analysis, ethnographic approaches involve unique ethical concerns. What are these concerns and how should researchers address them?
4   Collect written or spoken discourse from an educational setting. What features of the discourse require attention to the larger 'activity systems' in which they are produced?
5   Lin argues that micro-analysis of talk is not sufficient for understanding how people make sense of social interaction. What are some arguments that either support or refute her view?

Part III

Corpus-based discourse analysis

In recent years there have been exciting developments in corpus-based discourse analysis. As indicated in the introductory chapter to this volume, initial work in corpus-based studies focused primarily on lexicography and grammar. Only later did serious work start to be done in discourse analysis. A number of reservations, however, have been expressed regarding such applications (see e.g. Hunston 2002; Baker 2006). One such reservation is that corpus approaches focus on decontextualized examples. Discourse analysis requires the study of language in its full textual and situational context and this is lacking in corpus-based work, it is claimed. Another related criticism is that, in focusing on the concordance line, corpus-based approaches miss the structure of the text, a vital prerequisite for discourse analysis. A third criticism is that corpus-based analysis is a-theoretical, relying on a post-hoc analysis of frequency data and then deciding what can be said about it. While these criticisms hold some truth (although see Tognini-Bonelli 2001 for a defence of the post-hoc approach, which she refers to as 'data-driven'), it should be borne in mind that they do not undermine the whole enterprise. Rather, we would argue here, they indicate how corpus-based discourse analysis is to be placed on the textual side of the text-context dichotomy that needs to be considered in any form of discourse analysis.

The three contributions in this part, in their different ways, offer answers to the particular issues just mentioned (see also Stubbs, 2002 for more direct answers to some of these criticisms). Lee, in his chapter, begins by noting a perceived gap on the part of corpus linguists, on the one hand, and discourse analysts, on the other, in the work they do and what he sees as the many uncertainties surrounding the nature and scope of both of these groups of linguists. Lee then examines some of the work that has been done so far that can quite comfortably be labelled 'corpus-based discourse analysis' (CBDA), discussing some of the uses to which current corpora can be put and examining the characteristics of such work. Throughout, the focus is on how we can fruitfully bring together insights from those who see themselves primarily as 'corpus-based linguists', and those who are first and foremost 'discourse analysts'.

In his chapter, Biber introduces his multi-dimensional (MD) analysis, which is a corpus-based approach to discourse that characterizes the patterns of register variation in a language. The approach was originally developed to analyse the general patterns of variation among spoken and written registers in English and other languages. Surprisingly, these studies have found some striking similarities in the underlying 'dimensions' that distinguish among spoken and written registers in these diverse languages. It is even more surprising, Biber claims, that MD studies of restricted discourse domains have also uncovered dimensions that are similar in linguistic form and function to the more general studies of register variation.

Biber then presents a study which further investigates variation within a restricted discourse domain, presenting an MD analysis of a single register: conversation. Biber's expectations were that a unique set of dimensions would emerge to characterize the variation among conversational texts. Instead, the three dimensions identified turned out to be closely related to dimensions identified in previous analyses of general register variation. Taken together with previous studies, Biber's study of conversation thus raises the possibility of universal dimensions of register variation. It thus shows how corpus linguistics can identify discursive features across large bodies of text and thus responds to the second of the criticisms levelled at corpus approaches referred to above i.e. that it misses the structure of the text.

L. Flowerdew, in her chapter, addresses the second and third of the issues identified above, the question of context (or lack thereof) and the role of theory. Noting that, traditionally, corpus linguistics has focused most of its attention on frequency counts of lexical and grammatical items, she describes recent work which aligns corpus linguistic methodologies with genre-based approaches to discourse analysis. She argues that in this work corpus-based methodologies have been informed by genre theory and principles of text analysis, while at the same time genre theories have profited from corpus-based methodologies. In the empirical part of her chapter, L. Flowerdew examines this relationship between corpora and context through a study of a specialised corpus of environmental reports, focussing on semantic prosody and epistemic stance, both highly context dependent features.

Useful further reading on corpus-based approaches to discourse analysis can be found in Baker (2006), Hunston (2003), Sinclair (2004) and Stubbs (1996).

References

Baker, P. (2006) *Using Corpora in Discourse Analysis*, London: Continuum.

Hunston, S. (2002) *Corpora and Applied Linguistics*, Cambridge: Cambridge University Press.

Sinclair, J.M. (1991) *Corpus, Concordance, Collocation*, Oxford: Oxford University Press.

—— (2004) *Trust the Text: language, corpus and discourse*, London: Routledge.

Stubbs, M. (1996) *Text and Corpus Analysis*, Oxford: Blackwell.
—— (2002) 'On text and corpus analysis: a reply to Borsley and Ingham', *Lingua Franca*, 112: 7–11.
Tognini-Bonelli, E. (2001) *Corpus Linguistics at Work* (Studies in Corpus Linguistics 6), Amsterdam: John Benjamins.

6 Corpora and discourse analysis

New ways of doing old things

David Y.W. Lee

> I continue to believe that one should not characterize linguists, or researchers of any kind, in terms of a single favorite tie to reality [...] I would like to see the day when we will all be more versatile in our methodologies, skilled at integrating all the techniques we will be able to discover for understanding this most basic, most fascinating, but also most elusive manifestation of the human mind.
>
> (Chafe 1992: 96)

Introduction

By most accounts, the field of 'corpus-based approaches to discourse analysis' would seem to have a rather slim bibliography: an informal, small-scale survey of opinion that I conducted in March 2005 among several corpus-based linguists[1] revealed a consensus of opinion that was surprising in its unanimity: the experts agreed that very little discourse analytic work had been done by corpus linguists[2] (even with 'discourse analysis' deliberately left vague and undefined in my survey question). From a complementary perspective, most discourse analysts would probably agree that few research studies in their field have been based extensively on computerized text databases. One reason could be that a lot of discourse analysts focus on spoken language, and there are not many corpora of spoken English available (or those that are do not meet analysts' requirements). However, discourse analysis (DA) is certainly not exclusively restricted to spoken texts, so there must be other reasons for this scarcity of corpus-based discourse studies. One reason, of course, is that the 'corporist' approach is a relative newcomer to the scene and has yet to make its mark. The seeming lack of work in corpus-based discourse analysis (henceforth CBDA) is surprising, given Kirk's (1996) summary, more than a decade ago, of the work that had been done up until then. His personal comment at that time was that:

> Corpus linguistics and discourse analysis have been good partners, not least because they tend to have come from the same stables, e.g., Birmingham, Lund, and Santa Barbara. Exhaustive discourse analyses

of entire spoken corpora as well as quantified results would make them ever better partners.

(Kirk 1996: 276)

As far as I know, this challenge of doing 'exhaustive discourse analyses of entire spoken corpora' has not been taken up by many people so far. A quote from a personal correspondence with Michael Stubbs (2005) on this issue should prove quite revealing: 'Despite the fact that I have published a book entitled *Text and Corpus Analysis* [Stubbs 1996], I have to admit that the two things are relatively poorly co-ordinated.'

What is corpus-based linguistics?

To look at how corpora and discourse may be brought together in a more fruitful marriage, perhaps it would be helpful to clarify first some basic concepts and boundaries. First, it is worth pointing out that the label 'corpus linguistics' is something of a misnomer, and one that linguists should best avoid using. Phoneticians focus on speech sounds, sociolinguists focus on the social aspects of language use, but there is no separate 'corpus' aspect of language for linguists to focus on. Instead, what we have is what Larsen-Freeman (2000) would classify as a *methodological innovation* (not 'method', which refers to a fixed set of practices), which also simultaneously incorporates an *approach* to language. By 'methodological innovation', I mean 'a new way of accomplishing old goals', and by 'approach', I mean 'a set of theoretical positions and beliefs about the nature of language and how we can study it' (e.g. that large-enough amounts of real, empirical data should be the source of theorizing).

The more accurate term 'corpus-based linguistics' puts the focus on linguistics: i.e. what is done is language study – it just happens to be corpus-based (the related terms 'corpus-induced', 'corpus-driven', and 'corpus-informed' will be discussed later). Corpus-based linguists study the same aspects of language as other linguists (grammar, sociolinguistic variation, discourse phenomena, etc.) – we just happen to use banks of computerized text and certain computer techniques. Our interest is in language itself, not corpora.

It is therefore somewhat unfortunate that in many conference calls for papers, a separate strand 'corpus linguistics' is usually listed, giving the impression that this is an independent and separable approach to discourse analysis in the way that 'genre analysis' or 'conversation analysis' are. In fact, it is eminently possible for a corpus-based linguist to do genre analysis or conversation analysis. Being corpus-based only implies being familiar with a toolbox of techniques and procedures for dealing with textual datasets, in which computers are used in sometimes automatic, sometimes interactive ways. It means having a slightly 'technicist' approach to conducting language research, but the corpus enterprise is not just a box of tricks and techniques:

there are many theoretical contributions that a proper study of corpora can make that cannot come from other approaches within linguistics, as the research discussed below will testify.

To be a corpus-based linguist, then, is to have a particular orientation towards language ('real language is used language, or language in use'), a particular view of language data ('the more computerized data the merrier') and a familiarity with a set of techniques (e.g. part-of-speech tagging, concordancing, keywords analysis).

Most discourse analysts would probably concur with the corpus-based view of language: after all, what is discourse but actual, situationally embedded, used and re-used language? The more technical aspects of manipulating computerized data, and lots of it, however, are where some discourse analysts will part company with corpus-based linguists: for some, discourse analysis can proceed very well (thank you) with just one text, and manual (painstaking) analysis is almost *de rigueur* for some analysts. One challenge of this chapter, therefore, is to try to persuade more discourse analysts to take a closer look at what corpus-based linguistics has to offer: to see what data, software and techniques exist from which traditional discourse analysts might possibly profit.

Three ways of using corpora for discourse analysis

Setting aside the above claims about the paucity of CBDA, let us take a look at three broad ways that corpus data can be appropriated:

1   Mainly qualitative: some analyses of corpora are necessarily manual or qualitative in nature. Corpus data are used as the basis of careful, qualitative studies. We may call this type of research *corpus-informed*.
2   Both qualitative and quantitative: the vast majority of corpus-based research, contrary to stereotype, is actually both qualitative and quantitative in nature. Studies differ in how much the researcher actually lets the data determine the results. If the analyst comes to the task using, relying on or imposing prior linguistic intuitions or theoretical frameworks while examining the data, then we can call the research *corpus-supported*. If, on the other hand, the analyst approaches the task with fewer preconceptions, than we can say that the research is *corpus-driven*.
3   Mainly quantitative: here, corpora are used in large-scale, mainly automatic analyses, to obtain quantitative information about language for mainly practical (industrial) applications. For example, frequency information can be used to derive (or, to use the technical term, induce) rules or grammars that can then drive natural language engineering applications in text-to-speech synthesis, machine translation, information retrieval, automatic text summarization, etc. We may call this type of research *corpus-induced*.

If we take 'corpus-based' as a superordinate term, we can make a three-way distinction between corpus-based research that is *corpus-informed*, *corpus-supported*, or *corpus-induced* (although there is really a continuum). Below, DA using corpora will be categorized according to this scheme to illustrate the various types of research that has been done.

'Corpus-informed': corpora as text samples (mainly qualitative)

Corpus-informed genre analysis

In Swales' (2004) latest book on research genres, the otherwise hard to get data available in the MICASE corpus (e.g. dissertation defences) are used, but the analyses are essentially the same as in traditional genre analysis – done by hand, although some aspects of the searching and counting were undoubtedly speeded up by being done by computer. Such usage of corpus data will probably continue to be the biggest way in which corpora and corpus techniques contribute to discourse and genre analysis: they provide the raw data and tools,[3] but the analyses will be mostly manual, being dependent on not-entirely-automatable processes of classification, interpretation and generalization. However, in the section below on 'corpus-supported genre analysis', some examples of computer-aided analysis will be given.

'Corpus-supported, corpus-driven': corpora as the primary bases of theorizing

Corpus-supported genre analysis and corpus-based ESP research

As Swales (2002) has noted, the main corpus technique of using concordances to examine search items is a rather bottom-up approach to texts and thus somewhat at odds with the top-down genre analytic process of move structure analysis. Nevertheless, he has latterly admitted having a change of heart, and has successfully combined both approaches in teaching EAP to non-native speakers of English, as reported in Lee and Swales (2006). For this study, doctoral students explored the lexico-grammatical features of their own specialized discourse communities using self-compiled corpora, and made strong lexico-grammatical generalizations about the discourse practices of their fields. Similarly, Noguchi (2004) discusses how her Japanese science and engineering majors compiled their own mini-corpora and examined genre-rhetorical and lexico-grammatical issues using a concordancer.

As L. Flowerdew (2004) has rightly pointed out, corpora may not be useful for genre analysis if you do not put any larger structural units into the corpus first, perhaps by hand-tagging. An example of how to do this is given by Kanoksilapatham (2003), who combined a qualitative move analysis with Biber's (1988) quantitative multidimensional approach in order to linguistically characterize rhetorical moves in a corpus of 60 biochemistry research articles. While the 'moves' were identified manually, the multidimensional approach (Biber 1988) was used to find groups of linguistic features that co-occurred with greater than chance frequency (using the statistical procedure of factor analysis), on the assumption that such a grouping of features reflects a shared underlying function. Move analysis on its own has been accused of being too subjective and not linguistically grounded enough in terms of providing a full linguistic characterization of what an individual move is. Multidimensional analysis, on the other hand, had hitherto only been performed at the level of whole texts or aggregates of text[4] and is not inherently discourse-analytic. In Kanoksilapatham's research, each move was treated as a different text file, and this combination of qualitative familiarity with the data and quantitative analysis allowed her to make interesting findings with immediate pedagogical applications.

Corpus-supported critical discourse analysis (CDA)

One of the earliest corpus-supported CDA studies is Hardt-Mautner (1995), which is an analysis of a corpus of British newspaper editorials on the topic of the EC/EU (European political and economic integration). The author successfully combined the best of corpus techniques and qualitative CDA and summed up by saying that:

> concordancing effectively heralds a breaking down of the quantitative/qualitative distinction, providing as it does the basis for quantitative analysis without 'deverbalising' the data, that is, without transferring it, through human intervention, to the numerical mode.
>
> (Hardt-Mautner 1995: 24)

Similarly, Stubbs (1997) suggests that a corpus-based approach to CDA can help overcome one of the perceived weaknesses of CDA: the lack of substantive empirical support for some of its claims. In the past decade, increasing numbers of CDA studies have been appearing which draw on specialized corpora which analysts compiled themselves. J. Flowerdew (1997) examined the discourse of the colonial withdrawal from Hong Kong, with claims substantiated by corpus data. Fairclough (2000) did a keywords analysis of the discourse of the Labour party in Britain under Tony Blair's leadership, using the corpus technique of keywords analysis (Scott 1997; Scott and Tribble 2006), in which a computer program compares two corpora to generate a list of words whose differential frequencies of use are statistically significant. In a similar vein, Teubert (2000) looked at keywords in the discourse of 'Euroscepticism' in Britain, and Partington (2003) analysed the linguistic characteristics of political argument, a process he termed 'Corpus-Assisted Discourse Studies'.

My prediction is that the way corpora were used in these studies will be become more or less standard for CDA studies in the future, as evidenced by Coffin and O'Halloran's (2004) paper at recent conference (Teaching and Language Corpora, TALC 2004), entitled 'Teaching critical discourse analysis: the role of corpus and the concordancer'. With a corpus of authentic discourse and an easy-to-use piece of software such as Wordsmith Tools (Scott 1999) or the free program AntConc (Anthony 2006), corpus-supported CDA is now within reach of almost everyone.

Corpus-driven grammar: grammar as discourse; grammar is (prior) discourse

The theoretical contributions of corpus-based work are perhaps clearest when we consider the newly emerging theories of grammar that are built from the ground up on real corpus data, with few preconceptions. Thus, Hunston and Francis (2000) describe what they call Pattern Grammar, a grammar in which the basic premise is that much of language is prefabricated and pre-patterned, and which has implications for how discourse analysts should view texts. After all, the popular critical discourse analytic terms *intertextuality* and *interdiscursivity* are basically also referring to the same phenomenon: that language is never created fresh and from scratch, but borrows, repeats, quotes, implies and alludes to prior texts and prior ideas.

Hoey (1997, 2002, 2005) notes that what he calls the pervasiveness (ubiquity) and subversiveness (anti-creativity) of the concept of collocation have led to new ideas about the effect of *priming* and calls for a new view of grammar and discourse (usage-based grammarians (cf. Barlow and Kemmer 2000) have also discussed this fact). Hoey's corpus-driven observations about 'textual colligation', in particular, have implications for discourse analysis: from a frequency point of view, he claims, lexical items are primed for textual position (e.g. *x years ago* is primed by previous uses to begin both sentences and paragraphs). Hoey also proposes that paragraphing is essentially a lexical phenomenon since lexical items can be seen as being either negatively or positively primed with regard to paragraph boundaries (i.e. lexical items either like or avoid the beginning of paragraphs). This view of language chimes with the discoveries from the more technical, computational end of research (e.g. Bod 1998), and with more recent work by Sinclair and Mauranen (2006), who have postulated a 'linear unit grammar' that gives 'chunking' a central role in the description of discourse, especially spoken discourse. This corpus-driven discourse grammar is linear in the sense that it avoids the hierarchical structures of traditional grammars and concentrates on the combinatorial patterns of text. In summary, all the above studies together show how research on corpora is leading to new approaches to discourse.

'Corpus-induced': corpora as sources of statistical patterns for language processing

Corpus-induced research is generally the domain of what we nowadays call 'natural language processing' (NLP) or computational linguistics, and is distinguished by its heavy reliance on automatic procedures which are ultimately derived (or, more technically, 'induced') from texts themselves. For example, TextTiling is a technique in which a computer is used to automatically demarcate the discourse units of a text on the basic of surface-level features such as words (Hearst 1997; Biber and Jones 2005). Carletta *et al.* (2004), and Leech and Weisser (2003) are two other examples. They both use semi-automatic methods to analyse dialogue corpora, drawing on rules induced from corpora. This area is still relatively new, and so all that can be said now is that the methods look promising, and that traditional discourse analysts of all persuasions should keep an eye on developments in this area to see which, if any, of the contributions can be turned to real advantage.

Characteristics of CBDA: new things you can do with corpora

The divisions between the categories of 'corpus-informed', 'corpus-supported/driven' and 'corpus-induced' discourse analysis are, of course, not clear-cut. They are only meant to show the variety of discourse research that can be undertaken with corpora. What, however, are the unique contributions of a corpus-based approach?

Easier access to standardized, distributed data, and verifiable results

Existing corpora give us immediate and easy access to huge amounts of data. The variety and quantity of written data can be almost overwhelming, while the spoken data in available standardized corpora such as the British National Corpus (BNC) and the Michigan Corpus of Academic Spoken English (MICASE) are also substantial, and globally available rather than being exclusive to one researcher. Discourse analysts interested in spoken language should consider the considerable range of extant corpora before collecting and transcribing their own spoken data: analyses based on these corpora can be verified or contested by going back to the primary data.

More types of data, including less-studied genres

More types of text are now available, and much more of it. In addition to 10 million words of mostly unscripted speech, the British National Corpus also includes, for example, the almost mythical category of 'notes left on the kitchen table', and also lesser-studied genres such as 'postcards' and 'shopping lists'. Discourse analysts no longer have an excuse to study only the 'sexier', more popular genres such as casual conversation, classroom discourse, political speeches and advertisements. MICASE (the Michigan Corpus of Academic Spoken English; Simpson *et al.* 2002) contains 1.7 million words of academic discourse (some being accompanied by streaming sound files). Discourse analysts may well not be aware of the availability of these texts.

Quantitative, empirically-based information about frequency/ typicality/idiomaticity

Discourse analysts who want to say things about the typicality or atypicality of lexico-grammatical choices can now empirically quantify their statements instead of appealing to intuition or subjective gut feeling. Many software programs (e.g. Anthony 2006) now allow us to automatically identify statistically significant keywords, key-keywords (Scott 1997) and other types of textual patterns.

Easier, computerized coding, retrieval and analysis

Extensible mark-up language (XML) is the way of the future for all corpora, and qualitative, XML-based content analysis software now exists that will help you both *code* and *analyse* your data quickly and efficiently.[5] Data marked up in XML will also be highly portable (not tied to any one program or platform). There now exists a program called AntMover (Anthony 2003) that performs automatic move analyses on texts, giving a rhetorical (structural) label automatically to each sentence in a text file. At the very least, much time can be saved using automated tools to perform a 'first pass' analysis of the data, whether the annotations are parts of speech or higher-level categories. Human analysts can save themselves a lot of manual coding work and concentrate instead on making minor corrections to automatic analyses.

Bolder, fresher, data-driven observations and hypotheses about language

As mentioned earlier, if corpora are large enough, they can provide insights that cannot be obtained (or cannot be safely drawn) from intuition alone (especially a single analyst's intuition). Patterns emerge from sufficiently large amounts of data, and computerized texts make much of the analysis automatic, semi-automatic, or interactive. As Partington (2003: 6–7) points out, patterns of usage may be indiscernible to receivers of a text (and sometimes even to the author/speaker of a text), and it is only by computer analysis that we notice, for example, how an entity is always represented as an actor rather than a patient, thus creating a discursive effect. Keywords or key domains can be automatically generated, showing trends that would otherwise be hard to observe. The good news is that the optimal corpus size is dependent on the analysis: the more specialized the discourse, the less you need of it to get a representative corpus and generalizable results.

Review and prospects

To sum up, then, if we take a broad view of discourse analysis and include studies that have implications for discourse rather than those which are, strictly speaking, discourse analytic, then the amount of corpus-based discourse analysis done so far is quite considerable. These studies can be said to be corpus-informed, corpus-supported or corpus-induced. With the advent of mega-corpora such as the BNC, many genres of English are now represented in sufficient quantity in 'general language' corpora (Lee 2001), while discourse analysts who work with specialized discourses can benefit from compiling their own corpora and applying some of the techniques of corpus-based linguists to support their analyses.

What predictions can we make about the future of corpus-based discourse analysis? On the one hand, the pervasiveness of computers and electronic texts makes it easy to predict that more discourse analyses in the future will be corpus-based in one form or another, although the need for a human analyst, ethnographic knowledge of events and close textual readings will in no way be replaced because the nature of language is such that it is resistant to easy interpretations and automatized analyses. Nevertheless, the methods, tools and techniques that corpus-based linguists have built up in the past four decades or so (but particularly in the past 20 years or so, in terms of advances in computing technology and text encoding standards) have much to offer the 'traditional' discourse analyst who has hitherto steered clear of corpora (for fear of computers or because of perceived inadequacies of corpus-based methods). Software tools exist that can help automate and facilitate the tagging of discourse-level units and their retrieval (for closer qualitative analyses). Analytical programs can be used to induce keywords and other useful statistics, to make findings that would otherwise be difficult to obtain by hand, or even impossible, in the case of large amounts of data. And, finally, the rigorous procedural and theoretical knowledge that corpus-based linguists have built up over the years (from data sampling and collection to data coding, from precision and comprehensiveness in designing search algorithms to statistical methods for accurate analyses) can certainly complement the competencies which traditional discourse analysts already have.

Challenges ahead: new types of corpora for discourse analysis

I will now conclude with what we can expect (or hope) to see more of in the future:

Genre-representative corpora

Most mega corpora aim at representing 'general language' and are not sampled on the basis of genre. Lee (2001) categorized the BNC texts in terms of genre, but this was done after the fact, after the texts had already been sampled on other grounds. We need to see corpora designed around genres from the ground up, in order to help genre analysts support their qualitative analyses with observations that can only be derived from large amounts of data.

Multimodal corpora

People have been using the word 'multimedia' to describe the Internet for years, and yet a combination of still pictures and text is about as far as most web pages go in terms of being multimedia, with sound and video still not being used to any large extent on most web sites. When it comes to language corpora, the picture is even bleaker: practically none of the commonly used corpora are truly multimedia, and privacy and copyright concerns have kept most private sound recordings out of reach. For example, the sound recordings made for the BNC can only be listened to within the British Library. A notable exception is MICASE, which offers the sound files for some of its speech events as streaming downloads. At present, however, no standardized English language corpus contains video recordings of spoken events: this is a serious shortcoming, as huge amounts of information regarding the use of space, gaze, gestures, etc. are lost. Spoken corpora do record quite a lot of speaker and contextual information, and these may be sufficient for some purposes, but it is true that harder-to-get-at details such as how well the speakers know each other, and in what capacity, and other kinds of deeply personal, historical or contingent pieces of information tend to be left out of corpus files, along with non-verbal aspects of communication. All these, and this lack of immediacy of the discourses vis-à-vis the analyst, may be a hindrance for types of discourse analysis that rely on intimate knowledge of the data, participants and context. We can hope that multimodal corpora of the future will address some of these issues.

Uni-modal corpora of electronic discourse

By 'uni-modal' or mono-modal, I am referring to e-mail, bulletin board discourse, chat room discourse, mobile phone text messages, etc.: interactions lacking any real 'modality' other than a screen. With books, there is a printed page with physical texture, font choices, formatting, layout, headings, pictures and colours. Books also tend to have provenance: they come from certain publishers, are categorized in bookstores into certain genres, etc. In contrast, e-discourse is composed in the ether with the barest of context. Sometimes, the anonymity of the interactions means that even the identity and sex of the authors cannot be verified. E-texts of this kind, however, will constitute more and more corpora in the future.

Intercultural and NNS corpora: communication between cultures and co-cultures

Most corpora are designed to capture the output of native speakers (NS), and at present, there are not enough corpora containing the language of non-native speakers (NNS). The VOICE and ELFA corpora[6] contain interactions (for the most part) among non-native speakers using English as a lingua franca, but there is also a need for more (multimodal) corpora of NS–NNS interactions in English, to help discourse analysts working in the area of intercultural communication undertake detailed quantitative and qualitative research.

I believe that one thing that the above types of corpora will have in common is their relatively small size. Multimodal corpora, for example, will be technically more difficult to collect, store and analyse, and the same applies to corpora of intercultural communication. Putting in more metadata about the discoursal contexts of source texts implies a greater familiarity and closeness to the text producers, and this implies smaller-scaled, private projects. I thus agree with L. Flowerdew (2004) that the future will see the creation of more smaller-scaled, specialized corpora, which she calls 'localized corpora', and that we will see ever more corpus-based discourse analyses.

Notes

1 The author would like to thank Mark Davies, Tony Berber-Sardinha, Sebastian Hoffmann, Geoffrey Leech, Mike Scott, John Sinclair and Michael Stubbs for offering their personal assessment of how much of the corpus-based research so far may be categorized as 'discourse analysis'. In addition, John Swales was asked for his opinion as a discourse analyst on how much in his field has been corpus-based. The usual disclaimer about responsibility for representing other people's opinions, however, applies.
2 Partington, Morley and Haarman (2004), Aijmer (1996, 2002) and Aijmer and Stenström (2004) are good exceptions: they make a start at filling this gap in the literature, with their collections of papers relating to discourse markers and words and phrases used for evaluation and persuasion.
3 For software programs that assist in manual tagging of corpus data for discourse-level phenomena, see the section on software at http://devoted.to/corpora.
4 A single corpus text file can contain either an aggregate/composite of short texts (e.g. a group of short conversations), or a single complete text (e.g. a school essay), or just a text sample (e.g. the first chapter or section of a book or article).
5 See the software section of http://devoted.to/corpora.
6 See http://www.univie.ac.at/voice/ for VOICE and http://www.uta.fi/laitokset/kielet/engf/research/elfa/index.htm for ELFA.

References

Aijmer, K. (1996) *Conversational Routines in English: convention and creativity*, London: Addison Wesley Longman.

—— (2002) *English Discourse Particles: evidence from a corpus*, Amsterdam: John Benjamins.

Aijmer, K. and Stenström, A.-B. (eds) (2004) *Discourse Patterns in Spoken and Written Corpora*, Philadelphia, PA: John Benjamins.

Anthony, L. (2003) 'Mover: a machine learning tool to assist in the reading and writing of technical papers', *IEEE Transactions on Professional Communication*, 46(3): 185–93.

—— (2006) 'Developing a freeware, multiplatform corpus analysis toolkit for the technical writing classroom', *IEEE Transactions on Professional Communication*, 49(3): 275–86.

Barlow, M. and Kemmer, S. (eds) (2000) *Usage-based Models of Language*, Stanford, CA: Center for the Study of Language and Information.

Biber, D. (1988) *Variation across Speech and Writing*, Cambridge: Cambridge University Press.

Biber, D. and Jones, J. K. (2005) 'Merging corpus linguistics and discourse analytical research goals: discourse units in biology research articles', *Corpus Linguistics and Linguistic Theory*, 1(2): 151–82.

Biber, D., Conrad, S. and Reppen, R. (1998) *Corpus Linguistics: investigating language structure and use*, Cambridge: Cambridge University Press.

Bod, R. (1998) *Beyond Grammar: an experience-based theory of language*, Stanford, CA: Center for the Study of Language and Information

Carletta, J., Dingare, S., Nissim, M. and Nikitina, T. (2004) 'Using the NITE XML Toolkit on the Switchboard Corpus to study syntactic choice: a case study', paper presented at the Fourth Language Resources and Evaluation Conference, Lisbon, Portugal, May.

Chafe, W. (1992) 'The importance of corpus linguistics to understanding the nature of language', in J. Svartvik (ed.) *Directions in Corpus Linguistics*, Berlin: Mouton de Gruyter, pp. 79–97.

Coffin, C. and O'Halloran, K. (2004) 'Teaching critical discourse analysis: the role of corpus and the concordancer', paper presented at Teaching and Language Corpora (TALC) 2004 in Granada, Spain, July.

Fairclough, N. (2000) *New Labour, New Language*, London: Routledge.

Flowerdew, J. (1997) 'The discourse of colonial withdrawal: a case study in the creation of mythic discourse', *Discourse and Society*, 8(4): 493–517.

Flowerdew, L. (2004) 'The argument for using English specialized corpora to understand academic and professional language', in U. Connor and T. A. Upton (eds) *Discourse in the Professions: perspectives from corpus linguistics*, Amsterdam: John Benjamins, pp. 11–33.

Hardt-Mautner, G. (1995) '"Only connect": critical discourse analysis and corpus linguistics' (Technical Papers vol. 6), Department of Linguistics, Lancaster University: UCREL.

Hearst, M. (1997) 'TextTiling: segmenting text into multi-paragraph subtopic passages', *Computational Linguistics*, 23(1): 33–64.

Hoey, M. (1997) 'From concordance to text structure: new uses for computer corpora', in *PALC '97: Proceedings of Practical Applications of Linguistic Corpora Conference, University of Lodz*, pp. 2–23.

—— (2002) 'Lexis as choice: what is chosen?', paper presented at the International Systemics Congress, University of Liverpool, July.

—— (2005) *Lexical Priming: a new theory of words and language*, New York: Routledge.

Hunston, S. and Francis, G. (2000) *Pattern Grammar: a corpus-driven approach to the lexical grammar of English*, Amsterdam: John Benjamins.

Kanoksilapatham, B. (2003) 'A corpus-based investigation of scientific research articles: Linking move analysis with multidimensional analysis', unpublished PhD thesis, Georgetown University.

Kennedy, G.D. (1998) *An Introduction to Corpus Linguistics*, London: Longman.

Kirk, J.M. (1996) 'Corpora and discourse analysis: transcription, annotation, and presentation', in I. Lancashire, C.F. Meyer and C.E. Percy (eds) *Synchronic Corpus Linguistics*, Amsterdam: Rodopi, pp. 263–78.

Larsen-Freeman, D. (2000) *Techniques and Principles in Language Teaching*, 2nd edn, Oxford: Oxford University Press.

Lee, D. (2001) 'Genres, registers, text types, domains and styles: clarifying the concepts and navigating a path through the BNC jungle', *Language Learning and Technology*, 5(3): 37–72.

Lee, D. and Swales, J.M. (2006) 'A corpus-based EAP course for NNS doctoral students: moving from available specialized corpora to self-compiled corpora', *English for Specific Purposes*, 25(1): 56–75.

Leech, G. and Weisser, M. (2003) 'Generic speech act annotation for task-oriented dialogue', in D. Archer, P. Rayson, A. Wilson and T. McEnery (eds) *Proceedings of the Corpus Linguistics 2003 Conference* (Technical Papers, vol. 16), Department of Linguistics, Lancaster University: UCREL.

Noguchi, J. (2004) 'A genre analysis and mini-corpora approach to support professional writing by nonnative English speakers', *English Corpus Studies*, 11: 101–10.

Partington, A. (2003) *The Linguistics of Political Argument: the spin-doctor and the wolf-pack at the White House*, London: Routledge.

Partington, A., Morley, J. and Haarman, L. (eds) (2004) *Corpora and Discourse*, Proceedings of CamConf 2002, Bern: Peter Lang.

Scott, M. (1997) 'PC analysis of Key Words – and Key Key Words', *System*, 25 (1): 1–13.

—— (1999) *WordSmith Tools 3.0*, Oxford: Oxford University Press.

Scott, M. and Tribble, C. (2006) *Textual Patterns: key words and corpus analysis in language education*, Amsterdam: John Benjamins.

Simpson, R.C., Briggs, S.L., Ovens, J. and Swales, J.M. (2002) *The Michigan Corpus of Academic Spoken English*, Ann Arbor, MI: The Regents of the University of Michigan.

Sinclair, J.M. and Mauranen, A. (2006) *Linear Unit Grammar: integrating speech and writing*, Amsterdam: John Benjamins.

Stubbs, M. (1996) *Text and Corpus Analysis*, Oxford: Blackwell.

—— (1997) 'Whorf's children: critical comments on critical discourse analysis (CDA)', in A. Ryan and A. Wray (eds) *Evolving Models of Language*, Clevedon: British Association for Applied Linguistics and Multilingual Matters Ltd, pp. 100–16.

—— (2005) 'Discourse analysis etc.'. E-mail (11 March 2005).

Swales, J.M. (2002) 'Integrated and fragmented worlds: EAP materials and corpus linguistics', in J. Flowerdew (ed.) *Academic Discourse*, London: Longman, pp. 153–67.

—— (2004) *Research Genres: explorations and applications*, Cambridge: Cambridge University Press.

Teubert, W. (2000) 'A province of a federal superstate, ruled by an unelected bureaucracy: keywords of the Eurosceptic discourse in Britain', in A. Musolff, C. Good, P. Points and R. Wittlinger (eds) *Attitudes towards Europe: language in the unification process*, Aldershot: Ashgate, pp. 45–86.

7 Corpus-based analyses of discourse

Dimensions of variation in conversation

Douglas Biber

Corpus-based investigations of grammar, discourse and register variation

There have been numerous studies of grammar and discourse over the last few decades, as researchers have come to realize that the description of function is as important as structure. In most cases, these studies have focused on linguistic features that have two or more structural or semantic variants. By studying these features in naturally occurring discourse contexts, researchers have been able to identify systematic differences in the functional use of each variant (see, e.g. Prince 1978; Thompson 1985; Schiffrin 1981).

The earliest corpus-based studies that contributed to our understanding of discourse similarly focused the contextual factors that influence linguistic patterns of use, based on empirical analysis of large representative corpora (see, e.g. McEnery *et al.* 2006). A key factor for corpus-based research is the representativeness of the corpus. Two considerations are crucial for corpus design: size and composition (Biber 1993a; Biber *et al.* 1998: 246–50). A related factor is the influence of 'register': language varieties defined by contextual/situational characteristics (e.g. communicative purpose, interactivity, production circumstances). Speech and writing can be considered as two very general registers, but there are many more specified registers, such as formal lectures, conversations, e-mail messages, textbooks, etc. Registers can be defined at any level of generality. For example, 'academic prose' is a very general register, while 'methodology sections in experimental psychology articles' is a much more highly specified register.

Although registers are defined in situational terms, they can also be described in linguistic terms, because linguistic features serve important communicative functions associated with situational characteristics. For example, first and second person pronouns (*I* and *you*) are commonly used in conversation associated with high personal involvement and interactivity. Corpus-based studies of register adopt one of two general perspectives:

- focusing on particular grammatical features, showing how the feature varies in systematic ways across registers;
- focusing on the overall characterization of registers, analysed in terms of constellations of co-occurring linguistic features.

Studies of the first type have shown that discourse grammar cannot be accurately generalized to an entire language. Rather, each register has its own distinctive patterns of use (see, e.g. Biber 1999, on complementizer *that* omission in conversation versus newspaper prose). The *Longman Grammar of Spoken and Written English* (LGSWE; Biber *et al.* 1999) is an example of this approach, showing how grammatical features can be described for their patterns of use across four spoken and written registers: conversation, fiction, newspaper language, and academic prose.

Multi-dimensional (MD) studies of register variation illustrate the second perspective. The MD approach was originally developed for comprehensive linguistic descriptions of registers, comparing the range of spoken and written registers in English (Biber 1986, 1988). There are two major quantitative steps in an MD analysis: (1) identifying the salient linguistic co-occurrence patterns in a language; and (2) comparing spoken and written registers in the linguistic space defined by those co-occurrence patterns.

As noted above, almost any linguistic feature will vary in its distribution across registers, reflecting the discourse functions of the feature in relation to the situational characteristics of each register. However, comprehensive descriptions of register variation must be based on the *co-occurrence* and *alternation* patterns among the range of linguistic features (see Halliday 1988; Ervin-Tripp 1972; Hymes 1974; Brown and Fraser 1979).

The MD approach gives formal status to the notion of linguistic co-occurrence, by using a statistical factor analysis to identify underlying *dimensions* of variation. Dimensions have both linguistic and functional content. The linguistic content of a dimension comprises a group of linguistic features (e.g. nominalizations, prepositional phrases, attributive adjectives) that co-occur with a high frequency in texts. Based on the assumption that co-occurrence reflects shared function, these co-occurrence patterns are interpreted in terms of the situational, social, and cognitive functions most widely shared by the linguistic features. That is, linguistic features co-occur in texts because they reflect shared functions.

Several experiments have been carried out to evaluate the reliability (and to a lesser extent validity) of the original MD analysis of register variation in English. For example, Biber (1990) shows that factor analyses carried out on split corpora result in nearly the same dimensions of variation, as long as the texts in those corpora are sampled to include equivalent ranges of register variation. Biber (1993b) shows how these dimensions can be used to predict the register category of unclassified texts with a high degree of accuracy (using discriminant analysis). And Biber (1992) uses confirmatory factor analysis to test the goodness of fit of several factorial models determined on theoretical grounds, confirming the basic structure identified using exploratory factor analysis in the 1988 analysis.

While early MD studies focused on register variation in English, subsequent studies have applied the same approach to Somali, Korean, Tuvaluan, Taiwanese and Spanish. Although these studies all apply the same methodological approach, they are carried out independently. In each case, a corpus was designed to represent the range of spoken and written registers found in the target culture, and a computational tagger was written to capture the grammatical structure of the target language. The set of linguistic variables used in each analysis includes the full range of lexical/grammatical distinctions that are relevant in the target language. Despite this fact, the resulting MD analyses have turned out to be strikingly similar in some respects. In particular, the analyses of all languages have uncovered dimensions relating to interactiveness/involvement versus informational focus, the expression of personal stance, and narrative versus non-narrative discourse (see Biber 1995, especially Chapter 7; Biber forthcoming).

The MD methodological framework has also been applied to more restricted discourse domains.[1] These include analyses of elementary school registers (Reppen 2001), job interview language (White 1994), university spoken and written registers (Biber 2006), and written academic subregisters (Grabe 1987; Kanoksilapatham 2003). Many of these studies have identified dimensions of variation similar to those found in the cross-linguistic studies, relating to the same functional concerns of interactiveness/involvement versus informational focus, the expression of personal stance, and narrative versus non-narrative discourse.

This result is surprising because there was no a priori reason to assume that analyses of restricted discourse domains would yield similar results to the analysis of the full range of spoken and written registers. We would rather expect to find different linguistic features varying in a restricted domain, reflecting the specific functional priorities of that domain. However, these analyses have shown that some of the same basic dimensions of variation seem to be fundamentally important across both restricted and general discourse domains, raising the possibility of universal dimensions of register variation.

In the following sections, this possibility is explored further by undertaking an MD analysis of linguistic variation within a single spoken register: conversation. Factor analysis is used to identify the linguistic dimensions of variation operating in this discourse domain. Then, cluster analysis is used to identify conversation 'text types' that are well-defined in that multidimensional space: these are types of conversation that are distinguished by their linguistic characteristics, and that therefore turn out to be distinguishable in their typical communicative purposes.

Corpus and linguistic features

The corpus used for the present analysis is taken from the Longman Spoken and Written English Corpus (LSWE Corpus; see Biber *et al.* 1999, Chapter 1). Only the British English sub-corpus of conversation was analysed here (*c.*4 million words). In total, there were 2,166 individual conversations included in the study. Conversations ranged in length from 200 words to almost 14,000 words; on average, conversations in the corpus were about 2,000 words long. (An additional 760 conversations were dropped from the MD analysis because they were too short for reliable quantitative analysis.)

Each conversation was automatically 'tagged' using the Biber grammatical tagger. The current version of this tagger incorporates the corpus-based research carried out for the LGSWE. The tagger identifies a wide range of grammatical features, including word classes (e.g. nouns, modal verbs, prepositions), syntactic constructions (e.g. WH-relative clauses, conditional adverbial clauses, that-complement clauses controlled by nouns), semantic classes (e.g. activity verbs, likelihood adverbs), and lexico-grammatical classes (e.g. that-complement clauses controlled by mental verbs, to-complement clauses controlled by possibility adjectives).

Identifying and interpreting the dimensions of variation in English conversation

The multi-dimensional approach to register variation uses factor analysis to reduce a large number of linguistic variables to a few basic parameters of linguistic variation. In MD analyses, the distribution of individual linguistic features is analysed in a corpus of texts. Factor analysis is then used to identify the systematic co-occurrence patterns among those linguistic features – the 'dimensions' – and finally texts and registers are compared along each dimension.

Table 7.1 summarizes the important linguistic features defining each dimension in the analysis of conversation. (A complete description of the factor analysis is available in Biber 2004.) Only 27 of the original 120 linguistic features were retained in the final factor analysis. (Features were dropped or combined because they were redundant, rare, or did not vary in systematic ways in conversation.) The solution for three factors was selected as optimal. These three factors account for only 36 per cent of the shared variance, but they are readily interpretable, and subsequent factors accounted for relatively little additional variance.

Each factor comprises a set of linguistic features that tend to co-occur in these conversations. Factors are interpreted as underlying 'dimensions' of variation based on the assumption that linguistic co-occurrence reflects underlying communicative functions. That is, particular sets of linguistic features co-occur frequently in texts because they serve related communicative functions. Features with positive and negative loadings represent two distinct

Table 7.1 Summary of the factorial structure

Dimension 1: Information-focused vs. interactive discourse	Features with positive loadings: word length, nominalizations, prepositional phrases, abstract nouns, relative clauses, attributive adjectives, passive verb phrases, (likelihood adverbs, general hedges)	Features with negative loadings: present tense verbs, contractions, 1st person pronouns, 2nd person pronouns, activity verbs
Dimension 2: Stance vs. context-focused discourse	Features with positive loadings: *that*-deletions, mental verbs, factual/mental verb + *that*-clause, likelihood/mental verb + *that*-clause, likelihood adverbs, adverbial clauses, general hedges, factual adverbs	Features with negative loadings: nouns, *WH*-questions
Dimension 3: Narrative-focused discourse	Features with positive loadings: past tense verbs, 3rd person pronouns, non-factual/communication verb + *that*-clause, communication verbs, *that*-deletions	Features with negative loadings: present tense verbs

co-occurrence sets. These comprise a single factor because the two sets tend to occur in complementary distribution: when a conversation has high frequency of the positive set of features, that same conversation will tend to have low frequencies of the negative set of features, and vice versa. In the interpretation of a factor, it is important to consider the likely reasons for the complementary distribution between positive and negative feature sets as well as the reasons for the co-occurrence patterns within those sets.

For example, the positive features on Factor 1 (e.g. long words, nominalizations, prepositional phrases, abstract nouns, relative clauses, etc.) all relate to informational purposes. These features are mostly associated with elaborated noun phrases and a dense integration of information in a text; previous MD studies have shown these features to be typical of written informational registers (see, e.g. Biber 1995, 2006).

In contrast, the negative features on Dimension 1 reflect a focus on the immediate interaction and activities: present tense verbs, contractions, first and second person pronouns, and activity verbs. The overall interpretation of Dimension 1 is thus relatively straightforward, showing that conversations tend to be either 'informational' or 'interactive', but not both. The functional label 'Information-focused versus interactive discourse' is proposed for this dimension.

The positive features on Dimension 2 are mostly linguistic features that express 'stance': personal attitudes or indications of likelihood. In the 1988 MD study of spoken and written register variation, several of these features were shown to co-occur typically with interactive and reduced structure features (on Dimension 1). In contrast, the analysis here shows that stance-focused discourse is not necessarily highly interactive discourse, and vice versa. (This dimension also includes several specific features that were not distinguished in the feature set used for the 1988 analysis, such as likelihood/ mental verb + that-clause and factual adverbs.)

The negative pole of Dimension 2 shows a surprising co-occurrence of only two features: nouns and WH-questions. In past analyses, nouns have co-occurred with other stereotypically 'literate' features (like adjectives, prepositional phrases, etc.), while WH-questions have co-occurred with stereotypically 'oral' and interactive features. The interpretation here must consider why these two features would tend to co-occur in conversations, and why they would tend to occur in a complementary distribution to stance features. Consideration of texts with a high frequency of these two features indicates that they are used together to reflect a focus on the larger context. WH-questions – the 'what', who', 'where', 'when' and 'how' – directly ask about that context, and nouns are the primary device used to refer to it. Thus, considering both positive and negative poles, we propose the interpretive label 'Stance-focused versus context focused discourse' for Dimension 2.

Finally, Dimension 3 is composed of stereotypically narrative features – past tense verbs, third person pronouns, and communication verbs controlling that-clauses; the only negative feature on this dimension is present tense verbs. Given this grouping of features, the interpretation as 'Narrative-focused discourse' is uncontroversial.

Identifying and interpreting conversation text types

Most MD studies have been undertaken to investigate the patterns of variation among 'registers'. Conversation is an example of a register according to this definition, as is newspaper reportage, classroom lectures, personal letters, and academic research articles. Registers can be defined at any level of specificity, depending on the extent to which the situational characteristics are specified. For example, academic prose is a very general register, while academic research articles, psychology research articles and methodology sections in experimental psychology research articles are registers defined at increasing levels of specificity. The original MD studies (Biber 1986, 1988) analysed a wide range of general spoken and written registers in English, while many subsequent analyses have applied those dimensions to the analysis of other more specialized registers (see, e.g. the studies in Conrad and Biber 2001).

These analyses have shown that there are important, systematic linguistic differences among registers. Those linguistic differences exist because of the functional basis of MD analysis: linguistic co-occurrence patterns reflect underlying communicative functions. Registers differ in their situational/ communicative characteristics, and as a result, the dimensions identify important linguistic differences among registers. However, it is important to note that the register categories are defined in situational rather than linguistic terms.

A complementary perspective on textual variation is to identify and interpret the text categories that are *linguistically* well defined, referred to as 'text types'. Text type distinctions have no necessary relation to register distinctions. Rather, text types are defined such that the texts within each type are maximally similar in their linguistic characteristics, regardless of their situational/register characteristics. However, because linguistic features have strong functional associations, text types can be interpreted in functional terms.

Text types and registers thus represent complementary ways to dissect the textual space of a language. Text types and registers are similar in that both can be described in linguistic and in situational/functional terms. However, the two constructs differ in their primary bases: registers are defined in terms of their situational characteristics, while text types are defined linguistically.

In the MD approach text types are identified quantitatively using Cluster Analysis, with the dimensions of variation as predictors. Cluster analysis groups texts into 'clusters' on the basis of shared multi-dimensional/linguistic characteristics: the conversations grouped in a cluster are maximally similar linguistically, while the different clusters are maximally distinguished. This approach has been used to identify the general text types in English and Somali (see Biber 1989, 1995). The present section describes the text types that can be distinguished linguistically within the single register of conversation.

The dimensions of variation (see above) are used as linguistic predictors for the clustering of conversations. The individual feature counts are first standardized so that each feature has a comparable scale with a mean of 0.0 and a standard deviation of 1. (The standardization was based on the overall means and standard deviations for each feature in the conversation corpus.) Then, 'dimension scores' were computed by summing the standardized frequencies for the features comprising each of the three dimensions. The cluster analysis is based on the three dimension scores for each conversation.

The methodology in this analytical step can be illustrated conceptually by the two-dimensional plot in Figure 7.1. Each point on Figure 7.1 represents a conversation, plotting the scores for that conversation on Dimensions 1 and 2. The numbers in the figure show the cluster number for each conversation, based on the results of the cluster analysis. Conversations that are similar in their dimension scores are grouped together as a cluster, or

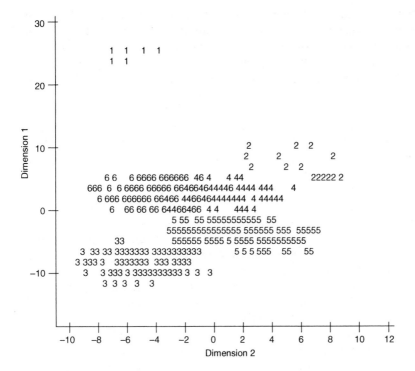

Figure 7.1 Plot of conversations along Dimension 1 vs. Dimension 2

'text type'. For example, the conversations labelled with a '1' on Figure 7.1 all have large positive scores on Dimension 1 (the vertical axis) and large negative scores on Dimension 2 (the horizontal axis). In contrast, cluster 2 has positive scores on both Dimensions 1 and 2.

Cluster analysis performs this grouping statistically, based on the scores for all three dimensions. Figure 7.1 shows the distribution across only two dimensions (1 and 3); these two dimensions were chosen because they provide a good visual display of how the conversations within each cluster are grouped based on their dimension scores. However, the actual cluster analysis uses all three dimension scores to identify the groupings of conversations that are maximally similar in their linguistic characteristics.

Cluster analysis is an exploratory statistical technique. The FASTCLUS procedure from SAS was used for the present analysis. Disjoint clusters were analysed because there was no theoretical reason to expect a hierarchical structure. Peaks in the Cubic Clustering Criterion and the Pseudo-F Statistic (produced by FASTCLUS) were used to determine the number of clusters. These measures are heuristic devices that reflect goodness-of-fit: the extent to which the texts within a cluster are similar, while the clusters are maximally distinguished.

Figure 7.1 shows the distribution of these six clusters in only a two-dimensional space, whereas the cluster analysis is actually based on a three-dimensional space. It turns out that the third dimension is also important in defining some clusters. For example, Cluster 4 is not sharply delimited in terms Dimensions 1 and 2, but all conversations in this cluster have large positive scores on Dimension 3 ('narrative').

Table 7.2 provides a descriptive summary of the cluster analysis results, showing the number of conversations grouped into each cluster plus descriptive statistics for the cluster dimension scores. The clusters differ in their distinctiveness: the smaller clusters are more sharply distinguished linguistically. For example, cluster 1 has only 40 conversations; linguistically, the conversations grouped in cluster 1 have extremely large positive scores on Dimension 1 ('informational'); large negative scores on Dimension 2 ('context-focused'); and scores near 0.0 on Dimension 3 ('narrative'). At the other extreme, cluster 5 is a 'general' text type: it is large (680 conversations) and relatively unmarked in its dimension scores.

The clusters can be interpreted as *conversation text types*, because each cluster represents a grouping of conversations with similar linguistic profiles. Figure 7.2 compares the linguistic characteristics of the four most distinctive of these conversation types, plotting their mean dimension scores. The 'general' conversation types – clusters 5 and 6 – are not plotted in Figure 7.2.

Taken together, Table 7.2 and Figure 7.2 provide the basis for the interpretation of each conversation type. (These interpretations are refined by consideration of individual conversations from each type.)

Type 1 is the most specialized, with the fewest number of texts (only 40, or about 2 per cent of the conversations in the corpus). Linguistically, these

Table 7.2 Cluster descriptive statistics for each dimension

Cluster means					
Cluster	No. of conversations	Dim. 1	Dim. 2	Dim. 3	
1	40	22.15	5.08	−0.99	(Informational context-focused)
2	116	7.67	5.87	0.93	(Informational stance-focused)
3	496	−8.04	−5.19	−2.88	(Interactive context-focused)
4	308	2.12	−0.31	5.61	(Narrative)
5	680	−4.15	1.74	0.55	(Unmarked interactive)
6	526	2.63	−4.46	−1.50	(Unmarked context-focused)

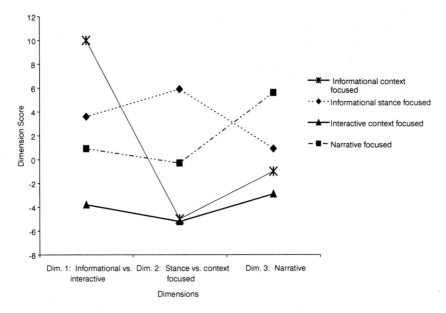

Figure 7.2 Multi-dimensional profile for conversational test types 1–4 (Note: Dimension 1 has been transformed to a scale of 10 for comparison)

conversations are extremely informational (Dimension 1) and focused on the context (Dimension 2). Text Sample 1 provides an example of a conversation from this cluster. This text illustrates the dense use of 'informational' features, such as nominalizations (e.g. *sophistication, agreement, possibility*), other long words (e.g. *paperwork, computer-wise, computerized*), attributive adjectives (*modern, massive, great*), passives (*be/getting inundated*), and prepositional phrases (*to you, about the conversation, with Alec*). Although texts from this cluster would be considered interactive and involved in comparison to written expository texts, they are highly informational in comparison to other conversational texts.

Text sample 1: conversation from cluster 1: informational, context-focused

A: I, I want to talk to you about er the conversation I had with Alec yesterday, he seems to be inundated with having to get details about <unclear> on his er, all his paperwork and so on, and he seems to be inundated and he sounded a bit low, quite frankly, to me yesterday on the phone that he was getting inundated with all this

B: Mm, mm

A: work. I said I'm quite sure there must be something that could be done computer-wise

B: Right

A: but he sort of pooh-poohed it and sort of said well you know, we're getting a bit too old for all this modern sophistication of computers and so on, well I said well quite frankly I am not totally in agreement with you, because as you probably know Clyde was looking into a program which will could alleviate a lot

B: Yes I know, I know

A: of the work, that I do, but I

B: yes it's on the <unclear>

A: would tell you right here and now, er I'm still retaining my bible you know the book

B: Yeah, yes, yes

A: that I have downstairs, because it's, if it was to be computerized, it would be a massive great bloody great volume

B: Yes

A: and I would be carrying this around and it just wouldn't be feasible

B: Quite, right

Type 2 is also relatively specialized (with only 116 conversations grouped into this cluster). Linguistically, this conversation type is relatively informational (Dimension 1) but especially marked for being highly stance-focused (Dimension 2). (This conversation type should be contrasted with Type 5: a much larger cluster that is stance-focused and highly interactive rather than informational.) Text Sample 2 illustrates the typical linguistic characteristics of Conversation Type 2. Notice especially the frequent mental verbs (e.g. *know, think, expect, want*), stance verbs controlling *that*-clauses, usually with the *that* omitted (e.g. *would have thought... , I think ..., I suppose ...*), and the frequent hedges and stance adverbs and adverbials (*surely, obviously, really, actually, probably, certainly*).[2] Texts from this cluster are informational, in that they are focused on discussion of a particular topic rather than the immediate interpersonal interaction, but they share the primary purpose of expressing personal stance in relation to that topic.

Text sample 2: conversation from cluster 2: informational, stance-focused

A: There is no, statutory obligation for the person organizing it

C: Oh, I know.

B: Well not the organizer surely oh I know I would have thought you'd have to, <unclear> shoot it

A: I'm sure that the social services require psychiatric or

B: Mm, I would've thought so

A: obviously medical <unclear> what you're doing. Mhm but they're to be qualified people involved. But I would have expected that the whole thing would have to be operated by, somebody who was qualified.

B: I don't know, because like, you know like the doctors <unclear>

A: <unclear> I think it sort of depends how big that you want to get involved in. If you're just somebody who's on the outside providing services, to keep the smooth running of it then you don't really have to know anything about it.

C: Mm.

A: But if you're actually involved in it, and you want to be involved in the people, then I think you have to know something about it.

B: Well the other evening they were showing something on TV, one of these doctors', doctors' practices that are opting out or whatever. And they got a stockbroker, someone who used to be a stockbroker, actually managing the whole practice.

A: Yeah.

B: I mean he's obviously not qualified as a doctor.

A: Mhm.

B: So I mean I suppose they'll look at it in the same kind of way [...]

In contrast, Type 3 conversations are much more common (496 conversations grouped into this cluster, or 23 per cent of all conversations in the LSWE Corpus). These conversations are extremely interactive and focused on the immediate context, as illustrated by Text Sample 3. The turns in this conversation are short and highly interactive (notice the dense use of *I* and *you*), and there is a dense use of common nouns together with WH-questions to express context-dependent information.

Text sample 3: conversation from cluster 3: interactive, context-focused (family riding in the car)

C: Can I go in the front?

A: Tie your belt up please. Tie your belt up. – Okay, speedily - now – can you er zip your zips up please? Keira. Can you zip your zip up?

B: I can't.

A: What do you think you'll be doing at school today?

B: Recorder concert!

A: Oh! Have you got your recorder? In school?

B: No! Er, yes, yes

A: Yeah.

B: yes.

A: Now, what you gonna be playing?

B: Joe Joe stubbed his toe. [...]

Finally, Type 4 conversations are also relatively common (308 texts). This cluster is relatively unmarked on Dimensions 1 and 2, but these conversations are extremely narrative in their Dimension 3 characterization. Text Sample 4 illustrates these characteristics. Note that these conversations are not necessarily extended stories (although some of them are). Rather, as in the present case, these conversations can be constructed out of extended discussion of past events (with frequent past tense verb phrases, third person pronouns, and communication verbs – especially *said* in this conversation), often coupled with commentary on their immediate relevance.

Text sample 4: conversation from cluster 4: narrative

A: I've just explained that to him. And he said he didn't know that, that he would get hold of Sen and ring me first thing, thing in the morning - er, to tell me why Sen hasn't paid. He's got the invoice and everything. I said well you've sent us twenty thou= - I said there is no VAT on it which it should be! Deary me! He says. Has he got the invoice? I said yes. And I said, we've been having, having the invoice outstanding since October at two and half thousand pound! I said, you actually owe me six thousand, one hundred and odd! And I said, you must realize I've a small company, and that's, in one respect that I've had to send those conditions because you're failing to meet the agreed thirty days payment!

B: Yeah.

A: And I said it's not on! I said we couldn't survive like that. And he said, well would you like to carry on with the contract? I said we're too far committed now to, I says to back out. [...]

Conclusion

The three dimensions identified by this factor analysis of a conversational corpus are surprisingly similar to the dimensions of variation found in earlier MD analysis of spoken and written registers (Biber 1988). Both analyses have a dimension that reflects the distinction between involved/interactive versus informational discourse; both analyses have a narrative dimension; and both have dimensions related to the expression of stance. The large-scale MD analyses of spoken and written registers in Somali and Korean similarly identified dimensions associated with these functions, composed of similar kinds of linguistic features.

Even more surprisingly, several MD analyses of restricted discourse domains have identified dimensions with similar correlates (e.g. Reppen's (2001) analysis of elementary school registers and White's (1994) analysis of job interviews). The fact that similar dimensions are found here in a corpus restricted to conversation suggests that these might be universal parameters of variation.

Comparing the present analysis to previous MD studies provides two complementary perspectives on the characteristics of conversation. In comparison to the full range of spoken and written registers, conversation is distinctive in being extremely interactive, involved, focused on the immediate context and personal stance, and constrained by real-time production circumstances. However, when conversation is considered on its own terms, we discover systematic differences among conversational texts. Interestingly, the present analysis indicates that the major parameters of variation internal to conversation are in part a microcosm of the dimensions of variation that distinguish among spoken and written registers generally.

Notes

1 There have also been several studies of specific registers that apply the dimensions that were identified and interpreted in the 1988 MD analysis of spoken and written variation in English (see, for example, the collection of studies in Conrad and Biber 2001). These studies do not entail separate MD analyses; rather they apply the dimensions identified in the 1988 MD analysis of English to some new discourse domain.
2 Note also the dense use of discourse markers (e.g. *I mean, you know*) supporting the expression of stance in this conversation.

References

Biber, D. (1985) 'Investigating macroscopic textual variation through multi-feature/ multi-dimensional analyses', *Linguistics*, 23: 337–60.

—— (1986) 'Spoken and written textual dimensions in English: resolving the contradictory findings', *Language*, 62: 384–414.

—— (1988) *Variation across Speech and Writing*, Cambridge: Cambridge University Press.

—— (1989) 'A typology of English texts', *Linguistics*, 27: 3–43.

—— (1990) 'Methodological issues regarding corpus-based analyses of linguistic variation', *Literary and Linguistic Computing*, 5: 257–69.

—— (1992) 'On the complexity of discourse complexity: a multidimensional analysis', *Discourse Processes*, 15: 133–63, reprinted in S. Conrad and D. Biber (eds) (2001) *Variation in English: multi-dimensional studies*, London: Longman, pp. 215–40.

—— (1993a) 'Representativeness in corpus design', *Literary and Linguistic Computing*, 8: 243–57.

—— (1993b) 'Using register-diversified corpora for general language studies', *Computational Linguistics*, 19: 219–41.

—— (1995) *Dimensions of Register Variation: a cross-linguistic comparison*, Cambridge: Cambridge University Press.

—— (1999) 'A register perspective on grammar and discourse: variability in the form and use of English complement clauses', *Discourse Studies*, 1: 131–50.

—— (2004) 'Conversation text types: a multi-dimensional analysis', in G. Purnelle, C. Fairon, and A. Dister (eds) *Le poids des mots: Proceedings of the 7th International Conference on the Statistical Analysis of Textual Data*, 15–34. Louvain: Presses Universitaires de Louvain.

—— (2006) *University Language: a corpus-based study of spoken and written registers*, Amsterdam: John Benjamins.

Biber, D., Conrad, S. and Reppen, R. (1998) *Corpus Linguistics: investigating language structure and use*, Cambridge: Cambridge University Press.

Biber, D., Johansson, S., Leech, G., Conrad, S. and Finegan, E. (1999) *The Longman Grammar of Spoken and Written English*, London: Longman.

Brown, P. and Fraser C. (1979) 'Speech as a marker of situation', in K.R. Scherer and H. Giles (eds) *Social Markers in Speech*, Cambridge: Cambridge University Press, pp. 33–62.

Conrad, S. and Biber, D. (eds) (2001) *Variation in English: multi-dimensional studies*, London: Longman.

Ervin-Tripp, S. (1972) 'On sociolinguistic rules: alternation and co-occurrence', in J.J. Gumperz and D. Hymes (eds) *Directions in Sociolinguistics*, New York: Holt, pp. 213–50.

Halliday, M.A.K. (1988) 'On the language of physical science', in M. Ghadessy (ed.) *Registers of Written English: situational factors and linguistic features*, London: Pinter, pp. 162–78.

Hymes, D. (1974) *Foundations in Sociolinguistics: an ethnographic approach*, Philadelphia, PA: University of Pennsylvania Press.

Grabe, W. (1987) 'Contrastive rhetoric and text-type research', in U. Connor and R.B. Kaplan (eds) *Writing across Languages: analysis of L2 text*, Reading, MA: Addison-Wesley, pp. 115–38.

Kanoksilapatham, B. (2003) 'A corpus-based investigation of biochemistry research articles: linking move analysis with multidimensional analysis', PhD dissertation, Georgetown University.

McEnery, A.M., Tono, Y and Xiao, Z. (2006) *Corpus Based Language Studies*, London: Routledge.

Prince, E.F. (1978) 'A comparison of *wh*-clefts and *it*-clefts in discourse', *Language*, 54: 883–906.

Reppen, R. (2001) 'Register variation in student and adult speech and writing', in S. Conrad and D. Biber (eds) *Variation in English: multi-dimensional studies*, London: Longman, pp. 187–99.

Schiffrin, D. (1981) 'Tense variation in narrative', *Language*, 57: 45–62.

Thompson, S.A. (1985) 'Grammar and written discourse: initial vs. final purpose clauses in English', *Text*, 5: 55–84.

White, M. (1994) 'Language in job interviews: differences relating to success and socioeconomic variables', PhD dissertation, Northern Arizona University.

8 Corpora and context in professional writing

Lynne Flowerdew

Introduction

One of the main concerns regarding corpus-based analyses is their lack of contextual features for interpretation of the corpus data. As Hunston (2002: 23) notes in her discussion of the limitations of a corpus, 'Perhaps most seriously a corpus presents language out of its context.' However, in recent years, more importance has been attached to the value of contextual features to aid corpus analysis, especially for those analyses of small, specialized corpora where the compiler-cum-analyst has access to valuable background information for interpretation of the data (see Flowerdew 2004a for an overview of such studies). In this respect, Tribble (2002) outlines an analytic framework for contextual analysis of corpus data, which he describes as derived from a synthesis of the three main approaches to genre (Swalesian, Australian systemic-functional linguistic, and the new rhetoric), to complement the linguistic analysis (see Table 8.1). Tribble's position, then, is to see the role of context as very much informing corpus-based analyses.

On the other hand, another perspective on this contextual dimension to the analysis of corpus data is to view the data as shedding light on the social and cultural context from which the corpus is extracted. Tognini-Bonelli (2001, 2004), taking a Hallidayan approach, argues that repetitions of linguistic patterns in the *co-text*, revealed by the co-selection of items on the vertical axis of the concordance lines, reflect the *context*, i.e. the situational and cultural parameters involved in the creation of meaning. Whereas individual texts are identified as unique, individual and coherent communicative events, corpora can be read for recurrent formal patterning, the repetition of which exhibits a sample of social or discursive practice (see Table 8.2). '... the way we can now look at text shows up the link between the individual instance of communication and the social tendency for a community of speakers to use particular patterns of language' (ibid.: 11).

Tognini-Bonelli (2001) illustrates the points made above by looking at the semantic behaviour of the words *largely* and *broadly* in a corpus made up of 13.81 million words of articles from *The Economist* and 6.36 million words of articles from *The Wall Street Journal*. The type of semantic behaviour under

Table 8.1 Analytic framework (contextual)

Contextual analysis	
1 *Name*	What is the name of the genre of which this text is an exemplar?
2 *Social context*	In what social setting is this kind of text typically produced? What constraints and obligations does this setting impose on writers and readers?
3 *Communicative purpose*	What is the communicative purpose of this text?
4 *Roles*	What roles may be required of writers and readers in this genre?
5 *Cultural values*	What shared cultural values may be required of writers and readers in this genre?
6 *Text context*	What knowledge of other texts may be required of writers and readers in this genre?
7 *Formal text features*	What shared knowledge of formal text features (conventions) is required to write effectively into this genre?

Source: Tribble 2002: 133

Table 8.2 Views of text and corpus

A text	A corpus
Read whole	Read fragmented
Read horizontally	Read vertically
Read for content	Read for formal patterning
Read as a unique event	Read for repeated events
Read as an individual act of will	Read as a sample of social practice
Coherent communicative event	Not a coherent communicative event

Source: Tognini-Bonelli 2004: 18

investigation is that of semantic prosody, i.e. the notion that in addition to its 'real' meaning, a word can also carry some type of evaluative meaning, usually negative, which is transferred from its habitual collocations. For example, the vertical concordance lines in Table 8.3 reveal that *largely* is seen to co-occur with words carrying a negative semantic prosody, an aspect speakers may be aware of only on a subconscious level.

Broadly, on the other hand, prefers sets of words denoting similarity and agreement with a more positive orientation.

The frequencies for *largely* (2,136 occurrences) and *broadly* (368 occurrences) in this specialized economics corpus were compared with their respective frequencies in the Birmingham Corpus, a 20-million-word general corpus, in which 1,084 instances for *largely* and 174 for *broadly* were recorded. The discrepancy between the frequencies of these two items

Table 8.3 Morphological and semantic negatives in the context of *largely*

gated for so long, blacks were left	**largely**	**illiterate** and without non-farmin
mercial banks, and – though this was	**largely**	**overlooked** – urged further flows of
Gary Condit from California. Having	**largely**	**shunned** the group, the Democratic
Kong have had enough. Legco, the	**largely**	**toothless** legislature, has vowed
previous regime doled out large and	**largely**	**unaudited** sums to homeland admin
industries. 'The government seems	**largely**	**unconcerned** about such complaints
The war caused one spectacular but	**largely**	**unforeseen** calamity: the mass flig

Source: Adapted from Tognini-Bonelli 2004: 16

Table 8.4 Broadly in connection with similarity and agreement

and visible breaks; and these breaks	**broadly**	**coincide.** They do so partly
Soviet Air Forces now had aircraft of	**broadly**	**comparable** performance to their
work of political activists working	**broadly**	**in unison** or at least with
with inter-union disputes now seem	**broadly**	**satisfactory.** But the Government
all English-speaking countries have	**broadly**	**similar** tenure patterns with
Scandinavian countries, which have	**broadly**	**the same** political and economic

Source: Adapted from Tognini-Bonelli 2001: 37

in a general and specialized corpus could therefore be seen as reflecting the discursive practices of the genre.

The purpose of this chapter is to examine in more detail these two differing standpoints regarding the relationship between context and corpora, i.e. in what circumstances it is necessary to rely on context for interpretation of corpus data, and on what occasions the concordance data can reveal institutionalized discourse practices. I have chosen to examine the areas of semantic prosody and epistemic stance as these are pragmatically motivated and therefore highly context-sensitive.

The items for investigation, *associated with* for its semantic prosody, and devices such as *It is expected that* ... for epistemic stance, have been extracted from a 250,000-word corpus of environmental impact assessment (EIA) reports. This 250,000-word specialized corpus consists of 60 summary reports, commissioned by the Hong Kong Environmental Protection Department from 23 different consultancy companies in Hong Kong. These reports document the potential environmental impacts of the construction and operation of proposed buildings and facilities and also contain a section on suggested measures to alleviate any possible adverse environmental impacts (see Flowerdew 2003, 2004b for further details and analysis of this corpus).

In the first part of the two following sections, I first review the notions of semantic prosody and epistemic stance with reference to key corpus literature in the field. I then discuss examples of these devices in my specialized EIA corpus in an attempt to clarify the complex relationship existing between a corpus and its context.

Semantic prosody

The concept of semantic prosody was first dealt with in depth in a seminal and oft-quoted article by Louw (1993), who acknowledges Sinclair (1987, 1991) as generating the first computationally derived 'profile' of this phenomenon. (Sinclair, himself, refers to Bréal (1897) for coining the term 'contagion' to signify the transference of meaning, usually pejorative, as the product of habitual collocations.)

Hunston (2002: 142) summarizes the key features of semantic prosody as follows:

- The semantic prosody of a lexical item is a consequence of the more general observation that meaning can be said to belong to whole phrases rather than to single words.
- Semantic prosody can be observed only by looking at a large number of instances of a word or phrase, because it relies on the *typical* use of a word or phrase.
- It accounts for 'connotation': the sense that a word carries a meaning in addition to its 'real' meaning. The connotation is usually one of evaluation, that is, the semantic prosody is usually negative or, less frequently, positive.
- It can be exploited, in that a speaker can use a word in an atypical way to convey an ironic or otherwise hidden meaning.
- The semantic prosody of a word is often not accessible from a speaker's conscious knowledge. Few people, for example, would define *SET in* as meaning 'something bad starts to happen', but when the negative connotation is pointed out in many cases it accords with intuition (*A spell of fine weather set in* sounds very odd, for example).

On the surface, semantic prosody seems to be a relatively straightforward concept to pin down according to its main features summarized above. Corpus-based studies such as the one by Tognini-Bonelli cited above, present it as a relatively unproblematic phenomenon, with the example of *largely* exemplifying Hunston's observations that identification of semantic prosody relies on the *typical* uses of a word and that it 'is often not accessible from a speaker's conscious knowledge' but is usually immediately realized by the speaker when pointed out, a phenomenen Louw (cited in Sinclair 1999: 4) refers to as 20/20 hindsight. Likewise, Stubbs (1995, 2001a) presents clear-cut evidence, based on an analysis of 40,000 examples across 120 million words of the Cobuild Corpus, showing that CAUSE is typically associated with nouns indicating 'something bad' (*anxiety, cancer, problems*) whereas PROVIDE collocates with mostly 'good things' (*care, food, help, money*).

However, one of the most contentious issues is whether semantic prosody is indeed a purely semantic phenomenon or also has a pragmatic orientation, which has implications for corpus interpretation. Sinclair (2004: 34) points out that semantic prosody carries attitudinal meaning, (as do Hunston and Stubbs), and is 'on the pragmatic side of the semantics/pragmatics continuum'. Widdowson (2004), on the other hand, seems to view prosody more as a semantic phenomenon recoverable from co-occurrences of collocations in the text. He agrees with the basic notion of semantic prosody, in that being a co-textual relation, semantic signification can be read off from concordance lines. In contrast to other linguists, Widdowson does not seem to view the assignation of pragmatic significance based on an analysis of concordance lines as so straightforward and maintains that it is somewhat problematic on the grounds that it does not exist in the text, but can only be fully ascertained from external contextual features and other features in the text beyond the immediate truncated concordance line:

> ... on the evidence of their customary collocates, particular words can be shown to have a typical positive or negative semantic prosody, and it can be plausibly suggested that facts of co-textual co-occurrence should be recognized as part of the semantic signification of such words. But this, of course, does not tell us about what pragmatic significance might be assigned to such a co-occurrence in a particular text. The point about these co-textual findings is that they are a function of analysis, with texts necessarily reduced to concordance lines. One might trace a particular line back to its text of origin, but then if it is to be interpreted, it has to be related not to other lines in the display but to the other features of the original text.
>
> (Widdowson 2004: 60)

However, in a chapter on corpus semantics Stubbs (2001b) argues that the conventionalized view that pragmatic meanings are usually inferred by the reader/listener, making them highly context-dependent, may be overstated and that large-scale corpus studies can provide evidence to show that pragmatic meanings, like semantic prosodies, can also be conventionally encoded in linguistic form. (In fact, Stubbs prefers the term 'discourse prosody' to 'semantic prosody' on account of the fact that prosodic information can often only be established by looking beyond the concordance line to more discourse-based extended units of meaning).

Evidence in support of Stubbs' view is provided by O'Halloran and Coffin (2004) who, based on a 45-million-word sub-corpus of the *Sun* newspaper drawn from the 450-million-word Bank of English, show how negative attitudinal meaning can be gleaned from multiple concordance lines. O'Halloran and Coffin maintain that an *accumulation* of negative co-texts for *United States of Europe* displays a regular negative attitude for 'United States of Europe', thus reflecting the anti-Europe stance of the *Sun* newspaper. Such an ideological stance may not be immediately obvious when encountered as a single instance, but can be retrieved from examining the co-textual environment of repeated occurrences of the search word in a large corpus.

In sum, Stubbs' argument seems to be in alignment with Tognini-Bonelli's view that recurrent patterns found in a corpus can reveal samples of social practice, which themselves are often pragmatically motivated. Widdowson, meanwhile, attaches greater importance to contextual features external to the corpus, such as those mentioned by Tribble, for interpretation of corpus data. Both these positions will be considered below in the interpretation of the phrase *associated with* and also in the interpretation of epistemic markers such as *It is expected that* ... in the specialized corpus of environmental reports.

Investigation and interpretation of *associated with* in the EIA corpus

The phrase *associated with* was found to occur 139 times in the corpus of environmental reports, and most significantly, across all the 23 different companies, indicating it was not just a feature of an in-house company style of writing. In 135 instances it seemed to be somewhat ambiguously involved in a causal effect with a negative semantic prosody.[1]

However, as Gavioli (2002) has shown in relation to medical texts, the language features found in specialized text may not necessarily be generalizable inside the wider domain of the specialized language. In order to substantiate my interpretation of this phrase and to see whether it also had a negative prosody involving a causal effect in general scientific texts, I consulted the 7-million-word Applied Science domain of the 100-million-word British National Corpus (BNC). In this sub-corpus, *associated with* was found to occur 1,327 times in 162 different texts. As it is not feasible to trawl through all 1,327 lines of concordance output to examine the data qualitatively, concordance lines were selected on a one-per-text basis. This examination revealed that in 40 per cent of cases this phrase clearly has

Table 8.5 Concordance lines for *United States of Europe*

leader's bleak plan for a	**United States of Europe**	came as a hammer blow to
the road towards a Federal	**United States of Europe.**	Hague has never tried to
forming into a giant	**United States of Europe**	– with the same tax and
The empire builders want a	**United States of Europe.**	Thank goodness you have
thirds say there will be a	**United States of Europe**	within the next 20 years.
for a hopeless dream of a	**United States of Europe.**	He is certain to pay the
was the first step to a	**United States of Europe**	– which would cost
or a state in a newly-formed	**United States of Europe?**	These are the central
Just as many are against	**United States of Europe**	under a federal

Source: Adapted from O'Halloran and Coffin 2004: 288

a negative semantic prosody, e.g.: *The commission is concerned about the possible risks associated with releasing genetically altered organisms ...*

This negative prosody of *associated with* is therefore most likely an attenuated form of 'caused by', in line with Hyland's (1998, 2000) observation that such hedging devices would be used when scientists would avoid claiming a direct causal effect, thereby forestalling any challenges from their peers, especially when controversial issues are involved. (In fact, this phrase is also one type of epistemic stance marker, other types of which are discussed in the following section.) Although Hyland's research is concerned with academic writing, it could be surmised that the same principles apply to writing in the professions, which have their own conventions and discourse practices. This view that *associated with* reflects the discourse practices of this genre is further strengthened by the fact that it was found in reports produced by 23 different environmental consultancy companies.

Where one is dealing with multiple texts from a particular discourse community with somewhat institutionalized practices, as in the case of the corpus of environmental reports, or known entrenched ideologies as in the *Sun* newspaper corpus, it may be possible, as Stubbs has noted, to establish pragmatic meanings based on regularly co-occurring instances of conventionalized attitudes in the text. However, as Widdowson (2004: 60) points out, such prosodic information does not tell us about what pragmatic significance might be assigned to a co-occurrence of items in just one particular text, and for such information it would be necessary to interpret the item with reference to not only other co-textual features, but also to external contextual information. For example, it could well be the case that a scientist might prefer to use the 'marked' form of causation, *caused by* instead of the attenuated form *associated with*, as outlined in Table 8.6, for some type of salient effect such as to express disagreement and provoke challenges in violation of the norm. Although *caused by* and *associated with* can both be regarded as displaying a negative semantic prosody, their pragmatic significance is not such a stable entity and could well vary depending on rhetorical purpose and other contextual factors not encoded in the text.

The dilemma for corpus linguists, then, in the interpretation of corpus data is to distinguish between what is *typical*, i.e. a 'repeated event', which can probably be 'read off' from the concordance lines, as claimed by Tognini-

Table 8.6 Concordance lines for associated with in EIA corpus

clamation footprint. Blasting activities	associated with	with the removal of the headland cou
ds. Suspended sediment concentrations	associated with	backfilling at the two MBAs (non-cu
. In view of the engineering difficulties	associated with	hydraulic dredging and vessel transfe
gh tension power lines. Health hazards	associated with	proximity to high tension power li
ct. Potential vehicular emission impact	associated with	The traffic from the roadworks, throu
the technical memorandum. The noise	associated with	tunnel drilling, or a tunnel boring ma
roundwater are in place. The problems	associated with	continued pollution of the beach and
Impacts. Some residual impacts remain	associated with	the stream works between Wong Nai

Bonelli, and what is *atypical*, which would be 'read as a unique event' for which context external to the text is required for interpretation.

Epistemic markers of stance

Epistemic markers of stance conveying the writer's certainty or doubt toward a proposition have been investigated in several corpus-based studies. For example, Biber and Conrad (2000) compare the use of adverbials (e.g. *perhaps, probably*) for marking epistemic stance across three different registers (conversation, academic and newspaper prose). Another corpus-based investigation by Charles (2003) looks at the use of epistemic nouns (e.g. *claim, theory, assumption*) to construct stance in theses from two different academic disciplines, politics/international relations and materials science. Charles's focus is on their discourse-organizing role with an anaphoric function, encapsulating a previous stretch of text. She notes that when they have such an organizing role, they mark the writer's stance and how the discourse should be interpreted, e.g.:

> (8) Policies aimed at raising the stakes faced by a state ... are likely to produce convergence in these competition-related areas of state practice ... *This claim* is made on the basis of the conceptual analysis offered here. (mpoalch2)
>
> (Charles 2003: 318)

Meanwhile, Hyland's (1999) corpus-based study on stance markers in academic text takes a broader perspective by looking at over 300 items expressing stance across eight different disciplines. The modal verbs, *may, would, could* and *might*, and hedging verbs *suggest, indicate, seem* and *assume* were found to be the most frequent devices to express stance across the whole corpus, and were represented more in the humanities / social sciences disciplines than in the science ones, e.g.:

> (9) I suggest that certain ways of thinking about social movements are likely to be very fruitful ... (Soc)
>
> (Hyland 1999: 117)

One interesting feature regarding epistemic markers is whether they mark attribution of stance to the writer explicitly or implicitly: 'Reference to the presence of the author can ... be explicit or disguised, with the writer taking responsibility for actions, or avoiding agency by transitivity selections which favour the passive and non-specific subjects' (Hyland 1999: 102).

In the corpus-based *Longman Grammar of Spoken and Written English*, Biber *et al.* (1999: 972–8) note that verbal markers of stance (e.g. *believe, expect, suggest*) are ambiguous as to whether they mark the stance of the speaker/writer or that of some third party, when involved in a short passive or as a passive verb in an extraposed *It* construction controlling a complement clause, as illustrated by the two following examples:

> The allegations **are believed** to involve several teenagers aged from 12 to 18. (NEWS)
> **It was expected** that they would interview him later today. (NEWS)
> (Biber *et al.* 1999: 977)

Significantly, such markers are found to occur more frequently in the news register than in fiction, conversation or academic prose, with Biber *et al.* (1999: 977) positing thus: 'In news, this seems to be a deliberate strategy to avoid direct responsibility for the reported stance'.

In the following section, I examine such types of ambiguous stance markers and how they may be interpreted in relation to co-textual and contextual features.

Investigation and interpretation of passive construction epistemic markers in the EIA corpus

In contrast to previous corpus-based studies in this area, I did not deliberately set out to investigate epistemic markers in my EIA corpus. Rather, this particular type of epistemic marker of an ambiguous nature regarding the attribution of stance surfaced during the analysis of the lexico-grammatical patterning of the key words, i.e. words of unusually high frequency when compared with a large-scale reference corpus (see Scott 1997; Scott and Tribble 2006), with the 100-million-word British National Corpus used as the reference corpus in this study. One keyword, *problem*, was found to occur in the environment of causative verbs and in phrases with *be* (see L. Flowerdew 2003). Closer examination of these phrases with *be* revealed that this verb took on the semantics of a causative verb. *Be* was also found to occur in complement clauses, mirroring the two types of passive constructions (short passive and passive verb controlling a complement clause) discussed in the previous section, e.g.:

> Increased noise levels **are not expected** to be a problem.
> ... **it is considered unlikely** that septicity would be a problem.

Having noticed these ambiguous markers of stance in the main clauses preceding complement clauses containing *be* + the key word *problem*, which were always used to indicate that a problem would *not* arise, or be unlikely to arise, I decided to investigate their overall use in this sense more closely. To this end, I selected the verbs *expect* and *consider* in the two types of passive constructions for examination.

In the short passive of the pattern *Increased noise levels are expected / are not expected* ... nearly 40 per cent, i.e. 47 out of 123 occurrences, were found to be in a negative construction, indicating lack of any potential environmental problem arising from the projected construction activities (see Table 8.7). Another 10 per cent, i.e. 12 instances, of the short passive were found to contain a modal (*could, would, may*) e.g. *sound absorption could be expected to be significant*, mitigating further the epistemic stance. The remaining 50 per cent were of the pattern ... *is / are expected to ...*, e.g. *the pollutants emitted are expected to increase in quantity*. It is interesting to observe that the environmental reports seem to attach as much importance, or nearly as much importance to environmental problems that are not expected to occur, but I have no means of knowing why this should be so.

Likewise, the patterning *It is expected* + negative, or *It is not expected that ...* was found to occur in 40 per cent of the 18 occurrences of this structure, with four instances of each, e.g.:

> ... **it is expected that** there will be no significant residual impacts.
> **It is not expected** that the reclamation will have any effect on the hydrodynamics of the Rambler Channel or ...

With regard to the patterning of *considered*, the short passive was found to be far more common than the extraposed *It* construction (70 occurrences compared with 38), with around a third of the short passives used with a negative, e.g.:

> ... the impacts **are not considered** to be ecologically significant.

Moreover, a third of the extraposed *It* constructions, 11 out of all 36 occurrences, indicated that a problem would not arise or would be unlikely, with the common patterns shown in Table 8.8.

In sum, an examination of the corpus data for the verbs *expect* and *consider* in both the short passive construction and in an extraposed *It* construction reveals consistency across all the reports. Almost equal weighting is given to environmental issues that are not considered likely to occur as those that are, but the reason for this phenomenon is not immediately obvious. Through consulting a specialist informant, the director of the atmospheric, marine and coastal environment programme at the university where I work, who is

Table 8.7 Concordance lines for *expected* in a short passive construction

onstruction of the afteruse facilities	is not expected to	result in any adverse environmental
e construction of Kam Tim bypass	is not expected to	cause any significant dust impacts
r quality. The operation of the CIF	is not expected to	generate any effluent likely to exceed
ite.Construction of the seawall	is not expected to	give rise to any significant rise in noi
tion. In general dust concentrations	are not expected to	Exceed the HKAQO. Landuse; impa
d the mainly bored piling activities	are not expected to	cause disturbance. During the constr
oved is very small. These activities	are not expected to	create significant adverse effects as
i Wo will also be containerized and	are not expected to	result in significant odour problems.

Table 8.8 Concordance lines for *considered* in extraposed It construction

it is considered	unlikely that storage drum containment will be breached within the LRWF
it is considered	extremely unlikely that these areas will be subject to dust impacts from the c
associated with	highly unlikely that any element of the effluent export scheme will create a
associated with	that agglomeration and subsequent sedimentation will not be of great concer
it is considered	that propeller scour or general wash will not have significant effects at any
it is considered	that casting operations will not result in an increase in noise levels in the vill

familiar with the discursive practices of the genre, I learnt that, in this genre, writers would go out of their way to mention the effects that would *not* arise in order to counterbalance any negative view of the construction project, and that they would do so in a somewhat indirect way. (In contrast, expected problems were expressed in a much more direct way, e.g. *Works at the tunnel portal will create a noise problem.*)

These insights from a specialist informant can thus be viewed as answering the following questions in Tribble's contextual analysis framework:

> *Social context*: what constraints and obligations does this setting impose on writers and readers?
> *Formal text features*: what shared knowledge of formal text features (conventions) is required to write effectively in this genre?

In the above case, it is not possible to 'read off' the social practice of the genre from an accumulation of concordance lines. The lines can be read for formal patternings, but these can only be fully interpreted with reference to the institutionalized practices of the genre.

Concluding remarks

In the above discussion, I have examined whether pragmatically motivated phrases can be interpreted solely through the accumulation of concordance data or whether a contextual dimension, such as that proposed by Tribble, is necessary for their faithful interpretation. As the discussion of *associated with* and passive construction epistemic devices have revealed, Stubbs and Widdowson are both right in their own ways. The investigation of *associated with* in a specialized and large-scale sub-corpus has provided evidence to show that pragmatic meanings may be conventionally encoded in text. On the other hand, in cases where a writer exploits semantic prosody to use a word in an atypical fashion, or the analyst is unfamiliar with the institutionalized practices of the genre, then it is a more difficult task to 'read off' and infer the discursive practice of the genre from the concordance data. Bhatia (2004) and Swales (2004) have underscored the importance of a contextual perspective for the interpretation of genre. In future, as discussed in Flowerdew (2005), it is expected that the field of corpus linguistics will become more attuned and sensitive to this perspective, taking a more socio-rhetorical approach to the analysis of corpus data.

Note

1   In the other four instances *associated with* was found with budget considerations with the meaning of 'in connection with', e.g. *The recurrent cost associated with the operation and maintenance of* ...

References

Bhatia, V.K. (2004) *Worlds of Written Discourse*, London: Continuum.

Biber, D. and Conrad, S. (2000) 'Adverbial markers of stance in speech and writing', in S. Hunston and G. Thompson (eds) *Evaluation in Text: authorial stance and the construction of discourse*, Oxford: Oxford University Press, pp. 56–73.

Biber, D., Johansson, S., Leech, G., Conrad, S. and Finegan, E. (1999) *Longman Grammar of Spoken and Written English*, London: Longman.

Charles, M. (2003) '"This mystery...": a corpus-based study of the use of nouns to construct stance in theses from two contrasting disciplines', *Journal of English for Academic Purposes*, 2: 313–26.

Coffin, C., Hewings, A. and O'Halloran, K. (eds) (2004) *Applying English Grammar: functional and corpus approaches*, Milton Keynes: The Open University.

Conrad, S. and Biber, D. (2000) 'Adverbial marking of stance in speech and writing', in S. Hunston and G. Thompson (eds) *Evaluation in Text: authorial stance and the construction of discourse*, Oxford: Oxford University Press, pp. 56–73.

Flowerdew, L. (2003) 'A combined corpus and systemic-functional analysis of the problem-solution pattern in a student and professional corpus of technical writing', *TESOL Quarterly*, 37(3): 489–511.

—— (2004a) 'The argument for using English specialised corpora to understand academic and professional settings', in U. Connor and T. Upton (eds) *Discourse in the Professions: perspectives from corpus linguistics*, Amsterdam: John Benjamins, pp. 11–33.

—— (2004b) 'The problem-solution pattern in apprentice vs. professional technical writing: an application of appraisal theory', in G. Aston, S. Bernardini, and D. Stewart (eds) *Corpora and Language Learners*, Amsterdam: John Benjamins, pp. 125–35.

—— (2005) 'An integration of corpus-based and genre-based approaches to text analysis: countering criticisms against corpus-based methodologies', *English for Specific Purposes*, 24: 321–32.

Gavioli, L. (2002) 'Some thoughts on the problem of representing ESP through small corpora', in B. Kettemann and G. Marko (eds) *Teaching and Learning by doing Corpus Analysis*, Amsterdam: John Benjamins, pp. 293–303.

Hunston, S. (2002) *Corpora in Applied Linguistics*, Cambridge: Cambridge University Press.

Hyland, K. (1998) *Hedging in Scientific Research Articles*, Amsterdam: John Benjamins.

—— (1999) 'Disciplinary discourses: writer stance in research articles', in C.N. Candlin and K. Hyland (eds) *Writing: texts, processes and practices*, London: Longman, pp. 99–121.

—— (2000) *Disciplinary Discourses: social interactions in academic writing*, London: Longman.

Louw, B. (1993) 'Irony in the text or insincerity in the writer?', in M. Baker, G. Francis and E. Tognini-Bonelli (eds) *Text and Technology: in honour of John Sinclair*, Amsterdam: John Benjamins, pp. 157–76.

O'Halloran, K. and Coffin, C. (2004) 'Checking overinterpretation and under-interpretation: help from corpora in critical linguistics', in C. Coffin, A, Hewings, and K. O'Halloran (eds) *Applying English Grammar: functional and corpus approaches*, London: Hodder Arnold, pp. 275–97.

Scott, M. (1997) 'PC analysis of key words – and key key words', *System*, 25(1): 1–13.

Scott, M. and Tribble, C. (2006) *Textual Patterns: key words and corpus analysis in language education*, Amsterdam: John Benjamins.

Sinclair, J.M. (1987) *Looking Up: an account of the COBUILD project in lexical computing*, London and Glasgow: Collins.

—— (1991) *Corpus, Concordance, Collocation*, Oxford: Oxford University Press.

—— (1999) 'The lexical item', in E. Weigand (ed.) *Contrastive Lexical Semantics*, Amsterdam: John Benjamins, pp. 1–24.

—— (2004) *Trust the Text*, London and New York: Routledge.

Stubbs, M. (1995) 'Collocations and semantic profiles', *Functions of Language*, 2(1): 23–55.

—— (2001a) *Words and Phrases: corpus studies of lexical semantics*, Oxford: Blackwell Publishers.

—— (2001b) 'On inference theories and code theories: corpus evidence for semantic schemas', *Text*, 21(3): 437–65.

Swales, J. (2004) *Research Genres*, Cambridge: Cambridge University Press.

Tognini-Bonelli, E. (2001) *Corpus Linguistics at Work*, Amsterdam: John Benjamins.

—— (2004) 'Working with corpora: issues and insights', in C. Coffin, A. Hewings and K. O'Halloran (eds) *Applying English Grammar: functional and corpus approaches*, London: Hodder Arnold, pp. 11–24.

Tribble, C. (2002) 'Corpora and corpus analysis: new windows on academic writing', in J. Flowerdew (ed.) *Academic Discourse*, London: Longman, pp. 131–49.

Widdowson, H.G. (2004) *Text, Context, Pretext*, Oxford: Blackwell.

Suggestions for further work

1   Consider the relative merits of close attention to concordance lines in corpus approaches, on the one hand, and attention to context, on the other.
2   Consider the relative advantages and disadvantages of using small and large corpora.
3   Consider the potential contribution of corpus linguistics to the study of language above the levels of lexis and grammar, where it began.
4   To what extent do you agree with Lee's examples as instances of 'corpus-based' discourse analysis?
5   Consider the potential contributions of corpus-based analysis to genre analysis and genre analysis to corpus study, as claimed by L. Flowerdew.

Part IV

Multimodal discourse analysis

Multimodal discourse analysis is a fairly new and rapidly developing perspective on discourse which holds that meanings are created in texts and interactions in a complex interplay of semiosis across multiple modes which include but are not limited to written and spoken language. In seeking to understand this interplay it has integrated insights from a number of more established approaches to discourse as well as other social sciences.

Work on the analysis of static texts such as Kress and van Leeuwen's (1996) grammar of images and O'Toole's (1994) investigation of paintings, sculpture and architecture, for example, rely heavily on Halliday's (1973, 1978) systemic-functional theory of language (see also Baldry 2000; Lemke 1998). Work on the analysis of more dynamic interactions, what Norris (2004, this volume) calls 'multimodal interaction analysis', has benefited significantly from previous work in fields such as anthropology and psychiatry, especially the 'ecological perspective' pioneered by Scheflen, Birdwhistle, Bateson and others working in the Palo Alto research group in the 1950s (see, for example, Birdwhistle 1970; Ruesch and Bateson 1968 [1951]; Scheflen 1974), as well as those influenced by them like Kendon (1990). Ethnography, with its concern with the wider contexts in which texts and interactions are produced or performed, has also had a profound influence, as have conversation analysis and pragmatics with their concern for the sequential organization of semiotic cues (see, for example, Goodwin 2000). There have even been attempts to apply the methods of corpus-based discourse analysis to multimodal texts (see, for example, Baldry 2007).

Despite its relatively short history, multimodal discourse analysis has also had an important influence on other approaches and fields, most notably in the area of literacy and the growing interest in digital literacies (Jewitt and Kress 2003; Kress 2003; Lankshear and Knobel 2003) and the field of human-computer interaction (see, for example, Granström et al. 2002). Critical discourse analysis has also begun incorporating the analysis of modes other than text, evidenced by a recent volume on how ideology is mediated through text and image (Lassen et al. 2005), which includes chapters by both Fairclough and Wodak.

This multi-disciplinary scope of multimodal discourse analysis is especially evident in the chapters in this part that demonstrate its potential to contribute to our understanding not just of texts and interactions but also to the ideological contexts which surround them and the psychological constructs which give rise to them (see also McNeill 1992; Thibault 2004). In her chapter, Norris explores how attention to the ways various embodied and disembodied modes in interaction can help us to understand how different aspects of identity interact and affect one another in conversations. In doing this, she combines her multimodal methodology with theories of human cognition and attention, showing how identity elements that have been constructed prior to an interaction and stored in the 'historical bodies' (Jones this volume; Nishida 1958) of participants have a direct influence on new identity elements that are co-constructed by participants in real time.

Whereas Norris applies the insights from a multimodal perspective to psychological issues, Jewitt and Jones show, in their analysis of classroom interaction, how local practices of posture, gesture, gaze and object handling can be linked to larger issues of policy and politics. Attention to multimodal semiotics, they claim, can help to uncover 'silent' discourses of power, which are sometimes even more potent than those expressed more explicitly though writing and speech.

Both of these chapters underline a recent shift in multimodal discourse analysis (and indeed all discourse analysis) away from the abstract and often de-contextualized concept of 'text' and towards a conceptualization of discourse as integrated in the flow of concrete social actions that go to make up ordinary and professional human practices. In this regard, studies in multimodal discourse analysis like those offered here are increasingly exploring the relationship between multiple and interacting semiotic modes used in particular concrete settings (such as workplaces) and the kinds of identities, power relationships and opportunities for social action that they make available to social actors. Such studies have considerable practical potential in helping people to redesign their interactions in classrooms and workplaces in ways which could make them more beneficial or efficient.

Useful further reading in multimodal discourse analysis can be found in Kress and van Leeuwen (1996), Jewitt (2006), O'Halloran (2004) and van Leeuwen and Jewitt (2001).

References

Baldry, A. (ed.) (2000) *Multimodality and Multimediality in the Distance Learning Age*, Campobasso, Italy: Palladino.

—— (2007) 'The role of multimodal concordances in multimodal corpus linguistics', in T.D. Royce and W.L. Bowcher (eds) *New Directions in the Analysis of Multimodal Discourse*, Mahwah, NJ and London: Lawrence Erlbaum Associates, pp. 173–94.

Birdwhistle, R.L. (1970) *Kinesics and Context*, Philadelphia, PA: University of Pennsylvania Press.

Goodwin, C. (2000) 'Action and embodiment within situated human interaction', *Journal of Pragmatics*, 32: 1489–522.

Granström, B., House, D. and Karlsson, I. (2002) *Multimodality in Language and Speech Systems*, Norwell, MA: Kluwer Academic Publishers.

Halliday, M.A.K. (1973) *Explorations in the Functions of Language*, London: Edward Arnold.

—— (1978) *Language as a Social Semiotic*, London: Edward Arnold.

Jewitt, C. (2006) *Technology, Literacy and Learning*, London: Routledge.

Jewitt, C. and Kress, G. (eds.) (2003) *Multimodal Literacy*, New York: Peter Lang.

Kendon, A. (1990) *Conducting Interaction*, Cambridge: Cambridge University Press.

Kress, G. (2003) *Literacy in the New Media Age*, London: Routledge.

Kress, G. and van Leeuwen, T. (1996) *Reading Images: the grammar of visual design*, London and New York: Routledge.

Lassen, I., Strunck, J. and Vestergaard, T. (2005) *Mediating Ideology in Text and Image: ten critical studies*, Amsterdam: Benjamins.

Lankshear, C. and Knobel, M. (2003) *New Literacies*, London: Open University Press.

Lemke, J.L. (1998) 'Multiplying meaning: visual and verbal semiotics in scientific text' in J.R. Martin and R. Veel (eds) *Reading Science: critical and functional perspectives on discourses of science*, London: Routledge, pp. 87–113.

McNeill, D. (1992) *Hand and Mind: what gestures reveal about thought*, Chicago, IL: University of Chicago Press.

Nishida, K. (1958) *Intelligibility and Philosophy of Nothingness*, Tokyo: Maruzen.

Norris, S. (2004) *Analysing Multimodal Interaction: a methodological framework*, London: Routledge.

O'Halloran, K. (2004) *Multimodal Discourse Analysis: systemic functional perspectives*, New York and London: Continuum.

O'Toole, M. (1994) *The Language of Displayed Art*, London: Leicester University Press.

Ruesch, J. and Bateson, G. (1968 [1951]) *Communication: the social matrix of psychiatry*, New York: W.W. Norton and Company, Inc.

Scheflen, A.E. (1974) *How Behaviour Means – Exploring the Contexts of Speech and Meaning: kinesics, posture, interaction, setting, and culture*, New York: Anchor Press/Doubleday.

Thibault, P. (2004) *Brain, Mind, and the Signifying Body: an ecosocial semiotic theory*, London and New York: Continuum.

van Leeuwen, T. and Jewitt, C. (2001) *Handbook of Visual Analysis*, London: Sage.

9 Some thoughts on personal identity construction

A multimodal perspective

Sigrid Norris

> The self is not something that exists first and then enters into relationship with others, but it is, so to speak, an eddy in the social current and so still a part of that current.
>
> (Mead 1974: 182)

Introduction

Identity construction is a widely covered topic in studies of discourse and a topic that has interested me for some time (Norris 2002, 2004, forthcoming). As in my other chapters, my focus in this chapter is a methodological one that allows the investigation of identity construction from a slightly new perspective. In this chapter, I take up the topic of personal identity construction and illustrate what a multimodal approach can offer to grasp such a complex, fluid and ever-changing notion. While these pages centre around one social actor in particular, I would like to emphasize that the reader needs to keep in mind the quote above, which alludes to the fact that one social actor can never act alone or have a personal identity without the collective.

My work is grounded in the methodological framework of multimodal interaction analysis (Norris, 2004) and with this, my writing is first of all an extension of Scollon's (1998, 2001) mediated discourse analysis. Second, this framework is strongly influenced by the work of Kress and van Leeuwen in multimodality (1998, 2001; and van Leeuwen 1998). Besides these two merging directions, the framework of multimodal interaction analysis draws on and builds upon the micro analytical aspects found in interactional sociolinguistics of Goffman (1959, 1961, 1974), Gumperz (1982) and Tannen (1984); discourse analysis as in Hamilton (1996, 1998) or Schiffrin (1994, 2005); and the macro analytical aspects of a historical approach of Wodak *et al.* (2001).

Some background

There is much current research from various perspectives on personal identity construction and it is not possible to review even a very small aspect of what has been written on the topic in this short chapter. However, in order to show some of the breadth, I give a brief eclectic overview without trying to discuss the many interesting chapters and books on personal identity construction or the breadth of research.

For example, we find that some scholars in discourse analysis are focusing on the individual side of personal identity construction – here I am thinking of studies like the ones done by Schiffrin (2005) or Hamilton (1998), who investigate micro discursive constructions such as pronoun use and show how individuals establish themselves as belonging to one group or another.

Other researchers focus on the social and historical side of identity – and here I am thinking of the work by Wodak *et al.* (2001), and their book on national identity construction, which combines text analysis with narrative and interview analysis and places it all into a historical perspective.

Again other scholars approach identity construction from a broader angle, trying to encompass social psychological and sociocultural forces when analysing a person's use of language – an example of this would be the work by Hall and Bucholz (1995).

What all of these approaches to identity have in common is their concentration on language (spoken or written). With such a focus on language, language is automatically assigned supremacy over other modes, leading analysts to analyse conversations as focused interactions. It is this point that creates the opportunity for this chapter on multimodal personal identity construction. In other words, all of the studies mentioned above (and many more not mentioned here) feed into the proposed perspective, making this slightly new investigation possible.

Theoretic argument

As I have argued elsewhere (Norris 2006), the prioritizing of language may limit our understanding of interaction; and here I will argue that it also may limit our understanding of personal identity construction, as a focus on language may in fact tell us little about which role language actually plays in everyday identity construction. Thus, my argument is that when we view language unquestioned as the primary mode of communication for identity construction, we may in fact assign too much value to what is being said or written and therefore analyse identity in quite obscured ways.

I utilize, draw and build on the micro analytical approach that Hamilton, Schiffrin and Tannen, for example, use to analyse spoken language, but take multiple embodied modes such as posture, gesture and head movement into consideration. Further, I investigate disembodied modes such as layout and objects. However, while findings in language-centred studies are highly accentuated by chiefly assigning primacy to the mode of language and by investigating mainly what people say/write, this chapter decentralizes language by integrating an abundance of modes without assigning supremacy to any one of them. Such integration of multiple modes points the analyst to look beyond focused interaction and to incorporate complexities of identity construction that have often been left out.

Just as Wodak *et al.* (1998) emphasize the need to take a historical perspective when investigating national identity construction, I would like to emphasize the need to account for the fact that every social actor carries with them a historical body (Nishida 1958) or habitus (Bourdieu 1998). Such a historical body allows social actors to co-construct themselves in their own lives in specific ways. These specific ways depend upon the actual happenings around the social actor on different time scales and on different vertical levels of action encompassing multiple identity elements. Here, in this chapter, I will only take a look at historical snippets, looking at the very specific ways in which one social actor co-constructs tidbits of identity elements.

I argue here that identity is not formed in cohesive wholes but as situationally grounded and co-constructed 'identity elements'. When speaking of identity elements I am thinking of an analogy with chemical elements such as oxygen, hydrogen, or gold. These elements are 'whole' in and by themselves, but they can also combine to make larger and/or different 'wholes'. Taking this analogy a bit further we can say that different elements are found in different ways: gold, for example, can be found free and unattached in the natural world, while other elements like oxygen or hydrogen are highly volatile when free and must be combined with others.

When thinking of identity in this way, we could say that a person's gender identity is more like the element of gold – illustrating that the gender identity element is not necessarily as much situationally dependent; whereas a person's occupational identity element is probably more like oxygen (which is more often found in complex molecules) – illustrating that an occupational identity element would be greatly situationally dependent.

Certainly, identity elements are attributed to social actors by others and are constructed by social actors themselves. Furthermore, identity construction is shaped by larger societal norms that are constructed and re-constructed on every level of interaction from personal and family interaction to interactions in organizations and public spheres. Such normative prescriptions are taken on by a social actor when constructing their personal identity and the structures are enforced and re-enforced through limited choices given in the world. However, in this chapter, I will take much of this for granted and focus on the theoretical argument that we need to take multiple modes of communication into consideration and that we have to look beyond focused interactions when trying to gain insight (however minute) into personal identity construction.

In this chapter I show how identity elements are co-constructed in (what we may for the purpose of this chapter call) clock-time, are then moved in consciousness into memory and to a different level of attention and awareness. Here, I illustrate two aspects: one, that the identity elements that reside in memory can (and do) shape clock-time actions; and two, that there is a lag-time between the ending of one action and identity formation and the next.

Structure of the chapter

As my first point, I illustrate my multimodal analysis by looking at an example of a social actor speaking on the phone with her employee. Then, I offer some new thoughts about consciousness to allow me to move to my next point, the point of I- and me-identity elements. Only after this, do I discuss how memory or me-identity elements impact on I-identity construction and how there is a lag-time in movement from I-to-me identity. Once I move towards the discussion of I- and me-identities, I use three consecutive higher-level actions as my examples of which the phone conversation (explicating the multimodal framework) is the second.

The following excerpts that I will look at in detail come from an extensive ethnographic study of two co-owners of a web-design business that I conducted over a period of four months. During this time, I spent most of the days with the two women (whom I will call Tanya and Lucy) during work hours and also spent time with them at their homes. I have met many of their friends, caretakers of their children, husband and ex-husband, and their parents.

An example

Here, I focus on Tanya and her everyday identity construction, reviewing data pieces that are mundane and not special in any way, since I am interested in the everyday of identity construction. In order to make sense of the complexity involved, I will use the modal density foreground–background continuum that I have discussed in much of my writing.

When looking at the transcript of a video excerpt of Tanya and Lucy in the office in Figure 9.1, we see that Tanya is speaking on the phone with one of their employees. When looking at the first image, we can easily determine that Tanya is focused upon the action of speaking on the phone because of the multiple modes that she employs.

Figure 9.1 Image 1 illustrates that the modes of object handling (with Tanya holding the phone) and spoken language (with Tanya speaking into the phone, where Tanya's utterances are illustrated in black and Lucy's utterances are shown in grey) take on much weight for Tanya. However, object handling and spoken language are not the only modes that she employs.

Image 1: Spoken language

Image 2: Posture and gaze

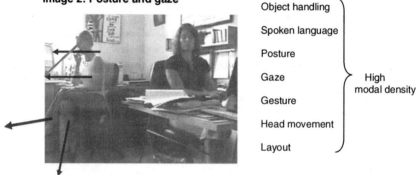

Object handling

Spoken language

Posture

Gaze   High
                        modal density
Gesture

Head movement

Layout

Images 3 and 3.1: Gesture   **Images 4 and 4.1: Head movement**

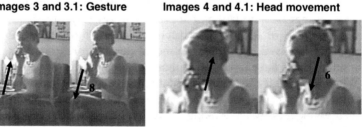

Figure 9.1

When we look at Tanya's posture in Figure 9.1 Image 2, we see that her posture is quite closed with her legs crossed, and that the directionality of her body (indicated by the black arrows) points away from Lucy. When looking at Tanya's gaze (indicated by a grey arrow), we can say that her gaze does not appear to be fixed on any one particular point and could be termed a middle-distance gaze. When we look at the gestures that Tanya performs as illustrated in Figure 9.1 Images 3 and 3.1, we notice that Tanya performs a great number of beat gestures, moving her hand up and down eight times in this same way during this brief section. These beat gestures are rhythmically organized with her spoken language, emphasizing particular words (*this* in line 2; *all* in line 3; *whatever* in line 4; *email, and, fax, everything* in line 5; *always* in line 6), and we may even be able to interpret these gestures as a way for Tanya to force herself to give clear instructions, speeding herself up to get to the point in lines 2–4 and slowing herself down in line 5, and speeding herself up again in line 6. Such gestures, both Kendon (1981) and McNeill (1992) have pointed out, help speakers and hearers to build greater discourse coherence. Six out of the eight times (lines 3 to 6), Tanya simultaneously performs beats with her head as indicated by the arrows in Figure 9.1 Images 4. and 4.1. Head movements start with *whatever* (in line 3), go through her point of instruction *email and fax everything* (line 4) and end with *always* (line 6). Thus, while the hand beats govern the coherence and speed of her utterances, the head beats bracket the actual point that she is trying to get across.

Here, Tanya utilizes what I call *high modal density* in order to co-construct the action of speaking on the phone with an employee: with object handling and spoken language as the most intense modes, which are at the same time complexly intertwined with the modes of posture, gesture, gaze and head movement. Looking at Figure 9.1, we also notice that layout plays a role, with desks, chairs and computers arranged as they are, making it easily possible for Lucy to overhear the conversation and to chime in when she deems it necessary. Tanya's use of the described modal configurations when constructing the higher-level action of speaking on the phone allow us to perceive this action to be constructed through high modal density, leading us to the conclusion that Tanya is focused on the phone conversation.

When we now take advantage of the modal density continuum, we can place the action that Tanya performs, namely her talking on the phone with an employee, in the foreground of her attention/awareness (Figure 9.2 Graph 1) and, as Scollon (1997) has noted, each action that a social actor performs also constructs their identity. Thus, by co-constructing this action together with her employee on the phone, Tanya is also co-constructing her identity element of an employer (Figure 9.2 Graph 2). But, of course, this is not all that is going on when Tanya is speaking on the phone.

When we revisit Figure 9.1 Image 1, you will see that Tanya is actually interacting with Lucy as well as with her employee: here we see that Lucy is listening to Tanya's call and chimes in at the appropriate time, giving Tanya the sentence 'and then follow up with a phone call', which Tanya repeats without losing her rhythm by saying 'and then ALways follow up with a phone call'. Accordingly, Tanya is interacting with two different people simultaneously. While she is interacting with her employee in the foreground of her attention, Tanya is certainly not as focused on the interaction with Lucy as Lucy is on the interaction with Tanya. For Tanya, this interaction

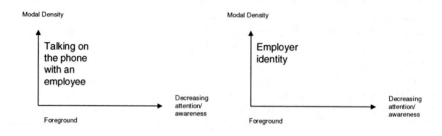

Graph 1 Focused action   **Graph 2 Focused identity element**

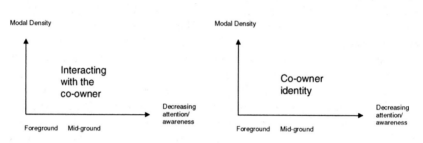

Graph 3: Mid-grounded action element   **Graph 4: Mid-grounded identity element**

Figure 9.2

happens in the mid-ground of her attention/awareness as illustrated in Figure 9.2 Graph 3. Furthermore, as every action also constructs a social actor's identity elements, Tanya then co-constructs her co-owner identity together with Lucy in the mid-ground of her attention awareness as illustrated in Figure 9.2. Graph 4.

Since I, as the researcher, was present during these interactions, video-taping the event, we should not forget that Tanya is also co-constructing a participant identity element in this excerpt. Besides these three identity elements, Tanya in fact co-constructs more identity elements at this very moment. However, at this point I would like to move first beyond the originally developed foreground–background continuum, as I believe that when thinking about personal identity construction, we cannot say that the social actor simply and only phenomenally co-constructs each identity element as they move through clock-time. When trying to delve deeply into identity construction, we need to consider the psychological mind as well.

Some thoughts about consciousness

For the purpose of this chapter, I will use the terms 'mind' or 'consciousness' interchangeably without trying to reach a full understanding of either one in its complexity. While I will have to speak of a social actor's mind or consciousness as if it was contained within the social actor themselves,

I believe that there is no distinction between a social actor and their environment (including other social actors and objects).

Here then, I am concerned about an apparently common assumption that the graph illustrates a part of a social actor's 'contained mind'. This is a wrong assumption, as the reader, who is familiar with my earlier work, will know. When looking at Figure 9.3 Graph 1, you will notice that each higher-level action that can be placed on the x-axis of the graph is located in the real world and is phenomenally displayed through mediational means or modes. In other words, this is what Middleton and Brown (2005) would call the 'actual'. Thus, what I term consciousness in this graph, is first of all made up of the actual ongoing actions located in the real world.

I believe, for the purpose of discussing personal identity construction, we have to also try to understand what is going on in a social actor's psychological mind (however we may want to define the term). Thus, when you read on, please take into account that these are only tentative thoughts and possible heuristic constructs that *may* allow us to understand a tiny piece of personal identity construction and maybe a minute piece of what we may want to call 'mind' or 'consciousness'.

Heuristically speaking the psychological mind (following Chalmers 1996) runs parallel to the phenomenal mind and, of course, there is a constant exchange going on between what a social actor thinks, feels, perceives, and processes psychologically and what the social actor performs phenomenally,

Graph 1

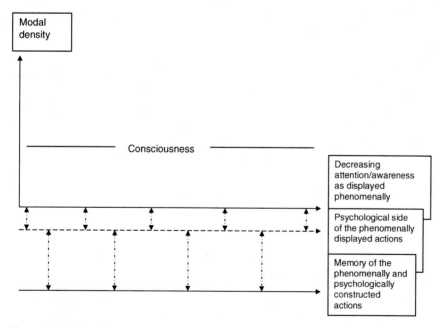

Figure 9.3   Consciousness

so that we could say that consciousness – again, just heuristically speaking – includes the phenomenally displayed attention/awareness levels and the psychological side of these phenomenally displayed actions.

However, as you can see in Figure 9.3 Graph 1, I believe that the psychological aspect of mind really has to be visualized as having (at least) two parts. One part is the psychological aspect of the phenomenally constructed actions and the other is the psychological part that can be called memory or the virtual, following Middleton and Brown (2005).

'I' and 'me' identity elements

Personal identity has been theorized by Mead (1974), Erickson (1973) and Ricoeur (1996), to name a few, and all of them propose some differentiation within the self. Mead (1974: 177–8) explains:

> the 'I' gives a sense of freedom, of initiative. The situation is there for us to act – in a self-conscious fashion. We are aware of ourselves, and of what the situation is, but exactly how we will act never gets into experience until after the action takes place.
>
> Such is the basis that the fact that the 'I' does not appear in the same sense in experience as does the 'me'. The 'me' represents a definite organization of the community there in our own attitudes, and calling for a response, but the response that takes place is something that just happens. There is no certainty in regard to it. There is a moral necessity but no mechanical necessity for it. When it does take place then we find what has been done.

With this passage, Mead claims that the 'I' is the novel self that acts in the present. This 'I' then corresponds to the phenomenally and psychologically co-constructed actions in Figure 9.3 Graph 1. The 'me', on the other hand, which according to Mead has been co-constructed within society and which regulates the 'I' to some extent, corresponds in part to the memory of the phenomenally and psychologically co-constructed actions.[1]

At this point, I would like to go back to the example of Tanya in the office. I believe that we can all agree that Tanya acts when conducting her phone conversation and when listening to Lucy – and we can see (in Figure 9.1) that her actions are performed by her 'I'. We also know that these actions are being turned into the performance of her 'me' as the phone call moves along. Thus the higher-level action of the phone call and the lower-level actions that make up the phone call clearly are constructed as Tanya's 'I' as they are being co-constructed phenomenally (with the concurrent psychological counter-actions). Then, these 'I' identity elements are moved into Tanya's memory as 'me' identity elements, as soon as the phenomenal construction is complete. I believe that these memories of prior 'I' constructions – me-constructions – can be accessed, shaped, and reshaped (see Middleton and Brown (2005) on reshaping memory); and I will now show that me-identity elements may also be accessed and can then shape the following actions constructed by the social actor. Further, I will show how there is a lag in movement when I-identity elements become me-identity elements.

In order to illustrate how a me-identity element can shape the construction of an I-identity element, I will now review the higher-level action that happened just before Tanya received the phone call: Lucy's ex-husband had stopped by the office to pick up their daughter. As soon as he left (the time exactly prior to the phone call) Lucy started telling the researcher about her ex-husband wanting to grow his hair long and Tanya chimes in. At this moment, both women are whispering, co-constructing what I call a friend identity element through spoken language and other modes.

A me-identity element shaping an i-identity element: the moment before the phone call

My focus here, will again be on Tanya: she uses several modes, including posture, proxemics, head positioning, gesture and language together with pitch variation when co-constructing the identity element of being a friend:[2]

TANYA:	IT LOOKS GOOD NOW,
	i do.
	i like it now,
	but literally,
LUCY:	[he looked like a porn star
TANYA:	[before work,
	he looked like a porn star
	i mean
	i thought i was gonna die laughing
	i called her up and
	oh mY GOD?

Thus, here we find some repetition, where Lucy speaks the utterance 'he looked like a porn star' and Tanya repeats the exact same utterance just a moment later.

Next, when we now look at Figure 9.4 Images 1 and 2, we find that Tanya slowly rotates with her chair 90 degrees. This rotation takes her about 3 and 1/2 seconds from the beginning to the end of her rotating movement. Tanya's posture is quite relaxed with her arms resting on her chair. Her gaze is focused on Lucy, her facial expression is open and relaxed; and her pitch, while consistently flat due to the whispering as long as the story is being told, ends in a sharp phrase mid-final pitch rising as she says 'oh mY GOD?' ending the story. Here, Tanya constructs a friend identity element in the focus of her attention.

Slow 90-degree rotation – 3.4 seconds   Focused gaze
Relaxed posture   Relaxed facial expression
                                                                   Phrase mid-final pitch rising

Figure 9.4 Friend identity element

Right after this, Tanya receives the phone call. At this moment, the friend identity element – now a me-identity element – is moved back in Tanya's consciousness and is available on the psychological level. Thus, while the friend identity element is not being co-constructed at this moment, it is present, nevertheless, in some vaguely established form within Tanya's memory. Next, I would like to argue that the construction of the co-owner identity – with Lucy's listening to the phone conversation and with Tanya's employing the words given to her – is influenced by the prior established friend identity element, which is further back in Tanya's consciousness. Accordingly, we can say that there appears to be a structuring of actions and identity formations coming from the background of a person's consciousness towards the focus.

The phone call

When looking at the phone call in this light we see that Tanya uses verbal repetition much in the same way as she had just a moment prior when constructing the story about Lucy's ex-husband:

TANYA: whatever you do,
                 email and fax everything.
LUCY: and then follow up with a phone call.
TANYA: [and then
                 always follow up with a phone call.

Here, Tanya repeats what Lucy says much as she had repeated Lucy's utterance when constructing the friend identity element, displaying a smooth overlap.

In the third line (Figure 9.1 Image 1) Tanya says 'this is all I'm gonna tell you', employing a phrase mid-final pitch lowering when talking on the phone. When we now look at the very next moment in interaction, we find that this interaction is again influenced, and to some degree structured, by the preceding interactions; and the identity construction is influenced by the prior identity constructions. But in this case, we also find phenomenal evidence of I-to-me movement that is apparent in the lag-time of the social actor's actions.

Evidence of I-to-me movement of identity elements: the moment after the phone call

Right after the phone call, the two women are working together, constructing a co-worker identity element. The reason that I distinguish between their co-owner and co-worker identity elements is that these elements are differently conceptualized. At this very moment it is not important to either one of them that they own the company, here they are interested in working out a particular problem. However, my point here is really not to go into the terminology of identity elements, but to show that we can find phenomenal evidence of movements in the lag-time of social actor's actions. Further, I will show that the friend identity, the co-owner identity and the employer identity now all shape Tanya's I-identity construction.

At this point, Tanya constructs a co-worker identity element that is strongly influenced by the other interactions and the other identity constructions which are now residing in her psychological consciousness on different levels as her me-identities. As you can see in Figure 9.5 Graph 1, her employer identity element is closest to her current focused identity construction, and appears to have the greatest influence in the beginning of the clip: verbally, she lowers her voice when saying 'you're probably right' (Figure 9.5 Image 1) and her pitch contour is very similar to the pitch contour when she was speaking with their employee on the phone, just moments before; non-verbally, her quick movements when she turns around to look at Lucy (Figure 9.5 Image 2), turning 180 degrees in just a little over one second, remind us of the quick beat gestures that she was performing just a moment earlier. Then, Tanya relaxes her posture, focuses her gaze and slows her movements.

Here, we can clearly see that there is a lag-time between the performance of one higher-level action, the fast-paced action of speaking on the phone with an employee and the coexisting identity formation, and another higher-level action, the more relaxed action of working with Lucy and that coexisting identity formation. In other words, although the fast paced higher-level action of speaking on the phone with her employee is completed and a new more relaxed higher-level action is unfolding, Tanya begins the

Graph 1 Identity elements and their influence on I-constructions

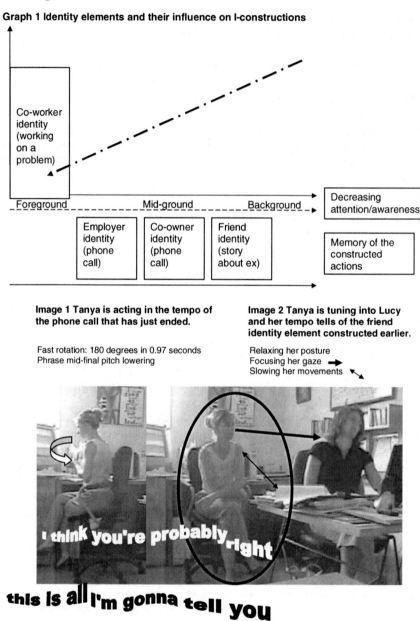

Image 1 Tanya is acting in the tempo of the phone call that has just ended.

Fast rotation: 180 degrees in 0.97 seconds
Phrase mid-final pitch lowering

Image 2 Tanya is tuning into Lucy and her tempo tells of the friend identity element constructed earlier.

Relaxing her posture
Focusing her gaze
Slowing her movements

Figure 9.5

construction of this new higher-level action with the same pace as she had co-constructed the prior higher-level action, utilizing movements that are rhythmically located in the prior higher-level action and using the same pitch in her first utterance in the new higher-level action as in her utterance requesting attention in the prior higher-level action. Thus, both rhythm in her motion and pitch in her utterance are indicative of the prior higher-level action and the prior I-identity element that is now moving into the memory as a me-identity element.

Conclusion: me-identity elements shaping the I-identity construction: evidence for structuring consciousness from back to front

Using a multimodal framework of interaction when investigating identity construction allows us to make the importance of multiple modes visible and to move beyond focused interaction. Only when viewing interaction and identity constructions in a modally holistic way can we see how identity elements that have been constructed in prior clock-time are later available on some psychological level, having a direct impact on new identity constructions.

In the case discussed above, we find evidence for consciousness to be structured from back to front.[3]

When we compare Tanya's co-construction of her employer and co-owner identity elements during the phone call with her co-construction of the co-worker identity (Figure 9.6 Images 1 and 2), we find that Tanya's posture – including the positioning of her shoulders, her left arm and her lowered foot tucked against the chair and only the tip touching the ground, as well as her lowering pitch – are very similar to the beginning of her co-worker identity element. Here, Tanya holds her shoulders in a similar way, slightly bent forward; her lowered foot is squarely positioned on the floor, while the other foot is rather relaxed; and her gaze is un-focused.

As the interaction evolves, the other me-identity elements play a role in the evolving identity construction. Here we find that a certain manner of constructing the friend identity element can also be found when Tanya co-constructs the co-worker identity element as shown in Figure 9.6 Images 3, 4 and 5: Tanya's way of listening to Lucy's list (Figure 9.6 Image 4), carries ingredients of the friend (and also the co-owner) identity element, where Tanya had repeated Lucy's utterances, had sat in a slightly bent position curving her shoulders forward, and had employed a focused gaze (Figure 9.6 Image 3). When Tanya is working with Lucy (Figure 9.6 Image 4) she reacts similarly by nodding and agreeing with what Lucy says, by sitting in a slightly bent position curving her shoulders forward and by focusing her gaze. Then, (Figure 9.6 Image 5), the women move into another form of repetition, both of them taking on a very similar posture and playing with their left earlobes, all lower-level actions that illustrate that this higher-level action is of a relaxed nature. With this, I would like to repeat my note of caution: while this chapter has mainly focused on Tanya and the identity elements that she constructs, the last image clearly illustrates that she does not construct these elements as a single social actor, but always and only co-constructs them in unison with other social actors and the environment.

Image 1 Employer and co-owner
identity elements during phone call

Image 2 Co-worker identity
element right after the
phone call

this is all I'm gonna tell you

I think you're probably right

Image 3 Friend identity element
before phone call

Image 4 Co-worker identity element
after rotation

Image 5 Co-worker identity element
Influenced by the friend identity element

Figure 9.6

Notes

1 In part, the 'me' also corresponds to Bourdieu's notion of habitus.
2 The spoken language transcript below utilizes the transcription conventions of Tannen (1984), with commas indicating slight utterance final rising intonation, the period indicating a 0.5 second pause, these kinds of brackets [ ] indicating overlap, CAPS marking emphatic stress, and question marks indicating mid-final pitch rising.
3 Such front-to-back structuring is only one case of possible structuring of actions and identity elements, but I will focus here on only this one and address other structuring in future writing.

References

Bourdieu, P. (1977) *Outline of a Theory of Practice*, Cambridge: Cambridge University Press.

Chalmers, D.J. (1996) *The Conscious Mind: in search of a fundamental theory*, Oxford: Oxford University Press.

Goffman, E. (1974) *Frame Analysis: an essay on the organization of experience*, Cambridge, MA: Harvard University Press.

Gumperz, J. (1982) *Discourse Strategies*, Cambridge: Cambridge University Press.

De Fina, A., Bamberg M. and Schiffrin, D. (eds) (2005) *Narratives in Interactions: identities and selves*, Cambridge: Cambridge University Press.

Hall, K. and Bucholz, M. (eds) (1995) *Gender Articulated: language and the socially constructed self*, London: Routledge.

Hamilton, H. (1996) 'Intratextuality, intertextuality and the construction of identity as patient in Alzheimer's Disease', *Text*, 16 (1): 61–90.

—— (1998) 'Reported speech and survivor identity in on-line bone marrow transplantation narratives', *Journal of Sociolinguistics*, 2(1): 53–67.

Kress, G. and Van Leeuwen, T. (1998) *Reading Images: the grammar of visual design*, London: Routledge.

—— (2001) *Multimodal Discourse: the modes and media of contemporary communication*, London: Edward Arnold.

McNeill, G.H. (1992) *Hand and Mind: what gestures reveal about thought*, Chicago, IL: Chicago University Press.

Middleton, D. and Brown, S.D. (2005) *The Social Psychology of Experience: studies in remembering and forgetting*, London: Sage.

Nishida, K. (1958) *Intelligibility and Philosophy of Nothingness*, Tokyo: Maruzen.

Norris, S. (2002) 'A theoretical framework for multimodal discourse analysis presented via the analysis of identity construction of two women living in Germany', Ph.D. dissertation, Georgetown University.

—— (2004a) *Analysing Multimodal Interaction: a methodological framework*, London and New York: Routledge.

—— (2004b) 'Multimodal discourse analysis: a conceptual framework', in P. Levine and R. Scollon (eds) *Discourse and Technology: multimodal discourse analysis*, Georgetown University Round Table on Languages and Linguistics, Washington, DC: Georgetown University Press, pp. 101–15.

Schiffrin, D. (1994) *Discourse Markers*, Cambridge: Cambridge University Press.

Scollon, R. (1997) 'Handbills, tissues, and condoms: a site of engagement for the construction of identity in public discourse', *Journal of Sociolinguistics*, 1(1): 39–61.
—— (1998) *Mediated Discourse as Social Interaction*, London: Longman.
—— (2001) *Mediated Discourse: the nexus of practice*, London: Routledge.
Tannen, D. (1984) *Conversational Style: analysing talk among friends*, Norwood, NJ: Ablex.
van Leeuwen, T. (1999) *Speech, Music, Sound*, New York: St Martin's Press.
Wodak, R., De Cillia, R., Reisigl, M., Liebhart, K., Hirsch, A. and Mitten, R. (2000) *The Discursive Construction of National Identity*, Edinburgh: Edinburgh University Press.

10 Multimodal discourse analysis

The case of 'ability' in UK secondary school English

Carey Jewitt and Ken Jones

Introduction

In this chapter we illustrate a multimodal approach (Kress *et al.* 2001; Kress and van Leeuwen 2001; Kress *et al.* 2005) to discourse analysis. We demonstrate that a multimodal approach opens up new possibilities for understanding the realization of discourses, including those that are produced and re-produced silently (such as ability) – a silence that often adds to their potency. We show how multimodal micro-descriptions of how discourses are realized in the classroom can contribute both to discourse theory and to educational practices. For instance the analysis of discourses of ability presented in this chapter serves to de-naturalize the realization of ability, which opens up the potential for teachers and students to reflect on and re-design their interaction in ways that re-make (reshape and resist) these discourses.

The illustrative example discussed in this chapter focuses on a lesson in which students are studying a poem, *A Letter to his Coy Mistress*, by Marvell (a seventeenth-century text that was required reading for a GCSE English syllabus). The lesson focus is on the rhetorical devices of argument and persuasion. This case study is drawn from a larger research study, *The Production of School English*[1] (Kress *et al.* 2005). Drawing on observations and video recordings as well as teacher and student interviews we analyse how classroom visual display and spatial arrangement, teacher and student posture, gesture, gaze, talk, and their interaction with pens and printed texts are 'orchestrated' in the lesson to realize discourses of ability.

The students are organized into small groups and each group is given one stanza of the poem to analyse. When first watching the video of the lesson we were struck by the difference in the teacher–student interaction between two groups she worked with consecutively during the group-work section of the lesson. The configuration of modes in the stages of the small group interaction (such as 'entering the group', 'opening the discussion' and 'establishing the meaning of the text') realize quite distinct discourses of ability between the two groups. We want to show how this works to 'produce' one group of students as less able than the other and to explore how this discourse of 'ability' shapes the kinds of activity that students are given access to in the English classroom.

Classroom discourses are realized through curriculum content (ideational meaning) and pedagogic interpersonal relations (interpersonal meaning). The teacher's work involves the continuous structured improvisation of subject knowledge and positioning students *differentially* in relation to that content. We argue that 'student ability' is at least partly constructed in social interaction, and may not be stable beyond the context in which it is produced. Out of this understanding comes a means for seeing how the teacher's perception of students in relation to ability gives shape to very different constructions of what English is or comes to be for different groups of students.

Ways of thinking

Pedagogical practices are political. Large-scale policy, as well as the texts that end up in the classroom and the organization and structuring of the interpretive relations students and teachers take to these texts, are all the result of choices – choices that connect discourses across policy and practices.

We can track the influence of these political choices, realized as policy, on some of the key elements of classroom organization and relationships. We are saying that an iterative move between the macro (local and national policy documents) and the micro (teacher and student interviews and classroom observation) illuminates the connections between policy and teachers – and how teachers translate policy into classroom practices. We are *not* saying that it is possible to 'read off' a policy directly from a multimodal analysis of classroom practice. We are aware that current policies are not the only influence in the organization of social relations and subject knowledge in the classroom. Classroom practices are shaped by other histories, past policies, the past and current experiences and desires of teachers and students among many other social forces all of which remain swirling around the classroom.

Points of intersection

It is possible to see elements of policy instantiated in classroom practices. Teacher and students are always agentive but policy impacts on the structuring of their agency – it shapes and underpins their interactions. We see macro policy instantiated in the micro practices of the classroom at specific 'points of intersection'. Sometimes the voice of policy is washed over by stronger histories and local concerns and the intersections are less 'present' in this complex flux – less apparent, indirect and unclear. At times, the point of intersection between these agentive forces of policy, teacher and student are clear to see: the line between policy and classroom practice can be so clear, the travel from A to B so swift and clear that the track between them looks unbroken by agency.

Our analysis focuses then on 'points of intersection' where the links, the connections, translations, echoes between policy and classroom practices can be heard and seen.

Multimodality and other social theory

Multimodal analysis can be used to get at the detail of how political policies become in the classroom. At the same time we are using social theories of discourse (Foucault 1991) and the (re) production of knowledge (Bourdieu 1973; Bernstein 1990, 1996) to try and explain the multimodal realization of social relations and content that we see in the classroom, to ask why does the classroom look like it does?

Using this iterative approach we examine the orchestration of semiotic resources in the work of the teacher, including movement, body posture, gesture (including gesture with objects), gaze, talk, and writing, in the context of the spatial arrangements of the classroom. In the illustrative example presented here we begin by looking at modes other than speech or writing by which discourses are realized. We then analyse ways in which official written texts – parts of the poem, the dictionary – are deployed. Subsequently, we attend to the written texts and to utterances produced by the teacher and by students. Of course, in the classroom all these resources are simultaneously in use. We focus on them separately for analytic purposes.

This initial descriptive analysis does not (cannot) answer the question of why the teacher and students behaved in such different ways, and why talk, gesture, gaze, writing, etc. feature as they did in Group 1 and not Group 2. Here we turn to the use of teacher interviews, policy and literature reviews to look at how the teacher talked about the students and her interaction with them in the classroom. For instance, the pressures of examinations, time and the notion of ability were repeatedly commented on and highlighted by the teacher. Ability was a key discourse of policy that informed the teacher's practices and her organization of the students in the classrooms – in this way the data provides a framework for explanation. We looked at the data and asked how the differences we had described related to the social relations and curriculum content, and in turn how these related to the idea of ability and the policies that weave around this contested term.

Moving along lines of connection

Central concepts of policy (e.g. the idea of 'ability' in the illustrative example discussed in this chapter) can be seen as a kind of gossamer thread to work along and to see how concepts spin through official policy and classroom practices connecting both. It is not a matter of *mapping* theoretical concepts like ability (or character, annotation, etc.) *onto* observational or video data. Nor is it a matter of *finding concepts* in the interview data and *matching* these to incidences of classroom practices. Our analysis moves along this line of connection in a dynamic way tracing and retracing multimodal discourses across moments of connection.

An illustrative case study: the multimodal construction of ability in the English classroom

To illustrate our approach to multimodal discourse analysis we look at how 'ability' was constructed by a teacher in an English lesson in a secondary school in London. As already mentioned the lesson is on the poem, *A Letter to his Coy Mistress*, by Marvell, with a focus on the rhetorical devices of argument and persuasion.

The students are seated at tables in groups of three or four; dictionaries are handed to each table. Following a whole class teaching episode in which the teacher models the process of textual analysis for the whole class – the kind of textual analysis required by the examination syllabus – each group is given a photocopy of one stanza of the poem to analyse, an activity that appears to include, in varying degrees, basic explication, interpretation and response. It is what happens in this part of the lesson that is the focus of our analysis.

Seeking explanations for the stark difference we observed between two groups that the teacher worked with consecutively, we explored the roles of teacher and students in constructing the terms of this interaction (and thus in constructing also their own subjectivities). That is to say, given the social constraints and possibilities that are at work in this classroom, it is both the teacher and the students who act, even if very differently, and with different means and resources. We want to insist that students themselves are involved as active agents in their own positioning in relation to English, and therefore also in relation to the category of 'ability', although their choices of ways of acting may not be to their own long term advantage. The episodes are co-productions involving all participants.

We illustrate this process through five points of intersection between official policy and the classroom practices that we observed in relation to discourses of ability.

Point of intersection 1: the choice and contestations of text

The lesson that we focus on here is the seventh in a series of 12 lessons over one month on the poems featured in the UK's Northern Examinations and Assessment Board (NEAB) GCSE anthology section *Hearts and Partners*. The subject of the lesson is Marvell's *A Letter to his Coy Mistress*, the only compulsory poem in the examination syllabus, for this unit. That fact gives it a central place in the curriculum, and in our analysis of English here.

The lesson objectives reflect the National Curriculum (1999) requirements for reading – the need for students to be able to 'read for meaning' and to 'understand the author's craft'. Specifically, successful students are required to extract meaning beyond the literal; to explain how the author's choice of language affects meaning; to analyse and discuss alternative interpretations; and how emotions and ideas are portrayed. These competencies will be assessed, of course, and the teacher feels the added pressures of teaching assessment strategies as well as literature, as she said when interviewed:

> I suppose at Key Stage 4, unfortunately it is quite exam orientated. I mean that is what those lessons are about really and I want them to know and understand the poems that they are studying and to be able to kind of also know what they need to do in an exam.

Point of intersection 2: the decisions about grouping

The teacher's decision to organize her class into small groups suggests that English, in the context of this particular school, is not intended to be a subject produced (solely) by the teacher and transmitted to students in a didactic form.

Rather, English is intended to be produced through the interaction of peers, through their engagement with previous knowledge and out of school cultural understandings over a text, with the teacher having more the role of facilitator.

This spatial arrangement of the classroom is a sign of this (interpersonal) process of producing English, with the students who are grouped around the tables facing each other rather than the teacher. However, spatial arrangement alone does not determine the specifics of the kind of English actually produced.

The school's decision not to 'set' students for English was mentioned as a cause for concern in an Ofsted Report produced shortly before the period of our research which stated, 'The very wide range of attainment within mixed-ability teaching groups makes it very difficult for teachers to ensure that all students are making appropriate progress.' Student ability, and the pedagogic strategies thought to be necessitated by ability differences, were also raised by the teacher in interviews. For example:

> I mean, that class does have quite a range of students and there is quite an able group at the top I think, which in some of the classes you don't have as much, I don't think. So I think I probably, I am not sure how, that definitely does influence how I teach, I think, and I know there are students that will explain things, so although I do try to get them to feedback into the classes, I tend to do a lot of group work. I think that helps students learn and I would do that with any group. Even with a

group that found it difficult I would persevere because that's ... where they learn.

When we viewed the video recording of interaction among the two groups, the difference between them was striking, both in the modes of interaction, but also in the kind of English teaching that characterized each. At this point we turned to interviews with the teacher, and noted that Group 1 is perceived by her to be a high ability group. She sees its members as capable of responding successfully to the demands of the curriculum and the examination syllabus. For them English is configured, at least to some extent, as conversation, in which dialogue, informality, the students' perspectives and expertise are all valued – though valued only in part. The teacher's position and posture is aimed at soliciting from them an articulation of their response to the text. But at the same time, aspects of the teacher's talk, those aspects of her gaze and gesture that involved (even at their table) the dictionary, the whiteboard and its instructions, tend in another direction.

As we will show the situation is very different for Group 2, whom this teacher does not recognize as able. Our analysis of the video recording reveals that in Group 1 the teacher's *gaze*, *movement* and *posture* produce a sense of English as that curriculum subject in which the text is the point of departure for engaged discussion, for personal involvement, for pleasure. In contrast, the same teacher's use of the same modal resources with Group 2 produces a kind of English which is about closure, about instruction in which the authority of the text, of the teacher and the dictionary as producers of its meanings are paramount.

Point of intersection 3: entering the two groups

In this first episode the teacher walks up to a group around one of the tables. By placing herself at one side of the table the teacher effectively locates herself within the group, as if she were one of the participants, for the time of her presence.

Her position provides a specific potential for engagement with this group. She leans across the table, opposite to one girl, whom we will call Sofia, making her, through positioning and gaze, the main focus of the interaction. A little later the teacher moves from her initial position directly opposite to Sofia, somewhat more to the side of the table, producing a shift in her relation to the group – maybe that from *member* more to *observer*, and, thereby invites a shift in the manner of engagement of the three students from *listeners* to *performers*.

The teacher's initial positioning of Sofia as her major interactant, through the position she assumed at the table, is also realized and reinforced through her *gaze*. Throughout, Sofia and the teacher engage in direct eye contact. The other students make eye contact with Sofia. Their gaze confirms Sofia's central role as representative for the group. Sofia herself uses *gaze* to indicate requests for teacher response, reassurance and help, without verbalizing her needs. Teacher and students use *gaze* to draw the text into their interaction throughout the episode.

Although there is a chair at her end of the table, throughout the interaction the teacher chooses to stand, or to lean rather, across the table – into the group. Her posture, combined with her smile and laughter, can be read as social signifiers of casualness, informality, friendliness and of being relaxed. By remaining standing she suggests the temporary nature of her visit and the interaction, as if she had merely dropped in, casually, for a pleasurable conversation. The body-posture of the students is also relatively open and expansive. Sofia leans back and stretches her hands behind her head, as does Iqbal later. The students sit relatively low in their chairs. These embodied signs both shape the interaction and provide a frame for all aspects of them. At this table, they are the material–bodily expression of a construction of English as the pleasure of engaging in discussion over a text.

Leaving Group 1, the teacher walks over to the second group of students, and without hesitation sits down at a corner of the table, next to one student, Tony, on her right. During the episode she does not alter her basic position, signalling 'permanency' by seating herself there (rather than dropping in as she did with the other group). This impression is clear, despite the fact that both interactions last for the same amount of time. In a seeming paradox, at Table 1 where she has merely 'dropped in' so to speak, her position signalled membership of the group; here, where she is seated, she is an outsider. Placing herself where she does also seems to suggest that she is preparing to work just with Tony, rather than engaging with the whole group.

Once seated, the teacher immediately leans forward to pick up a pencil. She then draws Tony's copy of the poem towards herself, putting her left elbow on the table and supporting her head on her hand as she starts to read the first line of the poem. Her upright, angular and tense body-posture contrasts with the first group. In the earlier episode she leaned in toward the students, here she leans in toward the poem. The position of her arms and head over the text close her off from interaction with the other students at the table; it is a posture that does not invite interaction. The teacher's posture actualizes a sign of authority and of directed instruction (or work).

Point of intersection 4: the technologies in the room

Here we are particularly interested in who holds the pen in the work of writing. For the lesson, students had been asked make annotations on the meaning of the poem, and this was the only writing expected during the group session. Throughout the interaction at Table 1, writing was a mode used by the students, not by the teacher.

In Group 2 likewise much writing is done. The difference here is that it is the teacher who does the work, appropriating Tony's pencil.

Throughout the interaction with Group 2, the teacher writes on the poem-sheet; none of the students writes themselves. The teacher underlines and writes single words from the poem and simple phrases on the poem-sheet (for example: Ganges = river; Thou = you; Flood = Noah's flood; Conversion of the Jews = ancient history and bible stories).

At Table 1 the students shared one dictionary. When the teacher joins Group 2, there are four dictionaries on the table, three of which, at the start of the episode, are open – although one student closes his dictionary as teacher sits down. This distribution of dictionaries itself suggests the teacher's expectations of each group's capacities in relation to the task in hand – clarifying the meaning of the poem. The dominant presence of the dictionaries on this table suggests that she regarded them as an essential resource for this particular group, indicating her different understanding of the pedagogic task of making sense of the poem for these students. Each of them is to undertake the work of finding words in the dictionary; it seems that the task that the teacher regards them as capable of doing is this relatively mechanical one.

Halfway through the episode with Group 2, the teacher taps on one of the dictionaries with the pencil, and instructs the students to 'look up *vegetable* in the dictionary'. The students pick up the dictionaries and – in a desultory manner – flick through the pages. While they do this, the teacher silently reads the poem and underlines *empire*. She asks the students, 'What's an empire?' One student responds: 'It's like a big kingdom.' The teacher leans forward and writes on the poem-sheet. However, one could not say that the teacher is simply acting as a scribe for the students, for while some of the meanings of words were offered by the students or co-produced with the teacher, nearly half of them were provided by the teacher directly, without attempting any interaction at all with the group.

At Table 2, *writing* interacts with other modes to signify the teacher's continuing possession of the text. With this group the teacher sees it as her role to write *for* the students, in contrast to her role in the previous interaction, where she looked up words in the dictionary for the students while allowing them to focus on relating the poem to their own experience.

For Group 1, the task seems different, so that the role of the dictionary becomes a different one: here the teacher facilitates discussion and speculation, and she herself quickly looks up words for them herself.

Point of intersection 5: the pedagogic options taken by the teacher, dialogue vs. instruction

If we look at teacher–student talk in bare numerical terms, we note that in Group 1, the teacher made 34 contributions, mainly focusing on the meaning of words and phrases. Sofia spoke almost as many times (33), largely concerned with the socio-cultural context of the poem and the emotional motivation of the female character, the addressee. While Najma, the third member of Group 1 contributes little more than any of the students in Group 2, the sort of English to which she and Iqbal have access at her table is of a different order from that constructed in the other group.

In Group 2, the numerical distribution of utterances is very different, with the teacher, at points, conducting a dialogue between herself-as-teacher and herself-as-spokesperson for the students. The teacher asks far fewer questions of the students here than in the previous episode. The students do not ask the teacher any direct questions (they ask two questions in response to her questioning). This lack of questioning is paralleled in the lack of eye contact between teacher and students.

With Group 2, the teacher spoke 22 times, focusing on the meaning of specific words. She asked 11 questions, with Tony answering 10 of them, all in response to these direct questions on vocabulary. The teacher and the students are involved in an entirely teacher-led interaction. The students do not express ideas about alternative or shared meanings about the poem, and the teacher does not invite a dialogue that goes beyond the barest requirements of the official curriculum.

Towards the end of this episode, as the last three lines of the poem are 'discussed', the teacher and the students are all looking at the text, although it is the teacher who writes, reads the poem, and offers a response to the poem. She appears to be modelling 'doing annotating a poem' for the students.

> Teacher: '*An age at least to every part*'. Erm, an **age**, that means like a sort of, a sort of, well I think he means there … like a period of time, like a generation or something. Yeah.
> '*And the last age should show your heart*'. So that's actually her revealing her love.
> '*For lady you deserve this state, nor would I love at lower rate*' OK, so that's just basically how much love … yeah.

As in the appropriation of the pencil in writing for the students, here the teacher also speaks for the students. Yet what she models for the group is atomistic, a starkly simplified version of 'comprehension', and one unlikely to help them achieve more than a basic grade in their GCSE assessment.

Point of intersection 6: interpretation and interaction with the text via gesture and gaze (silent modes of interaction)

In Group 1 the teacher and students both use *gesture* during their interaction, realizing their own constructions of the meaning and purpose of English. In this group students gestured at the poem, the dictionary, and at their body, indicating the focus of interest or term of reference of the gesture. The move from gesturing towards the poem to gesturing towards the body marked a shift in reference from the poem-as-text to their personal response to the poem. The teacher's gestures that were directed towards the text focus on the meanings of the words of the text. For instance, Sofia opens and waves her arms and hands to express 'sexual excitement' (a gesture which Iqbal fills in verbally with the word 'horny'), and later she makes a sweeping gesture over her shoulder to express 'the past'. Similarly, when the teacher opens her hand and moves it in a circular motion as she asks 'what is he trying to say there?' she is making an open gesture. Through gesture she embodies the text and asks for their explanation or response.

While the teacher's use of *gaze* and *posture* invite the students' personal responses, her gestures directed at the dictionary, by contrast, indicate and remind the students of her pedagogic intentions, of the job in hand. The teacher's holding of a page, finger pointing to a specific place while a student talked, was a sign of her listening whilst maintaining her pedagogic agenda.

In contrast within Group 2 it is primarily the teacher who gestures. As the episode begins, Tony points to a place on the poem/sheet in response to the teacher's request to know where they are 'up to'. When the teacher puts her own finger at this place, Tony removes his finger. The whole episode ends with Tony placing a finger on the text as if he were 'taking it back'. In between Tony's initial and final pointing with his finger, no student holds or touches the poem. In relation to gesture the text of the poem remains with the teacher throughout the rest of the episode. With the exception of Tony's opening and closing gestures, the students do not use gestures in this episode. They gesture neither towards the poem or the dictionary. Nor do they indicate their personal response to the poem by gesturing toward themselves, as the students in Group 1 had done.

Throughout the episode with Group 2, the teacher keeps control of the poem through her posture of leaning over the piece of paper, her body acting as a barrier to the students on her left, her gaze directed nearly exclusively at the poem, talking *for* the students as though speaking on their behalf, and scribing the talk that she has herself produced (though on their behalf), maintaining a near-constant physical contact with the copy of the poem, through its physical proximity to her. This is in stark contrast to the 'handing over' of the text in her interaction with the previous group of students, in which the students were able to share access to and even at times have control of the text.

Throughout the episode the teacher moves between the two postures of *leaning in towards the text*, and *sitting upright* in her chair. Through her first posture she models 'doing English' as work, an individual engagement with the text. Through her second posture she shifts back to a 'teacherly' role, checking students' understanding.

As with her movement, positioning and posture, the teacher's use of *gaze* differs between the first group and the second. With Group 2, the teacher spends most of the episode looking at the poem/text, focusing attention on the text, her head down, reading and annotating the text. When she looks up at the students to ask a question, her look is brief, wavering, and it quickly drops back to the text. The text, not the students, is the teacher's dominant object of gaze, and attention to the written text is the purpose of the sign of this interaction. At the same time the students gaze downward at the table in front of them, rarely looking at the teacher, even when the teacher is talking.

The teacher's eye contact with the text signifies her focus in her work with Group 2. The teacher is not intent on the work of producing interaction and debate, and the students are not engaged in the work of producing meaning. The lack of exchange between the teacher and students indicates a lack of co-production of interpretation and meaning in this episode.

Through the orchestration of modes and the intersection of policy and practices the students are positioned in relation to (and become a part of) the production of ability and school English.

Concluding comments

Taking a multimodal approach to discourse analysis is labour and time intensive but it can be analytically powerful particularly when research questions focus on an area that is rarely discussed. This applies to many aspects of education and social and cultural life, aspects that are quietly taboo. Approaching discourse from a multimodal perspective enables interaction that is usually filtered out by a linguistic lens to be included in a data set and to be analysed. Many things are never said and multimodality can offer a way to explore what might otherwise be seen only as silence – which often becomes non-data. Multimodality is important for discourse analysis as it looks beyond language at policies (such as ability) that show up or are reflected in many modes. Further, the mode of language is often the first language of those in power and in some situations this can lead to talk being a cleaned up and verbally sanitized interactional mode. A multimodal approach can implode this defence.

Note

1 *The Production of School English* (2000–3) was funded by the Economic and Social Research Council. The project team consisted of Carey Jewitt, Ken Jones, Gunther Kress, Jill Bourne, Anton Franks, John Hardcastle and Euan Reid.

References

Bernstein, B. (1990) *The Structuring of Pedagogic Discourse*, London: Routledge.
—— (1996) *Pedagogy, Symbolic Control and Identity*, London: Taylor & Francis.
Bourdieu, P. (1973) 'Cultural reproduction and social reproduction', in R. Brown (ed.) *Knowledge, Education and Cultural Change*, London: Tavistock, pp: 71–112.
Bourne, R. and MacArthur, B. (1970) *The Struggle for Education: 1870–1970*, London: School Masters Publishing Company.
DfES (1999) *National Curriculum*, London: HMSO.

Foucault, M. (1991) *The Foucault Reader*, P. Rabinow (ed.) London: Penguin.

Kress, G. and van Leeuwen, T. (2001) *Multimodal Discourse*, London: Arnold.

Kress, G., Jewitt, C., Ogborn, J. and Chararlampos, C. (200) *Multimodal Teaching and Learning: the rhetorics of the science classroom*, London: Continuum.

Kress, G., Jewitt, C., Bourne, J., Franks, A., Hardcastle, J., Jones, K. and Reid, E. (2005) *English in Urban Classrooms: a multimodal perspective on teaching and learning*, London: RoutledgeFalmer.

Suggestions for further work

1 Videotape and analyse a short interaction using Norris's concepts of 'modal density' and 'identity elements'. How are different aspects of participants' identities communicated in such modes as gesture, gaze, posture, dress and object handling? How do participants negotiate and co-construct their respective identities multi-modally?

2 Norris, following Mead, makes a distinction between 'I' and 'me' identities, the 'I' identity corresponding to the way we construct ourselves in the ongoing flow of interaction, and the 'me' identity corresponding to those aspects of the 'self' submerged in our memories and in the societal conventions that we follow. How is such a distinction useful for our understanding of the construction of identity in interaction? What kinds of evidence from discourse (spoken, written or multimodal) can help us to understand how these two aspects of identity interact?

3 One of the main points made by Jewitt and Jones in their chapter is that the subtle, non-verbal ways teachers communicate their attitudes towards their students can have an important impact on teaching and learning. The same can be said for the ways managers interact with their employees. Observe an educational or workplace situation and analyse how people in different positions of power use various modes to communicate such things as approval and disapproval, agreement and disagreement, using the methods and principles outlined by Jewitt and Jones.

4 Jewitt and Jones suggest that larger issues of educational policy manifest as concrete local practices in classrooms through such things as teacher and student positioning, object handling and the architecture of the classroom. Compare her points to those made by Lin in Chapter 5. In what ways might teachers and students redesign their interactions to make them more equitable and pedagogically effective?

Part V
Genre analysis

Genre analysis offers a grounded description and explanation of language use in academic and professional contexts in an attempt to answer the question: 'why do professionals use the language the way they do?' The evidence for necessary answers to this important question does not simply come from linguistic descriptions of texts or genres; more importantly, it comes from the investigation of a variety of text-internal as well as text-external factors that contribute to and influence the production as well as the reception of these generic artefacts (see Bhatia 2004 for details). So the important issue here seems to be to integrate the analysis of textual with contextual elements that often work in harmony to make a particular instance of textual genre pragmatically successful. Thus the conventional understanding of discourse analysis as analysis of texts can be misleading.

Recent studies (Swales 1998; Smart 1998; Bhatia 2004; Norris 2004) have pointed out that discourse and genre analysis is a complex multi-perspective and multidimensional phenomenon and it requires an equally complex methodological framework to understand and analyse discourse satisfactorily and comprehensively. This will require a continual effort to develop a multi-disciplinary, and hence a multi-perspective and multidimensional framework. The two chapters that follow in this part attempt and illustrate two rather different ways to extend textual analyses of professional genres from two very different contexts.

In the first chapter in this part Bhatia seeks to take the conventional view of genre analysis as textual practice (Swales 1990; Bhatia 1993) considerably further by demonstrating that a comprehensive and in-depth analysis of a relatively simple genre analysis of letters written by the corporate chairman as part of the annual report will require the analyst to go beyond the textual data to dig deep into intertextuality as well as interdiscursivity (Candlin and Maley 1997). The chapter then investigates a number of socio-pragmatic aspects of the construction, interpretation, use and exploitation of these letters to achieve a 'hidden' agenda or what Bhatia (1995) calls 'private intentions' through a conscious 'bending' of the generic conventions to 'promote' corporate interests, rather than to simply report on corporate results.

This chapter thus makes a strong case to integrate 'discursive practices' of professionals with their 'professional practices', which provide the real context for the enactment of genres, thus arguing for genre analysis to move toward 'critical genre analysis'. More generally it encourages investigation of how expert genre writers appropriate generic resources across academic and professional genres to create 'hybrid' forms, which include not simply mixing and embedding of genres, but also 'bending' of genres (Bhatia 2004). This perspective marks an interesting paradigm shift in the way conventional genre analysis tends to view genres, thus challenging the notion of 'generic integrity' as static and 'given' and encourages instead the notion of 'generic versatility', which is a significant advancement on the conventional thinking about genres.

In the second chapter in this part, Berkenkotter adds another dimension to the current literature on genre theory. In harmony with the earlier chapter by Bhatia, this chapter also underpins 'the importance in genre analysis of the relationship between structural properties of institutions and individual communicative actions'. However, Berkenkotter takes evidence from qualitative historical genre analysis, that is, from diachronic studies of the development of disciplinary and professional genres. Like Bhatia, she also argues for 'a multi-method approach to studying the textual dynamics of professional genres in their socio-historical contexts'. To illustrate her concept of historical evolution of genre, Berkenkotter focuses on psychiatric case reporting. She examines 'the rise and near demise of psychoanalysis through a genre-based historical lens' to suggests two 'revolutions' in psychiatry, and she tracks them by empirically examining the textual dynamics of the psychiatric case reports from the mid-eighteenth century, thus demonstrating that genre analysis needs a repertoire of techniques for capturing interactions between socio-historical, technological, demographic and epistemological factors in order to track and to interpret textual changes in disciplinary texts.

Looking at these and other similar developments in genre theory, we find a gradual movement away from purely textual analysis of academic and professional genres to incorporate contextual factors, including interdiscursivity and relevant aspects of professional culture and practices, although without undermining in any way the importance of lexico-grammar, which is extremely useful in pedagogical applications, especially in the teaching of English for Specific Purposes (ESP) and professional communication programmes.

Useful further reading in genre analysis can be found in Bhatia (1993, 2004), Bazerman and Paradis (1991) and Swales (1990, 1998).

References

Bazerman, C. (1988) *Shaping Written Knowledge: the genre and activity of the experimental article in science*, Madison, WI: University of Wisconsin Press.

—— (1994) 'Systems of genres and the enhancement of social intentions', in A. Freedman and P. Medway (eds) *Genre and New Rhetoric*, London: Taylor & Francis, pp. 79–101.

Bazerman, C. and Paradis, J. (eds) (1991) *Textual Dynamics of the Professions: historical and contemporary studies of writing in professional communities*, Madison, WI: University of Wisconsin Press.

Bhatia, V.K. (1993) *Analysing Genre: language use in professional settings*, London: Longman.

—— (1994) 'Generic integrity in professional discourse', in B-L. Gunnarsson, P. Linell and B. Nordberg (eds) *Text and Talk in Professional Contexts*, Skriftserie no. 6, Uppsala, Sweden: ASLA, pp. 61–76.

—— (1995) 'Genre-mixing and in professional communication: the case of "private intentions" v. "socially recognised purposes"', in P. Bruthiaux, T. Boswood and B. Bertha (eds), *Explorations in English for Professional Communication*, Hong Kong: City University of Hong Kong, pp. 1–19.

—— (1997) 'Genre-mixing in academic introductions', in *English for Specific Purposes*, 16(3): 181–96.

—— (2004): *Worlds of Written Discourse: a genre-based view*, London: Continuum.

Candlin, C.N. and Maley, Y. (1997) 'Intertextuality and interdiscursivity in the discourse of alternative dispute resolution', in B.-L. Gunnarsson, P. Linell and B. Nordberg (eds) *The Construction of Professional Discourse*, London: Longman, pp. 201–22.

Devitt, A. (1991) 'Intertextuality in tax accounting', in C. Bazerman and J. Paradis (eds) *Textual Dynamics of the Professions*, Madison, WI: University of Wisconsin Press.

Norris, S. (2004) *Analysing Multimodal Interaction: a methodological framework*, London: Routledge.

Smart, G. (1998) 'Mapping conceptual worlds: using interpretive ethnography to explore knowledge-making in a professional community', *Journal of Business Communication*, 35(1): 111–27.

Swales, J.M. (1990) *Genre Analysis: English in academic and research settings*, Cambridge: Cambridge University Press.

—— (1998) *Other Floors, Other Voices: a textography of a small university building*, London: Lawrence Erlbaum.

11 Towards critical genre analysis

Vijay K. Bhatia

Recent work in genre theory indicates a strong shift of emphasis from *text* to *context*, which has encouraged three interrelated developments. First, the analysis is becoming increasingly multidisciplinary, in that specific disciplinary concerns and methodologies are getting reflected in analytical frameworks, thus integrating professional and disciplinary practices with discursive practices of the professional and disciplinary communities. This integration of discursive and professional practices has made genre analytical insights more relevant and acceptable to the disciplinary and professional communities, which is also a useful development for applications of the theory, especially in English for Specific Purposes (ESP) and Professional Communication practices. Second, as a consequence of this increasing contextualization of genre analysis we notice more attention devoted to the complexities of professional genres rather than to a convenient selection of ideal examples of such genres for the design of ESP practice. This has encouraged genre theory to take note of different forms of appropriation of linguistic resources within and across generic domains, giving rise to mixing, embedding, and bending of professional genres (Bhatia 2004), thus highlighting the importance of interdiscursivity in genre theory. Finally, to support the study of these concerns, it has become necessary for genre theory to go beyond a textual analysis of linguistic data in order to incorporate a multidimensional and multi-perspective framework for the analysis of academic, professional, institutional and other workplace genres. This has prompted researchers (Smart 1998; Swales 1998; Bhatia 2004) to enrich their methodological frameworks by integrating ethnographic, socio-cognitive, institutional and other multi-perspective analytical measures, in addition to textual analytical procedures. In this chapter, I would like to illustrate these developments by analysing a selection of corporate disclosure genres, especially those written by corporate chairmen to their shareholders, reporting and interpreting financial and corporate performance. In doing so I would also highlight the implications of such analysis for the future development of genre theory arguing in favour of a shift towards *critical genre analysis*.

Corporate disclosure documents

Corporate disclosure procedures have been the subject of research and debate for some time; however, after the collapse of Enron and WorldCom in the last few years, they have become the focus of intense research, in particular the failure of corporate disclosure practices and procedures. These failures can be investigated from a number of different perspectives, some of which may include corporate accounting and finance, business law, financial accounting, free market economy, business ethics, financial markets, bankruptcies, banking and investment, stock market, financial gap analysis, etc. Corporate disclosure practices thus have implications for several areas of business and finance, such as corporate governance, economic management, financial investment and a number of others. An equally interesting investigation however could focus on the use of linguistic resources that often makes it possible for corporate writers to persuade and convince a varied audience of stakeholders, in particular, minority shareholders, to accept their accounts, estimates, and projections of the future performance of the corporation in question.

Unfortunately, however, very little attention has so far been paid to discourse analytical investigations of the use and exploitation of language in many of the regularly employed documents for corporate disclosure purposes, especially in the front matter accompanying the facts and figures about corporate performance; that is, the communication from the senior management to the various stakeholders through letters, reports, press releases, etc.

This study undertakes a detailed investigation of the use and abuse of linguistic resources in corporate periodic disclosure documents.[1] Using a critical genre-based approach to the analysis of the nature of some of these corporate disclosure genres and the use of generic resources (which include textual, intertextual, interdiscursive and socio-pragmatic) in a corpus of relevant corporate disclosure documents, the study attempts to demystify the appropriation of linguistic resources to obscure corporate performance, in particular, the negative aspects of corporate results, and to highlight instead the positive aspects of performance in order to enhance the company's image in the eyes of the shareholders, other stakeholders, and the business community as a whole. In order to investigate the use of language in this subtle and yet deliberate 'bending' of the socially expected generic norms of these corporate disclosure documents, the chapter also attempts to integrate the available analytical tools to illustrate a multi-perspective and multidimensional framework (see Bhatia 2004 for details) for 'critical genre analysis'.

Corporate disclosures documents such as corporate annual reports have long been considered the pulse of corporate realities. Their main purpose is to inform their shareholders about the performance and health of the company, specifically its successes and failures, current problems and prospects for its future development. In recent years however, the function of corporate annual disclosure documents, as in many others corporate genres, seems to have undergone a gradual shift from 'informing and reporting' to increasingly 'promoting' the companies to their audiences, by 'mystifying' corporate weaknesses through a subtle 'bending' of socially-accepted communicative norms of corporate disclosure genres. The main thrust of the study therefore is to focus on the appropriation of linguistic resources to *promote corporate interests* within socially accepted and hence expected procedures of *factual corporate reporting*. In this chapter I would like to consider some of the generic resources employed in a range of corporate disclosure genres to give expression to the 'private intentions' (Bhatia 1993) of promoting corporate interests against the background of established corporate disclosure procedures in the context of statutory requirements often imposed by government and other regulatory bodies. In doing so I hope to offer a grounded account of the discursive practices of the business community in corporate disclosure contexts by incorporating relevant insights from the conditions of production and reception of such documents by taking into account ethnographic reactions from a range of specialists in business, accounting, management and marketing, based on their convergent narrative accounts of first-hand experiences (Smart 1998), their lived professional experiences on 'who contributes and is responsible for what' to the process and the products of corporate reporting, including some reactions from media specialists who seem to know what goes on in the corporate world.

Data for the study

The focus of the study is on a selection of 15 Hong Kong listed companies categorized into three groups based on their corporate performance, that is, good, moderate or poor performance during the 1998 to 2005 period. The selection of the corpus, especially the performance of companies as revealed in corporate periodic and annual reports and several other documents, was made in consultation with two specialists in business and finance, keeping in mind overall turnover progress during the specified period, return on equity, among other indicators.

The main corpus for linguistic analysis consists of corporate disclosure documents, which included annual and other periodical performance reports, press releases by these companies about their corporate performance, and other communications from management to (minority) shareholders. These comprised sections of annual and other interim reports, press releases by these companies, earnings/results announcements, shareholder circulars, notes from general meetings, transcripts/slides from speeches/presentations, and a number of other corporate publications such as the company newsletters.

In addition to this primary corpus, the secondary data includes newspaper reports on corporate performance, journal articles highlighting or reviewing the performance of these companies, assessments of the performance of these companies by rating agencies, such as Standard and Poor's and other financial institutions, such as the Hong Kong Monetary Authority, etc. The main function of the secondary data, which is primarily drawn from newspaper and magazine articles, and through Internet websites of rating agencies and institutions, incorporating assessments, reviews and evaluations of performance by outside rating agencies, is to provide additional authoritative third-party perspectives on the performance of these companies.

Preliminary findings

One of the most important aspects of the present corpus is what is generally known as the President's or Chairman's letter to shareholders. As Kohut and Segars (1992) point out:

> ... annual reports to shareholders are fashioned as marketing tools highlighting the firm's mission, objectives, strategies, and financial performance. While financial portions such as the income statement, balance sheet, and changes in financial position are subject to the scrutiny of the firm's auditors, the narrative portions of the document are a direct consequence of corporate communication decisions. The president's letter should ... be viewed as downward communication to the firm's shareholders outlining past operating results and identifying new areas of potential corporate growth and profitability. Such a qualitative measure is an important ingredient in the investment evaluation process ... The information conveyed in letters to shareholders narrates the successes and failures of individuals (e.g., the CEOs), organizational subunits, and the entire company. These letters provide valuable but often overlooked information.

In one sense, it is a highly conventionalized and standardized genre, the purpose of which is to introduce and offer the company's perspective on its annual performance; in addition, it is also used to project the future expectations by the company, with some indication of evidence based on past achievements, sometimes pointing out the difficulties that the company might have faced and often promising the positive prospects that the company holds for its shareholders.

An interesting aspect of such letters to shareholders is the time sequence of events; they typically begin with present implications of past events and go towards future events or expectations. The amount of engagement with past events depends on how well the company has performed in the preceding year. If the company has performed financially well, we are more likely to find an elaborate account of the achievements, but if the company has gone through a lean period, then it is less likely to include a lengthy mention of past events. In such cases, however, we often find adequate compensation for this lack of discussion about past events in having a detailed and elaborate engagement with future and expected events. In this context, Subramanian *et al.* (1993), studying the performance and readability of the Chairman's letters to the shareholders of profitable and unprofitable corporations, claim that:

> The mean readability level of the annual reports of corporations that performed well was 10.1, indicating that a 10th grade education was required to comprehend the message in these reports. For corporations that did not perform well, the mean readability level was 14.1, indicating that the reader must have at least a 14th grade level of education to assimilate the message.

The corpus analysed in this study confirms the findings reported in Subramanian *et al.* (1993) that a low ROE (return on equity) firms 'tend to be more forward looking'. They further point out that this tendency is evidenced by the relatively high number of future references when compared to high ROE firms, thus emphasizing that future opportunities over poor past financial performance may be evidence of sound communication strategy at work.

As a typical instance of a letter genre, the Chairman's letter also has a number of conventional indicators; it has the opening address, the closing and, of course, the body of the letter. Considering it as a genre one may claim that the communicative purpose of this letter is to inform the readers, who are the stakeholders in the company, about the performance of the company in the past year.

In terms of regularities of organization, the letter often has a fairly standardized seven-move structure (although Move 5: *Expressions of gratitude* is not very common) with some scope for variation within this general discourse structure.

Move 1:   *Looking back* (overview of the review period)
Move 2:   *Identifying important themes* (claims made)
Move 3:   *Elaboration on themes* (evidence for claims)
Move 4:   *Expectations and promises* (projections for future)
Move 5:   *Expressions of gratitude* (thanks to staff and shareholders)
Move 6:   *Looking forward* (revisiting Move 1)
Move 7:   *Positive and polite closing*

One can also find typical use of lexico-grammar to signal movement between various rhetorical Moves. Figure 11.1 summarizes the rhetorical structuring of a typical Chairman's letter to the shareholders.

[Insert Figure 11.1 about here]

As one can see, it is common to have an adverbial of time, such as, '*Last year* was a ...', or '*This year* has been ...'. Similarly, in Move 2 themes of

			LEXICO-GRAMMAR
PAST EVENTS	Move 1:	**Overview of the review period** Oftern positive, occasionally cautious or negative mode	Last year was ... Year of value creation ...
	Move 2:	**Major themes**	Contraction of revenue ... Challenging environment ...
	Move 3:	**Achievements – measures (elaboration and explanation of themes** Major achievements, evidence and dtailing major contributing actors 9inside the company for success or outside factors for failures) Major steps or measures taken to ensure success	Has enhanced our reputation ... Expanded our coverage ... Reshaped the cost base ...
FUTURE EVENTS	Move 4:	**Expectations and promises** Detailed accounts of future actions Measures to be taken Intended and expected outcomes	We expect ... improvement Plans ... to maximize shareholder value ... to expand our businesses
	Move 5:	**Looking forward** Positive outlook Continued challenges (sometimes) Grim outlook (rare)	Prospects for ... are encouraging
	Move 6:	**Expressions of gratitude (optional)** Appreciation to management team, sometimes workers Congratulations to management for successful period	Thanks to the quality and talent of our staff and management
EXPECTATIONS	Move 7:	**Positive and confident closing** Revisiting themes from Move 1 Summarizing forward-looking, positive statements	As Chairman, I am working with the aim of making a signficant and positive impact on shareholder value

Figure 11.1 Corporate annual reports: analysis of move structure in the Chairman's statement

some significance are expressed by nominalized forms, such as *contraction of revenue, financial flexibility, productivity gains,* etc. In this context, it is interesting to note that Thomas (1997) in her study of the discourse of the marketplace found that business terms such as these 'together with nonhuman participants' give the appearance of 'objectivity' by suggesting a strong but subtle impression of a factual situation caused by circumstances not attributable to any person or persons who might otherwise be thought responsible, which is a very useful device for communicating weak performance. In Move 3 a typical use of perfect tense seems to be a common phenomenon when referring to achievements of the company in the past year, as in *have concentrated, have responded, have increased,* etc.

Similarly, expectations are often signalled by expressions such as a combination of the pronoun *we* and verbs such as *expect, hope,* and *will be able to,* etc. In addition, positive nominals such as *progress, challenges, expansion of business,* etc. are quite common. In Move 6: *Looking forward,* the most common expression seems to be *prospect, going forward,* etc. whereas in the optional Move 5: *Expressions of gratitude,* we find positive nominals such as *a world class team, quality, talent and commitment of staff and management team, strong leadership, broad industry experience,* etc. Occasionally we find a separate, final Move 7: *Positive closing* that often revisits the initial review of the previous year's main themes in Move 1, to promise significant gains and positive impact on the future performance of the company, especially the share value of company stocks.

Typical incidence of these two features of lexico-grammar, that is, nominals and the use of perfect and future tense forms interestingly cooperate to indicate that the text is embedded in a specific business context (particularly the use of nominals like *challenging economic environment, year of value creation, contraction of revenue, shareholder value, intense competition, financial flexibility,* etc.) and that it strongly projects a positive and forward-looking image of the achievements of the specific organization in question, especially through the use of *reshaped the cost base, has been positioned to prosper, will be able to exploit, have enhanced our reputation,* etc.

The identification and description of such lexico-grammatical resources within the move structure of the genre gives an insightful indication of the discursive resources employed in this professional genre; however this instance of discursive practice is also an integral part of the professional practice of corporate disclosure procedures, and one needs to explore further to understand the nature, function and execution of this corporate practice as embedded in business culture. No amount of linguistic description and analysis, however deep one may go, can explain why corporate communications in this context are written the way they are. In order to understand this issue better, one certainly needs to go beyond the textual or discursive description to incorporate contextual analysis, which may require the use of a multi-perspective and multidisciplinary framework of analysis (see Bhatia 2004 for details).

The rationale for writing this letter the way it has been written in such a positive tone is that businesses often downplay any indications of negative performance to highlight positive aspects for future growth. As an experienced public relations manager, in her specialist reaction, pointed out,

> ... the Chairman's Statement in a company report (is) the PR's job ... At times when profit is not so good, her role as a PR manager, is to manage the sentiments of the public and the shareholders so as not to make any dramatic share price movement. This involves management of tone and manner of writing the reports as well as meeting the expectations of the Management.

It is also important to point out that letters like these are often accompanied by annual reports, which are supposed to contain more realistic and objective performance indicators, such as the facts and figures of growth and achievement, indicating profit or loss, past weaknesses and future strengths of the company in question. One may argue that stakeholders often need to go beyond the rhetoric and interpret the results carefully interpreting the complexity of numbers in the annual report. However, these numbers often make little sense to many of the non-specialist readers, especially to the minority shareholders, who often depend on the accompanying rhetoric included in the report, including the Chairman's statement. Since the two discourses, the accountancy discourse and the public relations discourse are intertextually placed as part of the same document, it is natural for non-specialist readers to assume that the accounting details invariably certified by chartered accountants offer a reasonable basis for the PR discourse and the claims made therein. However, as a well-established chartered accountant giving his specialist reaction points out:

> The accountant's job is to note any inconsistency in the company reports and ... to go through the banking mechanism of the management ... Accountants are not responsible for the forecasting of the company's future.

Nevertheless corporations rarely hesitate in exploiting the intertextual as well as the interdiscursive nature of these two discourses by placing them in the same document, that is, the annual report. These features of contextual placement of the two discourses when interpreted in the context of the rationale for the genres in question, the lexico-grammatical features typically exploited in these genres, and also the nature of participant relationships, in particular between the insiders and the outsiders (i.e. minority shareholders), encourage a number of different and rather interesting interpretations of corporate disclosure practices. In addition, one may also find it useful to go beyond the analysis of the Chairman's letter and its relationship to the annual report, and consider a third genre, that is, the disclaimers, which tend to disclaim almost everything claimed in the annual report, in particular, the predictions, promises, expectations, etc. Without going further in this direction, I would like to argue for a critical look not only at the intertextuality and interdiscursivity in corporate disclosure documents because they tend to work together, but also at the much broader corporate context and culture that encourage a typical set of expectations which are fulfilled by a subtle bending of the typical corporate genres from 'information giving or reporting' to 'promoting corporate interests'.

Yet another text-external factor that has serious implication for the way corporate disclosure documents are interpreted and analysed is the issue of multiple perspectives, which any framework for critical genre analysis needs to take into account. In this study, an attempt was made to study the claims made by the corporations in their annual reports and other media announcements, such as the press releases, interim announcements, etc., against the perceptions of the media experts in business and corporate affairs.

There were several interesting cases of differing perspectives on annual results, especially in the area of promises and predictions. When a specific company ABC, for instance, (in their 2003 annual results press release) claimed that 'We are making the practical moves to prepare the company to pay a dividend ...', the media (*South China Morning Post* 17 July 2003) clearly pointed out that 'Earning per share of ABC's existing shareholders would be diluted by 8 per cent'. Similarly, in another instance the company (in their 2003 interim results) claimed that they were 'committed to making ABC a global leader in telecommunications technology to the benefit of our shareholders'; almost at the same time the media predicted that 'ABC remains a telecommunications company in an investor no man's land, neither offering the earnings of a growth stock nor dividend yield of a secure utility' (*South China Morning Post*, 4 March 2004). This aspect of multiple perceptions on interpretations of corporate discourses underpins the importance of intertextuality and interdiscursivity in critical genre analysis, on the one hand, and perhaps more importantly, in cases of potential 'bending of corporate genres', on the other.

To sum up, it is not only possible but also desirable in some contexts to explore deeper understanding of the immediate as well as the broader context, including intertextuality and more importantly interdiscursivity, in addition to lexico-grammar, textualization, and textual organization. Yet another factor that can play an important role is the asymmetry in the role relationship between participants, accompanied by the power distance between the company Chairman and shareholders, on the one hand, and social proximity between the Chairman and fellow directors, on the other. One may also notice the indications of one-way unequal interaction, with the writer providing general information to recipients who may not share the same awareness about the company's past performance.

The social or professional context in which this text or genre plays an important role, the social action that this particular example of text represents, and the institutional, social or professional culture it invokes when it is constructed and interpreted, are some of the important issues that need to be investigated. It is not simply that a professional genre is constructed and used for a specific professional purpose; it may be that a specific genre is deliberately and consciously bent to achieve something more than just a socially accepted and shared professional objective. One may need to investigate how and to what extent this seemingly harmless genre can be used to mystify corporate performance for (minority) shareholders and other stakeholders of the company.

Towards critical genre analysis

Focusing on genre-based corporate actions, this study has been able to identify and address a number of issues concerning the interaction between language use and corporate behaviour, and I hope, will make some contribution towards raising the awareness of stakeholders to a better understanding of the discursive practices of corporations in meeting the statutory demands as well as the social expectations of corporate disclosure practices. The study also contributes to the field of genre analysis by bringing into focus the conflict between discursive practices (constructing, interpreting and using professional genres) and professional practices (managing professional activities) in corporate contexts. At a more theoretical level, the study highlights the tension between 'generic integrity' (Bhatia 1993, 1994, 1995, 1998, 2000) and 'genre bending' (Bhatia 1997, 2004) in professional discourse. It also underpins the need to use a multidimensional and multi-perspective framework to better understand generic integrity of corporate disclosure documents through the analysis of appropriation of generic resources to achieve 'private intentions' within the context of 'socially accepted generic norms'.

The analysis highlights an important area of genre development, that is, the role and function of 'interdiscursivity' in genre construction, appropriation and interpretation, which I would like to characterize as a move towards critical genre analysis. Although the concepts of interdiscursivity are not entirely new and can be traced back to the works of Foucault (1981), Bakhtin (1986), Kristeva (1980), Fairclough (1995) and Candlin and Maley (1997), it has not been fully explored to investigate some of the complexities we find in academic and professional genres. To clarify the use of interdiscursivity here I would like to reiterate that whereas intertextuality refers to texts transforming the past into the present using prior texts often in relatively conventionalized and somewhat standardized ways, interdiscursivity refers to more innovative attempts to create hybrid or relatively novel constructs by appropriating or exploiting established conventions or resources associated with other genres. Interdiscursivity thus accounts for a variety of discursive processes, some of which include mixing, embedding and bending of generic norms in professional practice.

To conclude I would like to reiterate that genre analysis has until recently focused more on textual, intertextual and organizational aspects of genres (Swales 1990; Bhatia 1993), and very little on interdiscursivity and other wider aspects of contextualization. The analyses have generally been confined to 'textual space' (Bhatia 2004), focusing primarily on the use and application of lexico-grammatical resources, and more recently to 'tactical space' (Bhatia 2004), taking into account discourse or move structures, but rarely on contextualization that is often exploited for achieving specific objectives within shared or often contested perceptions of professional cultures.

In this chapter I have made an attempt to broaden the concept of contextualization to study professional genres as part of a much larger design in an attempt to establish a valid and useful link between the 'discursive practices' of a specific professional community and the 'professional practices' (Bhatia 2004) of that community, thus underpinning the importance of interdiscursivity in the development of genre theory. Viewing genres as reflections of disciplinary and professional cultures, I made an attempt to shift the focus more seriously on to corporate disclosure practices embedded in accounting and corporate management cultures. In order to have a satisfactory and insightful explanation of why corporate communication experts construct their disclosure documents the way they do, analysis of text internal resources is not sufficient. More importantly, one needs to investigate some of these corporate genres more critically to find out how the integrity of these genres is negotiated and exploited to serve some of the hidden corporate intentions.

To achieve this objective, genre theory needs to integrate a number of other perspectives and dimensions, such as the ethnographic perspective, which allows one to go to the heart of what Scollon (1998) refers to as 'critical sites of engagement' through 'lived narratives' of expert and experienced professionals, the socio-cognitive perspective, which will encourage interpretive behaviour of specialist and non-specialist audiences of corporate disclosure documents, particularly in the light of investment decision-making. A good and judicious integration of some of these perspectives and dimensions, I hope, will be useful in our critical understanding of the extent to which a particular set of generic resources are being creatively exploited to bend some of the socially shared generic norms to achieve what could be regarded as 'private' corporate intentions.

Note

1 The work described in this chapter was supported by a CERG grant from the Research Grants Council of the Hong Kong Special Administrative Region, China (Project No. 9041056 (CityU 1454/05H)).

References

Bakhtin, M.M. (1986) *Speech Genres and Other Late Essays*, Austin, TX: University of Texas Press.

Bhatia, V.K. (1993) *Analysing Genre: language use in professional settings*, London: Longman.

—— (1994) 'Generic integrity in professional discourse', in B.-L. Gunarsson, P. Linell and B. Nordberg (eds) *Text and Talk in Professional Contexts*, Skriftserie no. 6, Uppsala, Sweden, ASLA, pp. 61–76.

—— (1995) 'Genre-mixing and in professional communication: the case of "private intentions" v. "socially recognised purposes"', in P. Bruthiaux, T. Boswood and

B. Bertha (eds) *Explorations in English for Professional Communication*, Hong Kong: City University of Hong Kong, pp. 1–19.

—— (1997) 'Genre-mixing in academic introductions', *English for Specific Purposes*, 16(3): 181–96.

—— (1998) 'Generic conflicts in academic discourse', in I. Fortanet, J.C. Palmer, S. Posteguillo and J.F. (eds) *Genre Studies in English for Academic Purposes*, Bancaixa: Fundació Caixa Castelló, pp. 15–28.

—— (2000) 'Genres in conflict', in Anna Trosborg (ed.) *Analysing Professional Genres*, Amsterdam: John Benjamins.

—— (2004) *Worlds of Written Discourse: A Genre-Based View*, London: Continuum International.

Candlin, C.N. and Maley, Y. (1997) 'Intertextuality and interdiscursivity in the discourse of alternative dispute resolution', in B.-L. Gunarsson, P. Linnel and B. Nordberg (eds) *The Construction of Professional Discourse*, London: Longman, pp. 201–22.

Fairclough, N. (1995) *Critical Discourse Analysis: the critical study of language*, London: Longman.

Foucault, M. (1981) *The Archaeology of Knowledge*, New York: Pantheon Books.

Kohut, G.F. and Segars, A.H. (1992) 'The president's letter to stockholders: an examination of corporate communication strategy', *Journal of Business Communication*, 29(1): 7–21.

Kristeva, J. (1980) 'Word, dialogue and novel', in J. Kristeva (ed.) *Desire in Language*, Oxford: Blackwell, pp. 64–91.

Scollon, R. (1998) *Mediated Discourse as Social Interaction: a study of news discourse*, London: Longman.

Smart, G. (1998) 'Mapping conceptual worlds: using interpretive ethnography to explore knowledge-making in a professional community', *Journal of Business Communication*, 35(1): 111–27.

Subramanian, R., Insley, R.G. and Blackwell, R.D. (1993) 'Performance and readability: a comparison of annual reports of profitable and unprofitable corporations', *Journal of Business Communication*, 30: 49–62.

Swales, J.M. (1990) *Genre Analysis: English in academic and research settings*, Cambridge: Cambridge University Press.

—— (1998) *Other Floors, Other Voices: a textography of a small university building*, London: Lawrence Erlbaum.

Thomas, J. (1997) 'Discourse in the marketplace: the making of meaning in annual reports', *Journal of Business Communication*, 34(1): 47–66.

12 Genre evolution?

The case for a diachronic perspective

Carol Berkenkotter

In this chapter, I make a case for the theoretical and methodological importance of qualitative historical genre analysis for discourse analysis. 'Historical genre analysis' refers to diachronic studies of the development of disciplinary and professional genres. I also contend that taking a multi-method approach to studying the textual dynamics of professional genres in their socio-historical contexts provides a 'genre-based lens' (Bhatia 2004) through which to examine the historically developing practices of such jurisdictional professions as law, medicine, psychiatry, and the natural and social sciences.

I begin this discussion with a few theoretical questions: how literally – or heuristically – should we take the concept of 'genre evolution' and how might this concept be used to explain to the relationship between sociohistorical changes occurring within psychiatry as a clinical profession and changes to the case history's form and content? These two questions are related to the larger conceptual issue raised by Hyland (2002) of what the relationship might be between the structural properties of institutions (and their changes over time) and individual communicative action, namely in what ways can professional and disciplinary genres be said to *evolve*? Does importing a concept from the biological sciences serve to enhance our understanding of the relationship between discursive and social formation in such professions as law and medicine? Can scholars map such evolutionary processes as 'natural selection', random selection' or 'selection pressures' over the processes of textual change over time as disciplines become professionalized? Finally, how do applied linguists characterize the relationship between changes in a discipline's 'thought-style' and the subsequent alterations in the conventions of its knowledge-bearing texts?

Certainly in the way that Atkinson (1993, 1999) and Bazerman (1988) use the term, the idea of the 'evolution' of the scientific article as it developed in *PTRS* is *metaphorical*. Atkinson, for example, took some pains to discuss how some of the features of the scientific article emerged, specifically how the idea of 'virtual witnessing' (Shapin 1994) came to be instantiated in the conventions of the author's careful description of procedures and results. What Atkinson's study did not include, however, was a description of the external political, technological, and economic selection pressures resulting in either a gradual and continuous change in some feature or convention over time – or a relatively abrupt change in the lexico-grammar, for example, the emergence of a fused noun string (Gross *et al.* 2002).

Drawing on historian of science David Hull's (1988a, 1988b) theory of conceptual change in science, Gross *et al.* (2002) argued that just as conceptual change in science occurs as the result of various pressures producing 'natural selection' of successive predominating thought-styles, or paradigms, so too have scientists' representational practices (lexico-grammatical, visual/graphic) been subject to pressures in the discursive environment producing the selection of changes from the lexico-grammatical level to the macro-structural level. Gross and his colleagues went on to claim that from a historical perspective, the function of the scientific article has been to deliver cognitively complex information through a variety of characteristics that produce maximum syntactic and organizational efficiency, that is, features that maximize information finding. In other words, by the twentieth century the experimental article in science had become a master finding system.

In their last chapter, Gross *et al.* sum up the implications of the analysis of their data, arguing for a view of modern scientific prose as projecting 'a particular image – that of an objective, efficiently conveyer of cognitive complexity' (2002: 214). This image is communicated through successive changes in argument, presentation (i.e. the organizational conventions) and style. Summarizing changes in the scientific style over a 300-year period (1665–1995), Gross *et al.* conclude that the reader's attention has been focused *away* from people and *towards* things (2002: 219) through scientist–writers deploying such techniques as: (1) the [writer's] use of the suppressed person passive verb and verbs related to the activity of things rather than people; (2) the relative absence of the personal pronouns, I and we; (3) the use of hedges, a practice that signals that the style is object oriented; and (4) a set of stylistic features that make syntax more efficient, including more complex noun phrases in the subject position (2002: 215). This last development reflects:

> the increase in cognitive complexity [that] has forced the shift in scientific prose to the more complex noun phrase in the subject position, and as compensation ... a corresponding decrease in the length of sentences and in the number of clauses per sentence.
>
> (Gross *et al.* 2002: 215)

All of these changes conduce to syntactic efficiency. Regarding what they call *presentational elements* such as titles, introductions, headings, number of equations, figures and tables, the format and placement of citations, and the inclusion of the discussion/implications section, Gross and his co-authors conclude that the presentational features were introduced over time as the number of publications in the authors' fields multiplied. Finally, they suggest that the organizational features are designed to help the reader cull out the information she needs most efficiently from the abstract, figures and graphs, and references.

Taking their thesis one step further by drawing on Hull's theoretical argument that science is a *cultural* evolutionary process, Gross and his colleagues contend that these changes in the scientific article's discursive mechanisms suggest an evolutionary development that *parallels* the increasing cognitive complexity of scientific practices from the seventeenth to late twentieth centuries. Their argument, however, seems more to constitute an analogy between the evolution of species and the textual instantiations of the force of 'selection pressures', namely that in science – as in nature – species proliferate, and that the survival of the fittest results from discursive modifications in response to external selection pressures. Contextualizing their argument by referring to Hull's theory of science as an evolutionary process, they summarize his position, as follows:

> David Hull provides us with a theory that we can adapt to changes [we observed] in style, presentation, and argument. According to Hull, in biological evolution, individuals among species interact with one another and the environment. When they do, in sexual species at least, the genetic endowments of individuals combine to produce a next generation, a new cohort on which natural selection has operated and continues to operate in the direction of more nearly satisfactory adaptation to each other and the environment. Generalized and translated into Hull's terminology, selection theory takes the following form: When *interactors* interact, *replicators* create <u>*lineages*</u> by a *process of selection*. In Hull's words, 'when the interplay between replication and interaction causes lineages to change over time, the end result is evolution through selection'. [Hull 1988: 136]
>
> (Gross *et al.* 2002: 216–17; italics added for emphasis)

To sharpen their comparison between biological evolution and the changing textual activity of the scientific article, Gross and his co-authors bring into play the biological concepts of *phenotype* and *genotype*. Each organism is an instantiation of its overall phenotype, or general bodily design. The genotype, i.e. the set of generative structures by means of which an organism inherits phenotypes and suites of characters, is a *replicator*, or an entity that passes on its structure largely intact in successive replications (see Hull 1988a: 134). In other words, the genotype can be seen as a 'set of predispositions' when it comes to scientific prose. As Gross *et al.* contend,

> In the case of the scientific article, the genotype is a *set of predispositions*: to create arguments, the vehicles by means of which Hull's 'conceptual systems' are built, to transform these arguments into sentences and paragraphs, and finally, to organize these sentences and paragraphs

according to well-recognized organizational constraints. These predispositions are *behavioral tendencies* generally shaped by learning; they
function just like any skill we have, like violin playing or carpentry.
When the situation [or the rhetorical moment] calls for it – scientists
activate these predispositions to create a scientific article.

(Gross *et al.* 2002: 218; italics added for emphasis)

Gross and his colleagues' notion that genotypes can be reconceived as
scientists' *sets of predispositions* to create arguments requires a creative leap
of imagination, I will grant. But it is troubling that they offer only a single
example from mid-nineteenth Viennese science to support their claim. I also
find their formulation problematical, probably because it gives far too much
weight to argument (as rhetoricians so often do!) as the lever for conceptual
change – and, in the process, backgrounds the socio-historical contexts of
scientific thinking that have so interested the historians and sociologists of
science. For example, in the late 1980s the historian of science Peter Dear
borrowed the literary critic's and the rhetorician's tools to examine the
'literary structure of scientific argument' in the context of the social history
of the gentlemen scientists of the seventeenth century in England and Europe
(see Dear: 1989).

In his 1989 collection of essays on scientific and medical research writing,
The Literary Structure of Scientific Argument, Dear did, in fact, take his cue
from the rhetoricians in the late 1980s (e.g. Bazerman 1988; Miller 1984),
by determining that genres and the way they change over time are 'major
indicators' of change in the development of Western scientific thinking.
In order to undertake a cultural history of science, it was necessary Dear
argues, to study the cultures of scientific communities both in the *context of
their social history* and by *a close reading of scientific texts*. Such studies, he
suggests, necessarily 'recognize the relationship between textual and other
practices in scientific activities' by recognizing the importance of studying
scientific and medical genres – first of all, in relation to such factors as
the disciplines out of which they develop – and second, 'as a means for
examining a textually delineated shift in the epistemological posture of a
discipline' (Dear 1989: 5). Accordingly, the rhetorically oriented historian
of science examines scientific texts in their socio-historical contexts by being
concerned with such matters as: first, the role of genres in perpetuating,
changing, or subverting scientific research programmes; second, the role of
genre in defining disciplinary boundaries; third, the role of scientific texts
in embodying the cognitive assumptions or social structure of the sciences
to which they belong; fourth, the ways in which literary forms can direct
the cognitive content of a science through constraining problem-choice or
through requiring (via their own disciplinary entrenchment) particular kinds
of theoretical and experimental formulation (1989: 5).

By placing such concerns at the centre of their investigation into scientific
genres and the sets of cognitive assumptions that they instantiate, Dear and

his colleagues recognized the relationship between genre, discipline, and conceptual or cognitive change – or resistance to change via disciplinary entrenchment.

Given the preceding discussion of the proprietary interests of rhetoricians, historians of science, and applied linguists on the question of how scientific genres change over time, it's not unreasonable to assert that *genres – and their systems – often seem to be at the centre of disciplinary growth and professionalization.*

Not that the genres of medical and scientific writing are any richer as an object of study than studies of lexico-grammatical elements in scientific texts of the sort done by Halliday and Martin (1993) and by other linguists (see, for example, Taavitsainen and Pahta 2000). What is different is that the *unit of analysis* differs in each approach, as does the analyst's attention to contextual elements. Historians of science are absorbed by and attentive to socio-cultural, economic, political and ideological contexts, paying much more attention to them than to the changing textual features of scientific and medical texts over time. A historian might remark on these changes, but does not systematically attempt to describe them, as does the linguist.

In the previous section I described the biological concept of evolution as a heuristic for explaining changes in the scientific and medical research article, pointing to some key disciplinary differences between rhetoricians, linguists, and historians of sciences who have taken either a diachronic text-based (as in the case of Gross *et al.*) or context-based (Dear *et al.*) approach to analysing conceptual change in science, using scientific texts as the object of study. Although collectively these approaches advance our understanding of the textual side of the history of science, our understanding of the history of medicine, and particularly psychiatry as a text/context set of relationships is much more sketchy.

To address this gap, I would like now to turn to the history of psychiatric case reporting, first to make a number of general observations that are relevant to the concept of 'genre evolution'. Then I'd like to turn to Kuhn's notion of paradigm change, suggesting that from a diachronic perspective, changing 'thought styles' or paradigm shift is more powerful heuristically for characterizing what happened to the psychiatric case report in England and the United States between the late eighteenth and early twenty-first centuries. Kuhn's discussion (1970, 2nd edn; cf. Fleck 1979) of paradigm shift is a theory of conceptual change, as is Hull's (1988) adaptation of evolutionary theory to describe change over time in science.

The next section begins with two generalizations regarding the antecedents of today's clinical psychiatric case report in its latest manifestation as part of an institutional genre system in today's mental health clinic.

Psychiatric case reports: the genre next door

First, if we look closely at the history of case reporting in psychiatry, *form follows function*. For example, the *institutional* case report, which is based on the physician's oral interview with the patient, needs to be distinguished from the *published* case report. This institutional case report is both interdiscursive and intertextual, linked as it is to the physician's case notes, usually written during or after the oral interview between patient and physician, and being written for an entirely different purpose than is the published case history, written for an audience of peers and appearing in a professional journal. (I use the terms case history and case report interchangeably.)

Second, despite this difference, the published clinical case report in psychiatry as well as in other medical disciplines, is written from (and putatively based on) the institutional case report. The purpose of the published case report, however, unlike that of the institutional case history, has been pedagogical as well as epistemic. Early case reports appearing in the oldest medical journal, the *Edinburgh Medical and Surgical Journal*, in the late eighteenth and early nineteenth centuries were used to teach medical students how to recognize different kinds of mental illnesses based on the symptoms the patient presented. In this respect, the published psychiatric case report had not become differentiated from other kinds of medical case reports, and in the eighteenth and nineteenth centuries was printed side by side in medical journals such as the *Edinburgh Medical and Surgical Journal*.

Socio-historical context of the institutional case records

The institutional psychiatric case report, like the medical case report, consisted of the following sections: presenting symptoms, physical examination, patient history, diagnosis, descriptions of treatment, trajectory of illness and outcomes, discharge to family and friends, removal to another asylum or private hospital, or death, and post-mortem analysis of the morbid contents of the brain (in the late eighteenth and early nineteenth centuries). This format (without the post-mortem autopsy) became standardized in the mid-nineteenth century in England after Parliament passed a law requiring all insane asylums in England to maintain the same format for the patient record. These records were kept in large leather bound notebooks, and it was not infrequent that a patient remained in an asylum for lengthy duration – or more typically – was released, and then after a relapse returned to the asylum for several years. Thus the entries in a clinical history could span two or even three casebooks over a decade or more.

These records were a form of *local knowledge* to be read by the asylum superintendent (who might have also written in the case record), and other physicians, aides and the inspectors, appointed by parliament, who travelled from asylum to asylum to scrutinize the casebooks in order to protect patients from abuses from attendants and from neglect. It was for this reason that the format of the institutional case report became standardized in 1844 in England. By examining the socio-historical context in which case reports came to be prescribed, it is easy to see how the formal conventions followed the function of the asylum records.

The published case report, however, had other purposes and venues. As well as appearing in medical and later, psychiatric journals, case reports in truncated form could also be found in textbooks to illustrate the various classifications of mental disorder that were currently in vogue. They appeared as well in treatises on mental disorders, again as illustrations of particular types of insanity. In both textbooks and treatises, the illustrative case report was a rhetorical means for giving examples of *typical cases* of different forms of mental disorder and their treatment. On the other hand, the case report appearing in medical and – by the mid-nineteenth century – psychiatric journals had a pedagogical as well as an epistemic (Baconian) purpose. In addition to being often the *only* source of information about how the psychiatric examination should be conducted (in lieu of students making hospital or asylum rounds), the case report often provided a detailed account of unusual presentations of mania symptoms, or of mental disorders that were co-morbid with physical ailments, such as a patient with ovarian tumours presenting symptoms of mania.

Sigmund Freud, the analyst's couch and the curative power of talk therapy

By the end of the nineteenth century, once psychiatry became available to a middle-class outpatient population who were private patients, psychiatrists competed with neurologists for jurisdiction over this population. Thus a niche was created for a new kind of doctor–patient relationship, one that would provide therapy to the patient leading to a cure, rather than the essentially custodial care of the large numbers of patients warehoused in public asylums – the patients with severe and persistent mental illnesses. In the 1890s in Vienna, Sigmund Freud, the father of the talking cure and the founder of psychoanalysis, developed a much more complex case history than had been previously seen in the other venues of case reports described above. These case histories became the vehicle for Freud's 'new science of the mind'.

Although Freud still used the organizational conventions of the clinical case history – i.e. presenting problem, family history, physical examination – he developed the genre into something much more elaborate than its antecedents. Indeed, Freud's clinical narratives were populated with characters who spoke dialogue that was represented as *reported speech* most often (but not always) with quotation marks.

Freud himself was both narrator and actor in his case histories. The patient's past and the present were intermingled in the course of the Freudian narrative a study in which the denouement followed a climatic scene in which the patient experienced an important revelation, a scene very similar to the peripeteia of the novel or novella. Moreover, there were in Freud's case histories, elements of the fictional detective story, the Sherlock Holmes story with Freud as a Holmes surrogate, a sexual sleuth who ferreted out the patient's repressed desires and fears. This subterranean material, which was made available through the analyst's interpretation of the patient's dream symbols and significations, Freud mined for the dream's occluded logic. Once this logic was decoded it was understood to be the text of the patient's neurosis.

To summarize from these observations, psychiatry as a profession existed at the margins of the medical sciences, isolated as it was in the asylums of England and Europe. The expansion of the patient population to the nervous Viennese middle class with its anxieties, phobias, and obsessions, created a demographic niche for the first psychoanalysts and their new science of the mind. With this new set of practices, specifically, the talking cure and the psychoanalytic case history with its pedagogical purpose and new audience of psychiatrists, there appeared in print a greatly expanded case history, one that shows many similarities with the English and European novella and the British detective story.

In the following section of this chapter, I turn to describing in a very general way the psychiatric case report as an example of a genre that developed in the community of practice of eighteenth- and nineteenth-century 'mad doctors', those physicians whose training equipped them to be psychiatrists and superintendents of the nineteenth-century lunatic asylum. I will then briefly describe Sigmund Freud's revolutionary influence on psychiatry as the father of a new science of mind, psychoanalysis, with its unique and very non-medical form of representation – the literary case history.

Sigmund Freud and Emil Kraepelin

In the eighteenth century, epistolary case reports of patients with psychiatric problems, like other medical case reports of patients with physical problems, were based on the Baconian view that scientific (and hence, medical) knowledge grew out of the gradual accumulation of observations of nature and natural phenomenon. Whereas scientists' observations were written up in the eighteenth century as epistolary accounts of experiments, physicians' observations of their patients' illnesses, the treatment regimen, its success or failure, could as well be seen as 'natural histories' of diseases. Their interest to physician-readers lay in the 'news' of patients with heretofore undiagnosed maladies, the successful use of a new treatment and, occasionally, cases in which physical and mental symptoms were interwoven in such a way that the physical problem was seen as being the cause of a specific mental illness, for example linking a female patient's mania to a diseased uterus or ovaries. Such were the first of the medical and psychiatric case histories. Mental illness – or 'insanity' as it was called in the eighteenth and nineteenth centuries – was seen through a materialist perspective. Concepts of 'mind' or 'the psyche' were regarded with suspicion as being too close to the clergy's jurisdiction; thus, mental symptoms were seen as epiphenomena of bodily disorder – and were treated as such with emetics, purgatives and narcotics.

It wasn't until the end of the nineteenth century that two physicians – one, an Austrian (Sigmund Freud), the other a German (Emil Kraepelin) – were to develop two competing 'thought styles' about mental illness. Although ignored in the first half of the twentieth century, Kraepelin's classification system of mental disorders (1902, 1908) became the basis of the 'counter-revolution' in psychiatry which took place in the 1970s and 1980s. The rise of a 'new' research-based diagnostic classification system in 1980 was mainly directed against Freud and his followers with their 'metaphysics' of the unconscious and its mechanisms. By the last quarter of the twentieth century, Kraepelin's nosology became the prototype for the American Psychiatric Association's *Diagnostic and Statistical Manual of Mental Disorder*, 3rd edn (1980), whose classifications were based on empirical studies of large numbers of patients, individuals who had been separated into diagnostic groups based on presenting symptoms. In this newest iteration of a nosological system many Kraeplinian classifications re-appeared in modified form.

Although Kraepelin's empiricist approach was more consistent with and congenial to medical practices of the late nineteenth century, Freud's influence on psychiatry in Europe, England, and the United States was instrumental in many respects to the professionalization of the discipline. He provided both the intellectual means and the set of practices that constituted what was, arguably, the first full paradigm formation in psychiatry.

As generic innovations, Freud's case histories were hybrid forms borrowing conventions from both literary and scientific discourse. He appears to have drawn on the techniques of realist authors of fictional works, who were concerned not only with the origins of their fictional characters' personalities, but also with their inner lives. In the context of Freud's new science of mind, he was first and last concerned with the aetiology of his patients' neuroses, and therefore, a primary technique of his psychoanalytic method was to – with the help of the patient – unravel his or her personal history as a way to reach down to the roots of the illness. What he created in the first of his five major case histories, *Fragments of an Analysis of a Case of Hysteria* (1905) and then those that followed was a rich, multi-layered narrative that straddled a fine line between the scientism of his time and an alternative hermeneutic approach to the study of mind. The multiple techniques that Freud used to represent the speech of his patient, 'Dora', and the care he took to report his efforts to provide a verbatim account of what she reported laid the foundation for the modern case report in psychodynamic therapy. The patient's account of his or her life-world, reported verbatim, is still the *sine qua non* of the psychoanalytic case history. This attentiveness to the patient's speech in varying degrees of closeness or fidelity highlights the emphasis that Freud put on – for the first time in the history of the psychiatric case history – the idea of *talk* as the phenomenon that both reveals and conceals meanings that the psychoanalyst works to penetrate and uncover.

Freud's influence and his school of psychoanalysis dominated psychiatry in the United States for over 70 years. Even today, psychodynamically-oriented psychotherapy competes with cognitive-behavioural therapy, although psychoanalytic treatment lasting several years is much less common in this current era of short-term, solution-oriented therapy. Despite the reach of the psychoanalytic thought-style, several forces converged in the United States during the 1970s and 1980s that led to the decline of the psychoanalytic approach, as the biomedical approach to diagnosis and treatment supervened its psychodynamic predecessor.

The near extinction of the published case histories in psychiatry and medicine is an important part of that history. The case report nearly vanished from the pages of the *American Journal of Psychiatry* after 1984, when the journal's editorial board decided to stop publishing case reports in the 'Clinical and Research Reports' section, relegating them to the briefer and considerably more modest 'Letters to the Editor' section (Berkenkotter *et al.* 1999). The clinical case history languished until 2002 in the Letters section of the *American Journal of Psychiatry*, its status greatly reduced – as was its word count– from 2,200 words to a mere 600.

Genres and paradigm shift in psychiatry, an alternative to the conception of evolution in scientific writing

The history of psychiatry's case report does not parallel the development of the scientific article (Atkinson 1999; Bazerman 1988; Gross *et al.* 2002; Valle 1999). Because medicine as a profession was profoundly influenced by the natural sciences – botany having originally been an offshoot of the medical sciences – the history of medical research articles is not in fact, repeated in the history of psychiatry's case reports.

Although for most of its history as a profession, psychiatry maintained its identity as a branch of medicine, the humanistic influence of Sigmund Freud, and the growth and spread of psychoanalysis, with the case report as its favoured genre of reporting, resulted in a 70-year hiatus (see Shorter 1997). During this period, psychiatry as a discipline developed in the direction of the interpretive social sciences, until the positivist revolution occurred in the 1970s and 1980s in the United States and somewhat later in England and Europe. Thus psychiatry, as a branch of the medical arts, has had a chequered career in terms of its development as a profession. The single-subject case report mirrored for nearly 180 years changing conceptions of mental disorder, changes in the demographics of the patient population and changes in psychiatrists' jurisdiction, as they competed for patients with neurologists and members of the clergy.

Several researchers in rhetoric and applied linguistics (Bazerman 1988; Atkinson 1993; Taavitsainen and Pahta 2000) have used the concept of 'evolution' to characterize the development of the scientific or medical article. They used the concept metaphorically to characterize the diachronic processes of change in the genre. On the other hand, Gross *et al.* (2001) have taken a more literalist approach to explain changes in the experimental article over 250 years. These researchers enlisted David Hull's (1988a, 1988b) explanation of conceptual change in science as being an evolutionary process to argue such processes such as 'selection pressures' could be examined historically as acting on changes in the experimental article's stylistic features, presentation, and argument. In contrast, my research on the psychiatric case report leads me to a different and disconfirming position.

The development of case report genre in psychiatry during the nineteenth and twentieth centuries can be accounted for more parsimoniously by using a *grounded-theoretical approach* (Glaser and Strauss 1967; cf. Berkenkotter and Huckin 1995). By 'grounded-theoretical approach', I mean that the generalizations described above were arrived at through the process of my analysing case histories in the context of several socio-historical factors that converged during a particular period, factors that themselves were subject to change over time. This approach suggests that it is more helpful to think of a pre-paradigmatic era in the eighteenth and nineteenth centuries during which several schools and individual 'mad doctors' (as they were called) set the tone for their respective eras. Innovations in the published case report were made throughout the nineteenth century by some of the most well-known mad doctors, such as John Haslaam, John Conolly and slightly after mid-century, John Charles Bucknill and Daniel H. Tuke, most often reflected psychiatry's *materialist epistemology*, and can be seen as competing schools of thought constituting pre-paradigmatic activity.

Toward the end of the nineteenth century, Sigmund Freud developed an entire theoretical system of concepts and set of practices that constituted psychoanalysis. Psychoanalysis was no mere school of thought, but rather burst on Europe, England and later the United States with the force of a paradigm. And it was through the genre of Freud's major case histories that the new science of the mind could best be understood. Freud's case histories were a major departure from what had been previously published. The patient's speech – reported verbatim, putatively, and represented through direct and indirect quotations and other devices for reporting speech – became the evidence upon which Freud based his psychoanalytic interpretations. Freud was also the first psychiatrist to use literary devices in his case reports (cf. Marcus 1985), a set of techniques that resulted in a hybrid genre.

Freud's case histories were so well received within the newly emerging field of psychoanalysis (in the early twentieth century) that his writings and theoretical framework led to the efflorescence of many psychoanalytically trained authors (e.g. Bruno Bettelheim, Eric Erickson) who published case histories that were as likely to be reviewed in the *New York Times Review of Books* as the *American Journal of Psychiatry*.

The influence of psychoanalysis with its detailed case histories prevailed for nearly 70 years as psychoanalysts formed associations and constructed institutes, and the psychoanalytic method became the preferred set of techniques taught in medical schools in many countries, including the United States. However, Freud's influence was to wane dramatically in the 1970s (and somewhat later in Britain and Europe) as the biomedical model and the neo-Kraepelinian classifications of mental disorder (Feighner *et al.* 1972) became predominant. This new paradigm was textually instantiated in the American Psychiatric Association's *Diagnostic and Statistical Manual of Mental Disorder*, 3rd edn (hereafter, *DSM*), in 1980. A 30-year examination of the 'Clinical and research report' section of the *American Journal of Psychiatry* (Berkenkotter *et al.*1999) demonstrated that by 1985 the single-subject case report had been virtually replaced by large *n* statistical studies of the various classifications of mental disorder of *DSM–III* and its two revisions, *DSM–III-R* (1987) and *DSM–IV* (1994). By 2000 the case report had been retrieved from its lowly status in the 'Letters to the Editor' section of the *American Journal of Psychiatry*. It now appears in a separate section titled 'The clinical case conference', containing reports of an unusual case that is discussed by the reporting psychiatrist, then commented on by members of the journal's editorial board.

In examining the rise and near-demise of psychoanalysis through a genre-based historical lens, I am led to suggest that there have been thus far two 'revolutions', or paradigm shifts, in psychiatry. One way to track these revolutions empirically is to examine the textual dynamics of the psychiatric case report from the mid-eighteenth century to the present. The case report has been a workhorse in psychiatry; it remains so in the clinical mental health system. However, *published* clinical case reports have been supplanted by statistical studies of large *n* populations, following the much earlier trend in medicine (cf. Atkinson 1993; Taavitsainen and Pahta 2000).

Psychiatry is a set of clinical, research and discursive practices that developed into a bona fide profession within medicine from a pre-paradigmatic to paradigmatic stage, first as a result of Freud, his model of the science of mind and the burgeoning class of psychoanalysts who became his followers. Only 70 years later psychoanalysis was overthrown by a positivist group of research-based psychiatrists, the architects of *DSM–III*. These factors and processes make a strong case for a Kuhnian model, rather than the more complex evolutionary model elucidated by Hull and adapted by Gross *et al.* to account for changes over time in the experimental article. I hope that I have demonstrated in this essay that the genre analyst needs a repertoire of techniques for capturing the complex interactions between socio-historical, technological, demographic, and epistemological factors in order to track and interpret textual changes in disciplinary texts, especially in disciplines such as psychiatry, a profession that traverses the boundaries between the natural and human sciences.

References

American Psychiatric Association (1980) *Diagnostic and Statistical Manual of Mental Disorders*, 3rd edn, Washington, DC: American Psychiatric Association.
—— (1987) *Diagnostic and Statistical Manual of Mental Disorders*, revised 3rd edn, Washington, DC: American Psychiatric Association.
—— (1994) *Diagnostic and Statistical Manual of Mental Disorders*, 4th edn, Washington, DC: American Psychiatric Association.
Atkinson, D. (1992) 'The evolution of medical research writing from 1735 to 1985: the case of the *Edinburgh Medical Journal*', *Applied Linguistics*, 13(4): 337–74.
—— (1999) *Scientific Discourse in Sociohistorical Context: the philosophical transactions of the Royal Society of London, 1675–1975*, Mahwah, NJ: Lawrence Erlbaum.
Bazerman, C. (1988) *Shaping Written Knowledge: the genre and activity of the experimental article in science*, Madison, WI: University of Wisconsin Press.
—— (1998) 'Emerging perspectives on the many dimensions of scientific discourse' in J.R. Martin and R. Veel (eds) *Reading Science: critical and functional perspectives on discourses of science*, London: Routledge.
Berkenkotter, C. and Huckin, T.N. (1995) *Genre Knowledge in Disciplinary Communication: cognition/culture/power*, Hillsdale, NJ: Lawrence Erlbaum.
Berkenkotter, C., Heffron, B. and Madsen, A. (1999) 'Consensus formation or counterrevolution in psychiatry: the role of professional journals in the rise of a scientific classification system', paper presented at annual meeting of Society for the Social Studies of Science, San Diego, CA.
Bhatia, V.K. (2004) *Worlds of Written Discourse: a genre-based view*, London: Continuum.
Dear, P. (ed.) (1991) *The Literary Structure of Scientific Argument: historical studies*, Philadelphia, PA: University of Pennsylvania Press.
Feighner, J.P., Robins, G., Guze, S.B., Woodruff, R.A., Winokur, G. and Munoz, R. (1972) 'Diagnostic criteria for use in psychiatric research', *Archives of General Psychiatry*, 26: 57–63.
Fishelov, D. (1993) *Metaphors of Genre: the role of analogies in genre theory*, University Park, PA: Pennsylvania State University Press.
Fleck, L. (1979) *Genesis and Development of a Scientific Fact*, trans. F. Bradley and T.T. Tren, Chicago, IL: University of Chicago Press.
Fowler, A. (1971) 'The life and death of literary forms', *New Literary History*, 2(2): 199–206.
Freud, S. (1905) *Fragment of an Analysis of a Case of Hysteria*, standard edn, J. Strachey (ed.), vol. 7, London: Hogarth Press.
Glaser, B.G. and Strauss, A.L. (1967) *The Discovery of Grounded Theory: strategies in qualitative research*, New York: Aldine de Gruyter.
Gibson, J.J. (1979) *The Ecological Approach to Visual Perception*, Boston, MA: Houghton Mifflin.
Gross, A.J., Harmon, J.E. and Reidy, M. (2002) *Communicating Science: the scientific article from the 17th century to the present*, Oxford: Oxford University Press.
Halliday, M.A.K. and Martin, J.R. (1993) *Writing Science: literacy and discursive power*, Pittsburgh, PA: University of Pittsburgh Press.

Hull, D.H. (1988a) 'A mechanism and its metaphysics: an evolutionary account of the social and conceptual development of science', *Biology and Philosophy*, 3: 123–55.

—— (1988b) *Science as a Process: an evolutionary account of the social and conceptual development of science*, Chicago, IL: University of Chicago Press.

Hyland, K. (2002) 'Genre, language, context, and literacy', *Annual Review of Applied Linguistics*, 22: 113–35.

Kraepelin, E (1902) *Clinical Psychiatry: a textbook for students and physicians*, trans. A. R. Diefendorf from the 6th edition of Kraepelin's *Textbook*, London: Macmillan.

Kress, G. and van Leeuwen, T. (2001) *Multimodal Discourse: the modes and media of contemporary communication*, London: Arnold.

Kuhn, T.S. (1970) *The Structure of Scientific Revolutions*, 2nd edn, Chicago, IL: University of Chicago Press.

Marcus, S. (1985) 'Freud and Dora: story, history, case history', in C. Bernheimer and C. Kahane (eds) (1985) *In Dora's Case: Freud – hysteria – feminism*, 2nd edn, New York: Columbia University Press.

Miller, C.R. (1984) 'Genre as social action', *Quarterly Journal of Speech*, 70: 151–67.

Shapin, S. (1994) *A Social History of Truth: civility and science in seventeenth-century England*, Chicago, IL: University of Chicago Press.

Shorter, E. (1997) *A History of Psychiatry: from the era of the asylum to the age of prozac*, New York: Wiley & Sons.

Swales, J.M. (2004) *Research Genres: explorations and applications*, Cambridge: Cambridge University Press.

Taavitsainen, I. and Pahta, P. (2000) 'Conventions of professional writing: the medical case report in a historical perspective', *Journal of English Linguistics*, 28(1): 60–76.

Valle, E. (1999) 'A collective intelligence: the life sciences in the royal society as a scientific discourse community, 1665–1965', doctoral dissertation, University of Turku, Finland.

Suggestions for further work

1   Although we often identify and conceptualize genres in pure forms, in the real academic and professional world they are often seen in hybrid (mixed and embedded) forms. We often do this by identifying the communicative purposes they serve. Collect and analyse at least one example illustrating each of these hybrid forms (see Bhatia, 1995 and 1997).

2   Swales (1990) claims that society has given typical names to most of the conventionalized genres. Collect at least one example of the genres which has a misleading, ambiguous or in any way problematic name given to it.

3   Genres often cut across disciplinary boundaries, in that they are more or less similar in various disciplines, such as textbooks and research articles. Find one example each of the academic and professional genres that are typical of the discipline, which do not overlap across disciplines.

4   Berkenkotter suggests that genre 'evolves' over a period of time. Collect two examples of the same genre from two different time periods separating at least 20–30 years, and see if they show any development or changes over the period (see Bazerman, 1988 for a more detailed account).

5   Berkenkotter (this volume) mentions 'genre sets' and 'systems of genre'. How can one distinguish them? Read Devitt (1991) and Bazerman (1994) and Bhatia (2004) for more details.

Part VI

Critical discourse analysis

In recent years CDA has maintained its commitment to dealing with social inequality, focusing on real world problems and has remained problem-driven. In spite of its problem-driven approach, CDA nevertheless remains engaged with theory, Chouliaraki and Fairclough's *Discourse and Late Modernity* (1999) being an interesting examination of the relation of CDA to theories in the philosophy of science and social theory (although see Blommaert 2005 for critique). Blommaert's *Discourse: a critical introduction* (2005) (which is much more than an introduction) also draws on a broad range of social theories. With the development of multi-modality, CDA has increasingly developed to consider other semiotic modes, besides the textual. In this respect Chouliaraki's contribution to this volume is a good example.

In terms of critique, Blommaert has argued that CDA, in spite of its focus on inequality, has concentrated on the First World too much, both in terms of its object of analysis and of the theories which it typically draws upon (Baudrillard, Bourdieu, Foucault, Giddens, Habermas and Zizek). Bloomaert argues, on the one hand, that differences occur between societies located in different parts of the world, and that CDA has neglected the Third World. He wonders how the First World existential angst described by Chouliaraki and Fairclough might apply to a village in Tanzania, for example (2005: 36). On the other hand, Blommaert argues that theoreticians who might have more to say regarding Third World issues, such as Wallerstein, Arrighi, Amin or Frank, are absent from the CDA literature. Blommaert's own book goes some way to redressing this balance.

Another argument put forward by Blommaert is for a greater emphasis in favour of ethnographic analysis in CDA and away from text, stating boldly in his book that 'This is not a linguistic book' (2005: 3). At the same time, however, Fairclough (2003) has argued for textual analysis to play a greater role in social analysis. The jury would seem to be out on the relative emphasis to be given to text and context in CDA studies, as indicated in our introductory chapter, one of the fundamental distinctions to be made in any form of discourse analysis.

Meanwhile, Chilton (2005) has argued that CDA needs to address itself more to the cognitive aspect of communication, putting forward evolutionary psychology as a possible model. Others (e.g. van Leeuwen 2006) have argued for greater inter-disciplinarity. While Martin (1999) has argued for a positive discourse, focusing on emancipatory discourses, as an antidote to critical approaches.

The two chapters in this part both offer new directions for CDA. After an extensive review of the field, J. Flowerdew argues that while CDA has placed much emphasis on language power, it might fruitfully consider the issue of resistance, noting, with Foucault, that where there is power there is always resistance. Flowerdew reviews two studies in particular that demonstrate how discourse can be appropriated from those in power to be turned back on them by members of the general public, in both cases members of gay communities.

Chouliaraki, in her chapter, addresses one of the issues raised by Blommaert, the emphasis on First World issues. She does this in a consideration of depiction of suffering (in the Third World) by television (in the First World). Chouliaraki asks whether it is possible to talk about the media as agents of global citizenship or whether the media lead to compassion fatigue – a western denial of humanitarian problems. At the same time, in her focus on television and its associated phenomena of camera/visual, graphic/pictorial, as well as aural/linguistic features, Chouliaraki demonstrates how CDA is moving into the field of multimodal discourse.

Useful further reading on critical discourse analysis can be found in Blommaert (2005), Fairclough (1989, 2003), Fairclough and Wodak (1997) and Wodak and Meyer (2001).

References

Blommaert, J. (2005) *Discourse: a critical introduction*, Cambridge: Cambridge University Press.

Chilton, P. (2005) 'Missing links in mainstream CDA: modules, blends and the critical instinct', in R. Wodak and P. Chilton (eds) *A New Agenda in (Critical) Discourse Analysis*, Amsterdam: John Benjamins, pp. 19–51.

Chouliaraki, L. and Fairclough, N. (1999) *Discourse and Late Modernity*, Edinburgh: Edinburgh University Press.

—— (2005 *Discourse in Late Modernity*, Edinburgh: Edinburgh University Press.

Fairclough, N. (1989) *Language and Power*, London: Longman.

—— (2003) *Analysing Discourse: textual analysis for social research*, London: Routledge.

Fairclough, N. and Wodak, R. (1997) 'Critical discourse analysis', in T.A. van Dijk (ed.) *Discourse Studies: a multidisciplinary introduction*, vol. 1: 'Discourse as social interaction', London: Sage.

Martin, J.R. (1999) 'Grace: the logogenesis of freedom', *Discourse Studies*, 1(1): 29–56.

Meyer, M. (2001) 'Between theory, method and politics: positioning of the approaches to CDA', in R. Wodak and M. Meyer (eds) *Methods of Critical Discourse Analysis*, London: Sage, pp. 14–31

van Leeuwen, T. (2005) 'Three models of interdisciplinarity', in R. Wodak and P. Chilton (eds) *A New Agenda in (Critical) Discourse Analysis*, Amsterdam: John Benjamins, pp. 3–18.

—— (2006) *Introducing Social Semiotics*, London and New York: Routledge.

13 Critical discourse analysis and strategies of resistance

John Flowerdew

Introduction

The antecedents of critical discourse analysis (CDA) are usually said to lie in Critical Linguistics (CL), a movement developed at the University of East Anglia during the 1970s. Scholars working in this group, led by Fowler (e.g. Fowler 1991, 1996a), but also including names such as Kress, Hodge and Trew (e.g. Fowler *et al.* 1979) were concerned to develop a social approach to linguistics which recognized power relationships as a central theoretical issue and text as its main unit of analysis (Kress 1989). Wodak (2001) emphasizes the commonality between CDA and CL. In the same chapter she also describes what she sees as the coming together of CDA in a meeting in 1991 in Amsterdam involving van Dijk, Fairclough, Kress, van Leeuwen and herself, probably still the major names in the movement to this day (although Kress and van Leeuwen have not emphasized the critical dimension of their work so much in recent years).

Many social theorists, such as Bernstein, Bourdieu, Derrida, Gramsci, Foucault, Giddens and Habermas have drawn attention to the key role of language in society. However, as Fairclough (2003) has pointed out, these theorists have not examined the linguistic features of text. CDA, on the other hand, has sought to bring together social theory and textual analysis. As in mainstream critical social theory, the aim of CDA is to uncover hidden assumptions (in the case of the latter, in language use) and debunk their claims to authority. Following Hegel, however, criticism is not simply a negative judgement, but has a positive emancipatory function. CDA thus has a specific agenda in bringing about social change, or at least supporting struggle against inequality (van Dijk 2001).

CDA views language (and other semiotic systems) as a form of social practice (Fairclough 1989; Fairclough and Wodak 1997; Wodak 2001). According to Fairclough (1989), 'using language is the commonest form of social behaviour'. If language is a form of social behaviour, then there is a need to relate theories of society to theories of language. As Chouliaraki and Fairclough (1999: 16) put it:

> We see CDA as bringing a variety of theories into dialogue, especially social theories on the one hand and linguistic theories on the other, so that its theory is a shifting synthesis of other theories, though what it itself theorises in particular is the mediation between the social and the linguistic ...

In addition to the above, CDA has a number of other commonly shared precepts. First, as already suggested, CDA views discourse and society as mutually constitutive, that is to say that a society is not possible without discourse and discourse cannot exist without social interaction. That is not to say, however that all action is discursive. On the contrary, CDA allows for the interplay of discursive and material action (van Leeuwen (1996) in particular emphasizes this point). Second, because it is interested in power relations and is emancipatory in nature, CDA typically examines specific discursive situations where dominance and inequality are to the fore. Although CDA focuses on situations of inequality, however, analysis does not view discursive interaction as necessarily a question of *heroes* and *villains* (van Dijk 1993; Wodak 1999). Participants may not be aware of how powerful or powerless they are in discourse terms. Indeed, it is the role of CDA to reveal these relationships. In fact, CDA may play a role in bringing about change in social practices and relationships in, for example, teacher development, the design of guidelines for non-sexist language, or proposals to increase the intelligibility of news and legal texts (Titscher *et al.* 2000). The related movement of Critical Language Awareness, developed by Fairclough and his associates at the University of Lancaster (Fairclough 1992), argues for a systematic approach to the communication of a critical approach to language along the lines of CDA in the schools and in society at large. Perhaps because of the controversial nature of its findings CDA has not argued for the systematic feeding back of its findings to the subjects of the analysis, although this, done in the right way, remains a possibility. A further commonly held precept is that CDA is open to multiple readings (although this has been critiqued – e.g. Widdowson 2004; Blommaert 2005), as indicated by the following quotations:

> ... we should assume that no analysis of a text can tell us all there is to be said about it – there is no such thing as a complete and definitive analysis of a text ...
>
> Textual analysis is also inevitably selective: in any analysis, we choose to ask certain questions about social events and texts, and not other possible questions... There is no such thing as an 'objective' analysis of a text, if by that we mean an analysis which simply describes what is 'there' in the text without being 'biased' by the 'subjectivity' of the analyst.
>
> (Fairclough 2003: 14–15)

However, readings will be more plausible if grounded in the interplay of text and context (e.g. Fairclough and Wodak, 1997), including ethnographic analysis (Fairclough 2003: 15). Although Fairclough (2003) allows for an ethnographic dimension, along with most critical discourse analysts he does not employ it. For Wodak, on the other hand, ethnography is essential to her method (see below; see also Blommaert 2005). For Fairclough (e.g. 2003), an important dimension of context is intertexuality (Kristeva 1981, following Bakhtin, 1986), how one text inter-relates with other texts. In the study of context Fairclough and Wodak (1997) refer to the historical dimension, knowing about the historical socio-political situation in which a text is produced. They use an extract of an interview with Margaret Thatcher as an example of a textual analysis which needs an understanding of what was going on in Britain in the 1940s, for example, for a successful analysis. As well as being historical, in the view of this writer, CDA can be historiographic, that is to say, it can play a part in the writing of history (Fairclough 2001; Fowler 1996a). Indeed, history is one of the most obvious of disciplines which might make use of CDA as an analytical method (see chapters in Martin and Wodak 2003). As regards context, van Dijk (2005) adopts a rather different, 'socio-cognitive' approach, stressing how context is mediated through cognition; how individuals relate text and context through 'subjective mental models ongoingly constructed by the participants of the current communicative events ...' (p. 95).

Is CDA an approach, a theory or a method?

One area where there seems to be some confusion is whether CDA should be seen as an approach, a theory, or a method. The title of Wodak and Meyer's (2001) edited collection, *Methods of Critical Discourse Analysis*, emphasizes the method dimension. That is not to say, however, that because CDA has methods, it cannot also have a theory. Fowler (1996a: 9), as already mentioned, one of the precursors of CDA, refers to 'the theory of critical linguistics'. Fairclough (2001: 121) sees CDA as both theory and method: 'CDA is in my view as much theory as method.' Similarly Chouliaraki and Fairclough (1999: 16) state that '[w]e see CDA as both theory and method' and, as already mentioned, what constitutes the theory in CDA is 'the mediation between the social and the linguistic' (1999: 16). Meyer acknowledges both theoretical and methodological dimensions: 'CDA in all of its various forms understands itself to be strongly based in theory. To which theories do the different methods refer?' (Meyer 2001). Meyer lists the following as different theoretical levels: epistemology; general social theories; middle-range theories; micro-sociological theories; socio-psychological theories; discourse theories; and linguistic theories. Perhaps this is the key. CDA is not a theory *per se*, but it draws on a range of theories and uses a variety of methods. As such, CDA is perhaps better referred to as an approach which draws on various theories and methods. This would seem to be in keeping with the following statement from (van Dijk 2001: 96):

> CDA is not a direction of research among others, like TG grammar, or systemic linguistics, not a subdiscipline of discourse analysis such as the psychology of discourse or conversation analysis. It is not a method, nor a theory that simply can be applied to social problems. CDA can be conducted in, and combined with, any approach and subdiscipline in the humanities and the social sciences.

CDA and systemic–functional linguistics

A number of CDA practitioners have claimed allegiance to Systemic–Functional Linguistics (SFL) and a number of commentators have claimed it to be a preferred method. Fowler (1996a: 12), for example, advocates a simplified model of Hallidayan grammar (supplemented by concepts from pragmatics). Fairclough (2003: 5–6) adopts a similar approach, also mentioning the possible use of pragmatics, conversation analysis and corpus linguistics. Wodak (2001: 8), although not making consistent use of the model in her own work (see above), has stated as follows:

> Whether analysts with a critical approach prefer to focus on micro-linguistic features, macrolinguistic features, textual, discursive or contextual features, whether their angle is primarily philosophical, sociological or historical – in most studies there is reference to Hallidayan systemic functional grammar. This indicates that an understanding of the basic claims of Halliday's grammar and his approach to linguistic analysis is essential for a proper understanding of CDA.

Of the commentators, we can cite Renkema (2004: 284):

> In Critical Discourse Analysis more and more attempts are being made to ground analyses and interpretations of power relations on systematic descriptions of discourse. A promising perspective was developed by the founding father of the socio-semiotic approach ... Michael Halliday.

According to Halliday's systemic-functional linguistics (see Halliday and Matthiessen 2004 for the most recent exposition), language is conceived of as a resource for communication and making meaning rather than as a formal system as is the case in many other forms of linguistics. Linguistic structures, in this model, are viewed as interrelated choices (systems) which are available for the expression of meanings in situational contexts. Any utterance will simultaneously express meanings according to three (later four) 'macro-functions': the ideational function (language as an expression of the individual's experience of the world); the interpersonal function (how individuals relate to each other through language at the social level); and the textual function (how linguistic forms are used to relate to each other and to the situational context).

The case for SFL in CDA is put by Martin and Wodak (2003: 8):

> SFL provides critical discourse analysts with a technical language for talking about language – to make it possible to look very closely at meaning, to be explicit and precise in terms that can be shared by others, and to engage in quantitative analysis where this is appropriate.

There is no doubt there are many very good studies which make use of SFL (many of the analyses by Fairclough, for example, or the studies collected in Martin and Wodak 2003, or Martin's (2000) exemplificatory chapter on how SFL can be used in CDA) and some of the systems and concepts within Halliday's framework, such as transitivity (categories of verbal processes and participant roles), modality, thematic development, and grammatical metaphor have been used in CDA studies in the 'precise and explicit' way that Martin and Wodak describe.

However, there would be a number of problems with this approach if it were to be adopted as the only framework for CDA (which, as already should be clear, is not the case). First of all, to understand the grammar fully a lot of work is required. For example, in a recent talk, Halliday (2006) stated that some 17,000 systems would be required to analyse fully the meaning potential of just one transitive verb. Similarly, Halliday's best-known work, *An Introduction to Functional Grammar* (Halliday and Matthiessen 2004), extends to nearly 700 pages. This is why Fowler (1996a) states that this work 'offers both more and less than is required', 'more' in the sense that there is too much to absorb and 'less' in that it is not comprehensive enough to handle all the aspects of a text that one might want to analyse. Another problem with the SFL approach is that it is not designed to deal with pragmatic phenomena such as indirect speech acts and implicature. A third problem is that the model of context in SFL is relatively unexplored. None of these problems, however, implies that SFL cannot be employed in CDA along with other approaches. The other approaches are necessary, however, because SFL is concerned with developing a systematic linguistic description according to a set of formal categories. But in any given text, there may be structures and functions which do not fit neatly into these categories (see van Leeuwen 1996 for further discussion on this).

Tool-kits for CDA

In line with its eclectic approach various practitioners have presented 'tool-kits' for doing CDA. The term 'tool-kit' might not sound very scientific, but it is appropriate, given that the lists of features to look for in analysis are presented as suggestive rather than prescriptive, exhaustive taxonomies. Examples of these can be found in various sources.

To start with a simple one, van Dijk (2001: 99) has suggested the following as features of text to examine:

- Stress and intonation
- Word order
- Lexical style
- Coherence
- Local semantic moves such as disclaimers
- Topic choice
- Speech acts
- Schematic organization
- Rhetorical figures
- Syntactic structures
- Propositional structures
- Turn takings
- Repairs
- Hesitation.

In his early *Language and Power*, in Chapter 5, 'Critical discourse in practice: description' Fairclough (1989: 106) presented what he called a 'mini reference manual' in the form of a list of questions and sub-questions. The major divisions are as follows:

1 What experiential values do words have?
2 What relational value do words have?
3 What expressive values do words have?
4 What metaphors are used?
5 What experiential value do grammatical features have?
6 What relational values do grammatical features have?
7 What expressive values do grammatical features have?
8 How are (simple) sentences linked together?
9 What interactional conventions are used?
10 What larger scale structures does the text have?

Each of these questions has a set of sub-questions. For example question 5 has the following:

1 What types of *process* and *participant* predominate?
2 Is agency unclear?
3 Are processes what they seem?
4 Are *nominalizations* used?
5 Are sentences active or passive?
6 Are sentences positive or negative?

Another (unpublished) list is that of Huckin (2005), entitled 'Some useful tools and concepts for critical discourse analysis'.

Word/phrase level

- Classification, including names, labels
- Connotations, codewords
- Metaphor
- Lexical presupposition
- Modality
- Register, including synthetic personalization
- Politeness.

Sentence/utterance level

- Deletion, omission
  - through nominalization
  - through agentless passive
- Transitivity/agent–patient relations
- Topicalization/foregrounding
- Presupposition
- Insinuation, inferencing
- Heteroglossia.

Text level

- Genre conventions
- Discursive differences
- Coherence
- Framing
- Foregrounding/backgrounding
- Textual silences
- Presupposition
- Extended metaphor
- Auxiliary embellishments.

General

- Central vs. peripheral processing
- Use of heuristics
- Ideology
- Reading position
- Naturalization, 'common sense'
- Reproduction–resistance–hegemony
- Cultural models and myths; master narratives
- Intertextuality
- Context; contrast effects

- Communicator ethos
- Vividness
- Repetition
- Face work
- Type of argument
- Interests
- Agenda-setting.

As a final example, Jager (2001: 55–6) has the following set of categories as part of what he refers to as a 'little toolbox for conducting analysis' (this section is for 'processing the material for the sample fine analysis of discourse fragments of an article or a series of articles and so on ...' [p. 55]):

Word/phrase level

- Classification, including names, labels
- Connotations, codewords
- Metaphor
- Lexical presupposition
- Modality
- Register, including synthetic personalization
- Politeness.

Sentence/utterance level

- Deletion, omission
  - through nominalization
  - through agentless passive
- Transitivity/agent–patient relations
- Topicalization/foregrounding
- Presupposition
- Insinuation, inferencing
- Heteroglossia.

Text level

- Genre conventions
- Discursive differences
- Coherence
- Framing
- Foregrounding/backgrounding
- Textual silences
- Presupposition
- Extended metaphor
- Auxiliary embellishments.

General

- Central vs. peripheral processing
- Use of heuristics
- Ideology
- Reading position
- Naturalization, 'common sense'
- Reproduction–resistance–hegemony
- Cultural models and myths; master narratives
- Intertextuality
- Context; contrast effects
- Communicator ethos
- Vividness
- Repetition
- Face work
- Type of argument
- Interests
- Agenda-setting.

What all of these lists have in common is their emphasis on their indicative, as opposed to comprehensive, nature. One problem that they have, however, is that, while some of them include context, in their emphasis on textual features they present the danger of the user putting too much emphasis on textual features at the expense of context (see Blommaert 2005 for a critique of CDA's heavy emphasis on text at the expense of context). Perhaps what is needed is a tool-kit to help in the analysis of context.

Where is CDA going in the future?

In this final section, given the theme of this volume, *Advances in Discourse Studies*, I will consider the question of what direction CDA might take in the future. Toolan (2002: 230) has claimed that, on the one hand, because of too much theory and global contextualization, CDA practitioners have a tendency to make their analyses too complex. As he states, '... is it really that difficult, on many occasions, to demonstrate racism, sexism and so on in even the broadsheet ('quality') media' (2002: 230). In fact, there seem to be two issues here. On the one hand, analysis can be too difficult to comprehend, because it is too complex and, on the other hand, analysis may focus on texts which do not require deconstruction, because they are so obvious in their prejudices (Toolan 2002: 231 goes on to say that analysis should focus on 'the subtler and hence more insidious discriminatory and exclusionary discourses that abound ...'). Following these conflicting claims one way forward for CDA might be to develop more systematic frameworks for analysis. This could take the form of a simplified model of SFL, as called for by Fowler (1996a: 12), or might follow models such as those developed by Brown and

Levinson for their analysis of linguistic politeness, or this writer's framework for racist discursive practices (Flowerdew *et al.* 2002). Ultimately, however, it does not seem that there is any solution to the dichotomy between sophistication versus simplicity in analysis, except, as previously pointed out (namely van Dijk), through a diversity of approaches.

One future direction that has been called for is that of Martin (1999), who has suggested 'PDA', or Positive Discourse Analysis, as a possible development. 'The approach exemplifies a positive style of discourse analysis that focuses on hope and change, by way of complementing the deconstructive exposé associated with critical discourse analysis' (abstract: 29). In a later chapter Martin (2004: 197) states:

> I suppose it would be going too far to propose a 10 year moratorium on deconstructive CDA, in order to get some constructive PDA off the ground. But we do need to move beyond a preoccupation with demonology, beyond a singular focus on semiosis in the service of abusive power – and reconsider power communally as well, as it circulates through communities, as they re-align around values, and renovate discourses that enact a better world. Good question, of course, what better is! And how to achieve it? We can start to ask.

Instead of deconstructing a speech by Australian Conservative Prime Minister John Howard, Martin argues, work could be directed to the Australian 'Sorry Day' and analysis could focus on aboriginal elders, the impact of their stories of being taken from their families, and its effect in turn on migrant children and their families.

In a similar vein Luke (2002) has also called for an emancipatory form of discourse analysis: 'I have argued that to move beyond a strong focus on ideology critique, CDA would need to begin to develop a strong positive thesis about discourse and the productive uses of power.' To paraphrase Marcuse (1971: 106), we would need to begin to capture an affirmative character of culture where discourse is used aesthetically, productively, and for emancipatory purposes. Of course, one danger of proposals such as those of Martin and Luke would be that of the enterprise turning into a form of propaganda on behalf of the status quo. Another argument against PDA is that it sets up a false opposition with CDA. The term 'critical' incorporates both positive and negative, deconstruction and construction. One might argue, therefore, that CDA already incorporates a positive element, in arguing for a better world.

While Luke's call includes Martin's PDA, Luke (2002: 98), although not specific, seems to also want to include more resistant forms of discourses: 'subalturn, diasporic, emancipatory, local, minority, call them what we may – that may mark the productive use of power in the face of economic and cultural globalization'. This is a direction which this writer, personally, feels is in need of attention. If we accept that, following Foucault, 'there are no relations of power without resistances' (1980: 142) and that 'the latter are all the more real and effective because they are formed right at the point where relations of power are exercised' (ibid.), then resistance deserves far more attention than it has hitherto been given. If it is right that CDA has been interested in debunking the abuse of power by the powerful, it should also be appropriate for it to take up the position of the less powerful and to document their resistance in the face of the powerful.

What might the rationale be for a focus on resistance, apart from the argument just put forward? The sociologist Castells (1997: 69) has written powerfully on this issue, as follows:

> With the exception of a small elite of *globapolitans* ..., people all over the world resent loss of control over their lives, over their environment, over their jobs, over their economies, over their governments, over their countries, and, ultimately, over the fate of the Earth. Thus, following an old law of social evolution, resistance confronts domination, empowerment reacts against powerlessness, and alternative projects challenge the logic embedded in the new global order, increasingly sensed as disorder by people around the planet.

This is followed by an interesting insight by Castells on where the sites of resistance such as he has described might be found. They are not to be found necessarily in the traditional centres of power, but they 'come in unusual formats and proceed through unexpected ways' (Castells 1997: 69). This may lead us to the work of Scott (1990 – discussed quite extensively in Blommaert 2005). For Scott, those who are conventionally seen as powerless may have what he calls a 'hidden transcript'. The underprivileged may harbour powerful, but hidden (to the powerful) dissenting discourses. The example Scott gives is of the slave-owners and their slaves. On the outside the slave owner performs his rituals of brutality and dominance, while the slave, for his part enacts the role of dominated and brutalized subject. In private, however, the slaves could develop their own resistant discourses against their masters (at the same time, also, the slave owners might express their doubts and weaknesses through discourses in the privacy of their clubs). At moments of crisis these hidden transcripts may surface and become public.

It is possible to find some empirical studies of hidden transcripts, although not in the mainstream CDA literature. Through ethnographic procedures (which are well suited to rooting out hidden transcripts), in two studies, Lin (1999, 2000) has revealed the strategies of resistance employed by the teachers and pupils in the Hong Kong school which was the site of her research. Another example, again in the context of education, and again outside the mainstream CDA literature, is Canagarajah's (1999) book-length study of resistant discourse practices conducted by school pupils and teachers in Sri Lanka. Further examples are to be found in studies of gay men, one by Bunzl (2000) and another by Jones (2001, forthcoming), which will be reviewed in greater detail below.

Not all strategies of resistance are hidden in the way that Scott talks of them. In a paper published some years ago now (J. Flowerdew 1997), this writer, examined the (unsuccessful) resistance strategies employed by audience members in a public meeting. Of course, most resistance is not going to overturn the status quo (although there are many examples where this is indeed the case – the recent 'people's power' movement in Nepal or the toppling of the Berlin wall after many years of resistance in the countries of the former Soviet Union are two examples that easily spring to mind), but this does not mean that they are not worthy of study. To put it in everyday terms, one may learn by one's mistakes and therefore analysis of failed attempts at resistance may offer lessons for more successful attempts in future. In addition, the cathartic value of resistance and its role in identity formation should not be neglected.

This writer's earlier paper did not use the ethnographic methods which are perhaps best suited to examining hidden transcripts, but, because the meeting which was the focus of analysis was public, textual analysis (supported by a strong grounding in analysis of the historical and socio-political context) was appropriate. In such textually oriented analyses what are the sorts of discursive strategies that one might look for? This question, of course, can only be answered in a satisfactory way by empirical research. However, an initial brainstorming might include the following strategies:

- Open flouting of discourse/genre conventions
- Appropriation
- Euphemism
- Silence
- Irony
- Satire
- Lying
- Anti-language
- Quarrelling
- Laughter
- Slogans.

Here I will provide some examples of one particular resistance phenomenon, appropriation, situations where discriminatory speech forms are taken up by the discriminated and used as a counter-discourse, reversing the original intended discriminatory purpose. Well known examples are the use of the term 'nigger', or 'nigga', by members of the 'black' community (bearing in mind that the term 'black' was previously also a derogatory term which was appropriated by the civil rights and black power movement in the 1960s and 1970s and became naturalized as an accepted denotation and the term 'queer' claimed by the 'gay' community (bearing in mind again that the term 'gay' was itself an appropriation of an adjective which was previously devoid of any reference to sexual orientation) as a means of 'fighting back' against discrimination directed towards this group.

Ideally, this call that I am making for studies of resistance and appropriation in CDA would be exemplified in a textual analysis. In the space that is available to me, this is not possible. What I can do, however, is briefly review two studies (Bunzl 2000 and Jones 2001, forthcoming, referred to above), as examples of the sort of work that might be done.

First, I will consider Bunzl's (2000) paper concerning what the author refers to as 'inverted appellation', the use of feminine reference by male persons (and vice versa), a form of what he calls 'gender insubordination'. In this paper, by means of ethnographic data collection and analysis, Bunzl shows how gay men in Vienna, Austria, systematically undermine various gendered features of the language (Viennese German), appropriating them for their own purposes. These features include gendered third person personal pronouns e.g. *die* (she) referring to a man, gendered definite articles before proper names e.g. *die Sedlacek* and kinship terms such as *Schwester* (sister) and *Tante* (aunt). In this way, Bunzl (2000: 214) convincingly argues, 'A socio-discursive practice that, while structured by hegemonic forms, exposes normative gender and compulsory heterosexuality as discursively articulated, heteronormative fictions.' At the same time:

> In this manner, gay men can at once appropriate and resist their abject positioning in the larger socio-sexual field by contributing (along with lesbians, feminists and other critics of the heteronormative and patriarchical hegemony) to a resistive rearticulation and creative reimagination of the performative and socio-discursively transported construction of gender and sexuality.
>
> (Bunzl 2000: 211)

My second example, the paper by Jones (forthcoming), focuses on appropriation strategies adopted by gay men in China. Like Bunzl, using ethnographic techniques, Jones demonstrates through his data how Chinese men who have sex with men appropriate elements from dominant discourses of the Party–State and the mass media. 'This strategy', Jones argues, 'has opened up spaces within which gay men can claim 'cultural citizenship' in a society in which they have been heretofore marginalized' (abstract). Jones claims that emergent communities, such as that of gay men in China, 'begin to imagine themselves and claim cultural citizenship through 'poaching' the voices of more powerful communities and adapting them to their own purposes' (abstract: 9). The use of the term *tongzhi*, which means comrade, to refer to members of the gay community (a clear appropriation of an all-but-abandoned Communist party term) is the most obvious of these strategies of appropriation. In addition, the gay men with whom Jones interacted inserted themselves into the nation's mainstream narratives by appropriating stories and idioms from dynastic history (by referring, for example, to emperors and high officials of the past and present who are said to have had homosexual relations or by using fixed expressions that refer to these stories e.g. 'cut sleeves' and 'sharing a peach', and even referring to the teachings of Confucius). Furthermore, these gay men sought legitimacy through recourse to various criteria of 'quality' – by excluding, for example, certain types of individuals as sexual partners (e.g. men from the rural areas, or men who sell their services) in preference to others (e.g. men who are well educated, or men who are discreet). In this appeal to 'quality', these gay men are appropriating one of the prominent discourses in contemporary mainstream Chinese society, both past and present. Jones concludes by stating that:

> the appropriation of voices from mainstream discourse by Chinese gay men for imagining their identities is implicated in the formation of what Mendes-Leite (1998) calls 'imaginary protections', boundaries communities and individuals create through reassigning meaning to official knowledge in ways which conform more closely to the demands of their social lives.
>
> (abstract: 35)

In both of these accounts of appropriation strategies there is an important element of identity formation. Blommaert (2005: 165–6) makes a distinction between those resistance ideologies which operate within the boundaries of the general hegemony (these are not anti-hegemonic because they do not form a challenge to the overall system) and those which pose a genuine threat. It would seem that the examples of Bunzl and Jones are not anti-hegemonic in these terms. They do not form a threat to the mainstream status quo. While this may be the case, in their identity construction of these marginalized groups, these discourses may nevertheless be said to be successful. Instead of feeling marginalized, these groups, by means of their discursive practices, realize an individual identity which provides them with, in their eyes, legitimacy. These discourses can therefore said to be truly emancipatory for the groups concerned. The two papers together indicate just one way I think CDA may focus on strategies of resistance and how these strategies may challenge inequality and discrimination.

Acknowledgement

The work described in this chapter was supported by grants from the Research Grants Council of the Hong Kong Special Administrative Region, China (CityU Project No. 7001725 and Project No. 9041059 (CityU 1458/05H)).

References

Bakhtin, M. (ed.) (1986) *Speech Genres and other Late Essays*, Austin, TX: University of Texas Press.

Blommaert, J. (2005) *Discourse: a critical introduction*, Cambridge: Cambridge University Press.

Bunzl, M. (2000) 'Inverted appellation and discursive gender insubordination: an Austrian case study in gay male conversation', *Discourse and Society*, 11(2): 207–36.

Canagarajah, A.S.(1999) *Resisting Linguistic Imperialism in English Teaching*, Oxford: Oxford University Press.

Castells, M. (1997) *The Power of Identity*, London: Blackwell.

Chouliaraki, L. and Fairclough, N. (1999) *Discourse in Late Modernity: rethinking critical discourse analysis*, Edinburgh: Edinburgh University Press.

Fairclough, N. (1989) *Language and Power*, London: Longman.

—— (ed.) (1992) *Critical Language Awareness*, London: Longman.

—— (2001) 'Critical discourse analysis as a method in social scientific research', in R. Wodak and M. Meyer (eds) *Methods of Critical Discourse Analysis*, London: Sage, pp. 121–38.

—— (2003) *Analyzing Discourse: textual analysis for social research*, London: Routledge.

Fairclough, N. and Wodak, R. (1997) 'Critical discourse analysis', in T.A. van Dijk (ed.) *Discourse Studies: a multidisciplinary introduction*, vol. 12, 'Discourse as social interaction', London: Sage, pp. 258–84.

Flowerdew, J. (1997) 'Reproduction, resistance and joint-production of language power: a Hong Kong case study', *Journal of Pragmatics*, 27: 315–37.

Flowerdew, J., Li, D.C.S. and Tran, S. (2002) 'Discriminatory news discourse: some Hong Kong data', *Discourse and Society*, 13(3): 319–45.

Foucault, M. (1980) *Power/knowledge: selected interviews and other writings 1972–1977*, New York: Vintage.

Fowler, R. (1991) 'Critical linguistics', in K. Malmkjaer (ed.) *The Linguistics Encyclopedia*, London: Routledge, pp. 89–93.

—— (1996a) 'On critical linguistics', in C.R. Caldas-Coulthard and M. Coulthard (eds) *Texts and Practices: readings in critical discourse analysis*, London: Routledge, pp. 3–14.

—— (1996b) *Linguistic Criticism*, 2nd edn, Oxford: Oxford University Press.

Fowler, R., Hodge, B., Kress, G. and Trew, T. (1979) *Language and Control*, London: Routledge & Kegan Paul.

Halliday, M.A.K. (2006) Talk given at City University of Hong Kong, March.

Halliday, M.A.K. and Matthiessen, C.M.I.M. (2004) *An Introduction to Functional Grammar*, London: Arnold.

Huckin, T. (2005) Talk given at City University of Hong Kong.

Jager, S. (2001) 'Discourse and knowledge: theoretical and methodological aspects of a critical discourse and dispositive analysis', in R. Wodak and M. Meyer (eds) *Methods of Critical Discourse Analysis*, London: Sage, pp. 32–62.

Jones, R.H. (2001) 'Mediated action and sexual risk: discourses of AIDS and sexuality in the People's Republic of China', unpublished PhD dissertation, Macquarie University, Sydney.

—— (2007) 'Imagined comrades and imaginary protections: identity, community and sexual risk among men who have sex with men in China', *Journal of Homosexuality*, 53(3).

Kress, G. (1989) *Linguistic Processes in Sociocultural Practice*, 2nd edn, Oxford: Oxford University Press.

Kristeva, J. (1981) *Desire in Language: a semiotic approach to literature and art*, trans. T. Gora, A. Jardine and L.S. Roudiez, Oxford: B. Blackwell.

Lin, A.M.Y. (1999) 'Doing-English-lessons in the reproduction or transformation of social worlds?', *TESOL Quarterly*, 33(3): 393–412.

—— (2000) 'Lively children trapped in an island of disadvantage: verbal play of Cantonese working-class schoolboys in Hong Kong', *International Journal of the Sociology of Language*, 143: 63–83.

Luke, A. (2002) 'Beyond science and ideology critique: developments in critical discourse analysis', *Annual Review of Applied Linguistics*, 22: 96–110.

Martin, J.R. (1999) 'Grace: the logogenesis of freedom', *Discourse Studies*, 1(1): 29–56.

—— (2000) 'Close reading: functional linguistics as a tool for critical discourse analysis', in L. Unsworth (ed.) *Researching Language in Schools and Communities*, London and Washington, DC: Cassell.

—— (2004) 'Positive discourse analysis: power, solidarity and change', *Revista Canaria de Estudios Ingleses*, 49: 179–200.

Martin, J.R. and Wodak, R. (2003) 'Introduction', in J.R. Martin and R. Wodak (eds) *Re/reading the Past: critical and functional perspectives on time and value* Amsterdam and Philadelphia, PA: John Benjamins, pp. 1–16.

Meyer, M. (2001) 'Between theory, method, and politics: positioning of the approaches to CDA', in R. Wodak and M. Meyer (eds) *Methods of Critical Discourse Analysis*, London: Sage, pp. 14–31.

Renkema, J. (2004) *Introduction to Discourse Studies*, Amsterdam and Philadelphia, PA: John Benjamins.

Scott, J. (1990) *Domination and the Arts of Resistance: hidden transcripts*, New Haven, CT: Yale University Press.

Titscher, S., Meyer, M., Wodak, R. and Vetter, E. (2000) *Methods of Text and Discourse Analysis*, London: Sage.

Toolan, M. (2002) *Critical Discourse Analysis*, London: Routledge.

van Dijk, T.A. (1993) 'Principles of critical discourse analysis', *Discourse and Society*, 4(2): 249–83.

—— (2001) 'Multidisciplinary CDA: a plea for diversity', in R. Wodak and M. Meyer (eds) *Methods of Critical Discourse Analysis*, London: Sage, pp. 95–120.

van Dijk, T.A. (2005) 'Contextual knowledge management in discourse production', in R. Wodak and P. Chilton (eds) *A New Agenda in (Critical) Discourse Analysis* Amsterdam and Philadelphia, PA: John Benjamins, pp. 71–100.

van Leeuwen, T. (1996) 'The representation of social actors', in C.R. Caldas-Coulthard and M. Coulthard (eds) *Texts and Practices: readings in critical discourse analysis*, London: Routledge, pp. 32–70.

Widdowson, H.G. (2004) *Text, Context, Pretext: critical issues in discourse analysis*, Oxford: Blackwell.

Wodak, R. (1999) 'Critical discourse analysis at the end of the 20th century', *Research on Language and Social Interaction*, 32(1&2): 181–93.

—— (2001) 'What CDA is about – a summary of its history, important concepts and its developments', in R. Wodak and M. Meyer (eds) *Methods of Critical Discourse Analysis*, London: Sage, pp. 1–13.

14 Mediation, text and action

Lilie Chouliaraki

Introduction

In this chapter, I argue that one major concern for discourse analysis today is to engage in critical studies of culture under conditions of mediation. The key concern here is the de-territorialization of experience that mediation brings about in our culture: the experience of connecting us with people around the globe without, at the same time, giving us the option to respond to or act upon their situation.[1] In so far as we live in a world divided into zones of prosperity and poverty, safety and danger, peace and war, this concern is primarily ethical. It brings forth the questions: what sense of responsibility and caring action do the media cultivate vis-à-vis far-away others? Can the global visibility of suffering, a most common spectacle of our home screens, lead to forms of public action towards these distant others?

The connection between media texts and social action, however, remains under-theorized. Despite attempts to conceptualize the interplay between media texts and audiences, the question of how to describe the role of media texts in producing forms of public agency and proposing options for action is still inadequately addressed. In this chapter after reviewing three key approaches to this question, I then outline a discourse analytical approach, which conceptualizes media texts as instantiations of ethical values that propose options for action at a distance to diverse media publics. This approach seeks to study the conditions of possibility for action in our mediated culture by analysing the production of meaning in hybrid media texts, and the production of social relations of power in these texts.

Mediation, text and social action

The textual nature of mediation has long been the object of study within and outside the field of discourse analysis. The key question has been to establish a link between media texts and social action. Three approaches broadly address this link: audience interpretation studies (exemplified in the work of the Glasgow Media Group; Livingstone and Lunt 1994; McQuail 1997); text analysis in the critical discourse analysis tradition (e.g. van Dijk

1987, 1990; Fairclough 1995; Scollon 1998; Jewitt and van Leeuwen 2001, J. Flowerdew 2004) and media sociology studies in the broader contexts of mediation in which texts are disseminated and consumed (for example, Wodak 1996, 1999; Couldry 2005).[2] As always with social scientific methods, there are advantages and limitations to all three approaches.

Audience interpretation studies regard the media text as the immediate context for people's understanding of social events and emphasize the process by which people's own accounts of such events are both enabled and constrained by the discourse of the media. Analytical focus here falls on audiences 'retelling' the news (or other media genres) and it is these texts of interpretation that are taken as evidence of how the media influence social action. Critical discourse analysis work has taken both text production (the discourse of the news, for example) and text interpretation (audiences' accounts of the news) as its objects of study. Depending on the studies, analytical focus may fall either on the news text as a locus of social struggle over meaning or on texts of interpretation as the locus of people's active construction of meaning. Whereas for news text analysis, a conception of social action lies within the text, in the form of the construction of hegemony and the legitimation of 'common sense' through media discourse, for news interpretation analysis, a conception of social action lies with the audience's capacity for appropriating the meanings of the news – in reproductive, but also in resistant or subversive ways.

Despite their differences, audience interpretation studies, in both media and CDA approaches, are criticized for 'methodological individualism', that is for using a narrow conception of social action defined exclusively in terms of how people understand news stories. What is lacking from this conception is broader, societal explanations as to how the media may influence social action.[3] The text analysis of media discourse, on the other hand, captures the broad, societal dimensions of social action, using a Gramscian view of media power as hegemonic articulations of meaning, yet such work is still held accountable for not quite explicating how such struggles of meaning may affect social action in diverse and contradictory ways, in broader contexts of culture and society.

Media sociology, the third approach outlined here, attempts to link media and social action by reference to concepts such as habitus, naturalization and everyday life. 'Habitus', a concept originating in Bourdieu, refers to routine social practices that have become inculcated and embodied in people through socialization and habit – including the socialization of the media. Entailing a historicized conception of action as a 'structuring structure' that provides people with the categories by which they live their daily life, habitus seeks to explain how such categories become naturalized into 'taken for granted' patterns of behaviour and belief and how they tend to reproduce certain preferred distinctions among spheres of activity in our social life. For example, the mediated and the ordinary come to organize hierarchical spheres of activity, whereby the mediated carries more power, value and prestige than the ordinary; the 'rituals' of reality shows or the 'liveness' of broadcasting are just two instances of a conception of the media as the 'social centre' and the privileged locus of experience vis-à-vis everyday life. What such distinctions ultimately do is serve relationships of power; they come to 'naturalise further the concentration of symbolic resources in media institutions that characterise contemporary societies' (Couldry 2005: 7).

Right as it is in opening up media texts to broader contexts of social action, this type of media sociology does not adequately deal with the question of *social power*. Power is of course there. It is implicit in the terminology of naturalization, the 'taken for grantedness' of ways of seeing and acting upon the world and the effects of this naturalization in amplifying the power of the media. Yet, power is not thematized as an analytical category that can explain *how exactly* the media may naturalize certain categories as spaces of ordinary life rather than others and *how*, in so doing, the media reproduce divisions that exclude far away others from our sphere of responsibility and action (Silverstone 2004, 2006). In focusing on the mediated/ordinary distinction, this type of media sociology remains limited to the agendas and concerns of those in the zone of safety, prosperity and peace- those who are close to us. What it leaves aside is the key ethical question of how mediation may (if at all) enable and legitimize spheres of action towards the zone of danger, poverty and war – those far away.

Additionally, what is lost in this broad focus on routines, categories and ordinary life is precisely the *specificity of media texts* as loci through which media power may be produced and reproduced. The category distinction between the mediated and the ordinary, again, leaves open the analytical question of just *how* media texts may participate, through their systematic choices of word and image, in construing certain ways of being and acting as natural for audiences rather than others; how, for example, they may construe the audiences of distant suffering as disposed towards a passive voyeurism of human pain – as the compassion fatigue argument has it – or towards active charity and humanitarian action – as the 2004 tsunami catastrophe showed.

What I argue here is that, in order to theorize the link between social action and media texts, we need to provide more concrete accounts of how media texts inculcate dispositions to action for their publics and how social power is implicated in these processes of inculcation. Drawing on Aristotle's idea that engaging with the spectacles of public life, be these our contemporary media stories or the performances of Athenian antiquity, is an important part of our *moral education as citizens of the world*, I claim that the link between media texts and social action may usefully be explored through the ways in which such texts expose their audiences to specific *dispositions to feel, think and act* in their everyday lives.

From this perspective, it is not the hegemonic struggles of meaning within media texts nor is it the use of media stories as resources for audience 'retellings' that *per se* can adequately resolve the question of social action in the context of the media. It is rather the ways in which such struggles of meanings and the 'retellings' of these meanings cumulatively come to articulate and naturalize ways of being and modes of acting for the spectator as a social actor. The terms 'habitus' and 'naturalized category' can be understood, in this context, as conceptions of the systematic repertoire of dispositions that media texts propose to their audiences through the forms of agency they incorporate in their stories.[4]

To be sure, the forms of agency embedded in media stories of distant suffering are not enough in themselves to constitute the spectator as a public actor. For this to happen, a broader chain of links to action must take place. Rather, media texts are purely 'performative'. They propose forms of identification that may (or may not) subsequently link up with other forms of effective action in the public sphere. What this performative role of the texts points to, however, is that the media do not simply address a pre-existing audience that awaits to engage in social action but they have the power (institutional and symbolic) to constitute this audience as a body of action in the process of narrating and visualizing distant events. Media texts are, in this sense, conditions of possibility for social action.

The case of distant suffering best exemplifies how the media may use their performative capacity in order to call a group of spectators into a collectivity with a will to act – a public. Because of the practical impossibility to act on the scene of suffering, the forms of engagement and action that the media propose to the spectator have less to do with immediate, practical intervention and more to do with patterns of imaginary or projected action on the part of the spectator (Barnett 2003: 102). Such patterns, as we shall see below, belong to two historical modes of action at a distance: to feel for the sufferer or to contemplate the suffering objectively. Feeling for the sufferer is associated with the ancient public of the theatre and the imaginary agency of charitable action, political denunciation or passive voyeurism, whereas contemplating on the suffering is associated with the public of the agora and the rational capacities of the citizen to deliberate objectively on the suffering (Chouliaraki 2006: 88–93). In both these contexts, Aristotle reminds us that the spectacles of public life are infused with social value and ethical content. The key question then for the study of the link between social action and media texts is: which values of public conduct undercut specific media narratives of distant suffering? Which ethical dispositions (to action or inaction) does the portrayal of the distant sufferer propose to the spectator?

The analytics of mediation

Following, again, Aristotle's advice that our enquiries into public life should be driven by the practical consideration of social value and ethical content, of what 'is good or bad for man' in his words, I wish to approach media texts as particular manifestations of ethical values that open up concrete and local possibilities of action to the spectator.[5] This engagement with ethical values, what Aristotle calls *phronesis* (prudence), grasps the question of ethics from the pragmatic perspective of praxis.[6] This is the perspective that takes each particular case to be a unique enactment of ethical discourse that, even though it transcends the case, cannot exist outside the enactment of cases.

The term 'analytics', which Foucault borrows from Aristotle to distinguish his approach from a 'grand' theory of power, aims at describing how discourse manages to articulate 'universal' values of human conduct at any given moment in time and how, in so doing, discourse places human beings into certain relationships of power to one another (Foucault 1980: 199; Flyvbjerg 2001: 131–8). Media discourse on distant suffering, for instance, operates as a strategy of power in so far as it selectively offers the option of emotional engagement and practical action with certain sufferers and leaves others outside the scope of such engagement, thereby reproducing hierarchies of place and human life (Cohen 2001).

In this sense, the analytics of mediation is an approach to the study of the media that considers television both as a semiotic accomplishment, as text, and as a technology embedded in existing power relationships of viewing. The object of study of the analytics of mediation is various media genres (television news being the case in point here) as regimes of meanings. The term 'regime of meanings' refers to the bounded field of possible meaning relations that obey a certain regularity in the ways in which they can be combined and circulated and, as a consequence, in the possibilities they offer to make legitimate proposals of action to the spectator.

Two dimensions of mediation make up the grid of the analytics, the multimodal and the multi-functional dimensions of mediation. *Multimodality* refers to the study of the semiotic processes of language and image by which television manages to create a coherent regime for the representation of suffering, a regime of pity, that construes the event of suffering as the spectator's most immediate reality. *Multi-functionality* assumes, in turn, that every regime of pity creates meaning that fulfils more than one social function at once. The first is the social need to name and represent the world, the ideational meta-function of semiosis; the second is the social need to engage in interaction and relate to other people, the interpersonal meta-function of semiosis.[7] In so far both the representational and the interpersonal functions are caught up in historical relations of economic hierarchies and political divisions in our world, then the study of multi-functionality is simultaneously a study of the power relations of mediation.[8] Let me now briefly discuss the two categories of the analytics of mediation, looking, in turn, into the multimodality of mediation (in multimodal analysis) and to the multi-functionality of mediation (in critical discourse analysis).

Multimodal analysis

The methodological principle of multimodal analysis is that regimes of pity do not coincide with the specific image or language we watch on screen. The image and language of suffering, rather, follow a systematic pattern of co-appearance and combination, which organizes the potential for the representation of suffering under the generic conventions of the news broadcast. I take three aspects of the genre of the news to be relevant in the construal of regimes of pity: the 'mode of presentation' of the news text, the 'correspondence between verbal narrative and image' in the news text, and the 'aesthetic quality' of the news text.

Mode of news presentation

The mode of presentation of the news refers to the locations from which the news story is told and to the media that tell the story. Modes of presentation may include studio anchor, which secures the flow and continuity of the broadcast, usually accompanied by footage (archive or live) and commentary by reporter voiceover. Whereas studio presentation may include the commentary of invited experts, footage may include oral testimony of witnesses from the scene of action. Choices over the mode of news presentation have an impact upon the ways through which the spectator comes to evaluate the news on suffering. Depending, for example, on how the visual presentation relates to anchor speech or to voiceover, each mode of news presentation offers the spectator a distinct approach to the reality of the event, a distinct form of narrative 'realism' (Grodal 2002: 67–91; Ellis 2000: 193–200).

Narrative realism may evoke the tangible reality of facts based on the truth of what we see, on the power of perception. This is what we call 'perceptual' realism – or the realism of the 'raw' documentary. Narrative realism may also bring about the reality of the heart, a reality evoked through strong feelings rather than facts, giving rise to a form of realism that we call 'categorical' realism – or the realism of sentimentality usually encountered in stories of famine in Africa or war in the Middle East. Finally, narrative realism can make use of the reality of *doxa*, a reality appealing to our deep-rooted certainties about what the world is or should be like. This is what we call 'ideological' realism – a realism often used for political manipulation. The realities both of the heart and of *doxa* are versions of 'psychological' realism, a way of knowing about reality that appeals to our emotional and moral sensibilities rather than to our quest for facts. News realism, it follows, is not about presenting the spectator with the single reality of suffering but it is about presenting them with different realities about suffering – different meanings through which suffering can be represented (Chouliaraki 2006: 74–80; Nichols 1991: 87; 141–57).

Verbal–visual correspondence

The sense of reality that each news text attempts to evoke for the spectator cannot simply be identified through the mode of presentation. In order to be able to describe precisely how types of realism emerge through the multimodal combinations of the news text, we need to talk more specifically about the work that language and the image perform in the news text. The verbal entails three modes of narrating the suffering, what I term below 'descriptions', 'narrations proper' and 'expositions',[9] whereas the image entails three modes of portraying suffering, the 'index', the 'icon' and the 'symbol'.[10] Let me focus, in turn, on each one of the two semiotic modes.

The visual: the impact of any news text is almost always a function of its visual referent.[11] It is the 'seeing it happen' that makes the strongest claim to the authenticity of suffering in television and 'burdens' the spectator with the moral role of the witness.

In this sense, the shift from no visual towards an increasingly intensive visualization of suffering is a shift towards an increasingly intensive involvement with the sufferer and thus an invitation for the spectator to remember and to repeat the sufferer's misfortune. For example, video images of human figures with their backs to the camera place us in the scene of suffering but they do not engage us with the sufferer. In contrast, a sequence of close-ups of suffering children gazing at the camera invites us to respond urgently to their tragedy. The distinction between the former and the latter type of visualization is a distinction between news without pity that we hardly register as such and news with pity that make upon us a demand to speak up or do something about the misfortune (Chouliaraki 2006: 157–83 and 187–98).

The verbal: if visualization tells us something about the degree of authenticity of a piece of news, it is the verbal mode that establishes the distinct sense of reality that the story evokes for the spectator. In ordering and organizing the spaces and temporalities of events, the verbal narrative of the news performs fundamental classificatory activities: it includes and excludes, foregrounds and backgrounds, justifies and legitimizes. It separates 'us' from 'them'.

Three narrative functions of the news are responsible for this classificatory work: descriptions, narrations or story-telling proper, and expositions. The hard facts of suffering are mainly evoked through descriptive narratives that tell us what we see and so they make the strongest claim to objectivity. For example, in a news piece on an Indian boat accident, a descriptive report sounds like this: *Forty-four people drowned in river Baytarani.* In narration, the factual report of events is replaced by elements of fictional story-telling, such as a chronological plot (with moments of deliberate tension or suspense) as well as generic conventions of opening and/or closure: *It was the end of an ordinary school day, when the boat transporting the children in river Baytarani capsized; forty-four people drowned.* The term exposition refers to the verbal narrative that incorporates a point of view within the news and, in so doing, it explicitly articulates ethical judgement vis-à-vis the reported suffering: *Forty-four people feared drowned in river Baytarani.* Evaluation is here contained, in a suppressed form, in the use of the affective/impersonal process *feared.*[12]

The relationship between the verbal and the visual

Each type of realism, perceptual, categorical and ideological, brings together its own combination of linguistic narrative with image and, in so doing, also establishes three distinct types of meaning relations in the news text. These are indexical, iconic and symbolic meanings. The realism of each news text depends then upon the distinct claim to the reality of suffering that each of the three types of meaning makes: claim to the facticity of suffering, in perceptual realism, claim to the emotion of suffering, in categorical realism, claim to justice around the cause of suffering, in ideological realism.[13]

The claim to facticity is the claim of perceptual realism and builds upon an indexical relationship between the verbal and the visual. This means that perceptual realism relies heavily upon the image and uses descriptive language to tell us what we see on the screen. Indexical meaning signifies precisely by employing language to establish some direct connection to the image and thereby to offer the spectator a 'window' to the outside world (Nichols 1991: 171; Messaris 1997: xvi–xvii; Ellis 2000:193–4). Although hardly any news text relies exclusively on indexicality, not even paradigmatic cases of live news footage that show what happens right now, all news texts inevitably entail an element of indexicality that grounds them to the world out there.

The claims to emotion and, more explicitly, to the ethics and politics of suffering inform psychological realism, in its two manifestations: categorical and ideological realism. Claims to emotion and to justice depart from the reliance on physical perception, that is to say, on the link between what we see and what we hear. In the case of categorical realism, fact matters less and the welling up of the spectator's feelings towards the suffering matters most. In order to bring about emotions, categorical realism often relies on story-telling or narration proper, which frames the visual representation of suffering with dramatic urgency and sensationalism. This relationship between image and narration gives rise to iconic meaning, meaning that is related to its referent not through some direct or 'physical' connection, but through similarity or family resemblance. Iconicity, then, does not attach itself to a concrete reality but, rather, represents an abstract reality by using image as the key-signifier of whichever generic condition it seeks to capture. In the typical 'famine in Africa' news stories, for example, images of emaciated children evoke the referent 'starvation' and function in a cumulative way to overwhelm the spectator with the reality of children's imminent death by famine.

Ideological realism works, similarly to categorical realism, through the association of the image with an abstraction. But this time, abstraction does not take the form of a generic category such as famine. It takes the form of a specific ideological dilemma – for example, whether we are for or against humanity – and urges the spectator to take a public stance vis-à-vis this dilemma. Here, the relationship between visual and verbal semiotic mode gives rise to symbolic meaning. Symbolic meaning is related to its referent neither by direct connection nor by family resemblance, but through discursive associations based on conventional knowledge and value, such as the *doxa* of 'us' as humane, 'them' as the savage. For example, in a news piece on a Nigerian woman convicted to death-by-stoning, the visual contrast between a close-up shot of this young woman with her baby followed by a long shot of a crowd mobbing another woman in the streets evokes the cultural belief that Islam is an 'inhumane' culture.

Aesthetic quality

The aesthetic quality of the news is a consequence of both its mode of presentation and of the relationship that the news text establishes between language and image. The aesthetic quality describes the overall multimodal effect of the news in terms of three historical tropes for the public staging of suffering, what Boltanski describes as 'topics of suffering' (1999). These historical topics for the representation of suffering are pamphleteering, philanthropy and sublimation. Pamphleteering is associated with the genre of political denunciation and aims to address the spectator's affective potential for anger vis-à-vis the evil-doer who inflicted the pain upon the sufferer. Philanthropy is associated with genres of Christian care and aims to activate the spectator's affective potential of tender-heartedness towards the benefactor who comforts the sufferer's pain. Finally, sublimation distances the spectator from the actuality of suffering and orients her towards a reflexive contemplation of the conditions of human misery.

The broadcast genre may endow the reported event with a single aesthetic quality, say philanthropic appeal towards famine victims, or it may select and combine elements of many topics. For example, the aesthetic quality of terror attacks footage may draw simultaneously on tender-hearted philanthropy in the scenes of emergency aid, indignation against the perpetrators of evil in the public statements of eye witnesses and political figures, and voyeuristic sentiments over the remains of buildings, trains or buses in a city centre. In so doing, the event invites the spectator at once to denounce the attacks, empathize with the victims and indulge in the sublimated contemplation of the aftermath of the attacks.

To conclude, the study of multimodality in the media text seeks to identify the process by which a concrete representation of suffering comes to articulate 'universal' public values, the values that connect the feelings of the individual spectator with the space of public action – with the urge to 'do something' about this sufferer. But which are these values? Which are the options offered to the spectator to do something in the world out there? And how can the spectator be guided to endorse such values and articulate them as her own? In order to study the content of these public values, we must now turn to the multi-functional dimension of mediation and its analytical category, critical discourse analysis (CDA). CDA concerns itself with representations of proximity and agency, because it is these two dimensions of media texts that are responsible for rendering (or not) the spectacle of distant suffering into a case of emotional involvement and a cause for social action on the part of media publics.

Critical discourse analysis

The analysis of the multi-functionality of mediation, that is of the social relationships of power through which media texts operate, is critical discourse analysis.[14] CDA is a method of analysis of media texts that treats the linguistic and visual choices on screen as subtle indicators of the power of the medium to mediate the world to the world. This is, for example, the power of television to classify the world into categories of 'us' and 'the other' and to orient the spectator towards this suffering 'other'.

In the analysis of representations, CDA looks into the construal of the scene of suffering within a specific spacetime that separates safety from danger. The category of spacetime refers to the place and the temporality of suffering. This is an important category, because it crucially participates in proposing options for action to the spectator by telling us how close an instance of suffering is to the spectator and how urgent action on the suffering is. The analysis of spacetime then focuses on the axes of proximity/distance or urgency/finality.

In the analysis of orientations, CDA looks into the category of agency. Agency is about who acts upon whom in the scene of suffering: first, agency refers to how active the sufferer appears on screen and, second, it refers to how other actors present in the scene appear to engage with the sufferer. These two dimensions of agency come to shape how the spectator herself is invited to relate to the suffering, that is if she is supposed to simply watch, to feel for or to practically act on the 'other's misfortune. The study of agency, in this respect, focuses on the analytical axis of 'our own'/ other'.[15]

Spacetime

The spacetime of suffering is the category that analyses how the spectator encounters the reality of the distant sufferer in different degrees of intensity and involvement. In this sense, spacetime is responsible for establishing a sense of immediacy for the scene of suffering and for regulating the moral distance between spectator and sufferer. But spatio-temporal immediacy is a fragile construction. This is so not only because most pieces of news come from far-away places, but mainly because issues like famine, war or death-by-stoning fall outside the spectator's life-world, outside their structure of experience. Just how effectively each piece of news articulates the spatial axis of proximity/ distance or the temporal axis of urgency/finality in order to establish suffering as a reality for the spectator is the first of the two analytical priorities of the study of news of suffering. In order to respond to questions concerning *space*, we focus on the following semiotic choices of the news:

1   *visual editing* (how spaces are shown to come closer to each other or remain resolutely distant on screen);
2   *camera position* (for example, filming from within the scene of action or from a location above and afar);
3   *graphic specification* (such as a map, the presence of written text or the split screen); or
4   *linguistic reference* (such as the use of adverbs of space, geographical references).

Concerning *time*, we focus on the following semiotic choices of the news:

1   *visual intertextuality* (for example, combining archive film, and hence a past reference, with on-location reports, thus shifting to right-now action) and
2   *linguistic reference* (the use of temporal adverbials such as *simultaneously, previously* etc; the use of tense, present or past; or the use of modality or imperatives).[16]

Depending on the broader multimodal text in which these choices are embedded, the suffering may appear to be happening categorically in the right-here-right-now temporality or in the far-away-in-the-indefinite-past temporality. If emaciated children are placed in the time frame of a *fait accompli*, in the past tense, there is little to do about them; if they are represented in terms of an ongoing temporality where co-ordinated action develops as we speak, famine becomes an emergency and acquires a radically different horizon of action.

Suffering, however, may also be represented with a higher degree of ambivalence. It may appear to be happening simultaneously here and there, in the past and right now. In the September 11th footage, for example, long shots over Manhattan in smoke establish a voyeuristic distance from the scene of action, but paradoxically, they also establish a sense of proximity based on the temporality of reflection, on the chance they give to the spectator to ponder upon the circumstances and consequences of the terror attacks. I would argue that the difference between categorical and ambivalent representations of proximity is a difference in the degree of spatiotemporal complexity where the suffering is shown to occur – or in the degree of its *chronotopicity*.[17] I define chronotopicity as those variations of spacetime that increasingly expand to encompass four elements in the representation of suffering:

1   *concreteness*, which shows the minimal context of suffering as a physical space;
2   *multiplicity*, which moves the spectator through multiple physical contexts of suffering;
3   *specificity*, which shows the context of suffering as a singular space, by elaborating on its unique properties, or which individualizes the sufferer as a unique person with a array of attributes; and
4   *mobility*, which connects the contexts of safety and danger suggesting a specific relationship of action between them.

The move from news defined by a minimum of these properties to news defined by increasing spatiotemporal complexity (chronotopicity) is simultaneously a move from news with minimum potential for pity to news with maximum moral appeal and potential for engagement: the more complex the spacetime the less the 'othering' of the sufferer.

Agency

This is the analytical category that focuses on action upon suffering in terms of the agency of the sufferer herself and in terms of the system of other agents that operate in the scene of suffering. The type of action that these figures of pity play out on screen bears an effect on the spectator's own orientation to the sufferer and, in this sense, the category agency cannot be considered in isolation from the spatio-temporalities of suffering and the proximity to the scene of action. This is because the spectator of television news is by necessity separated from the scene of suffering and therefore can only respond to the misfortune of the sufferer through television's own proposals for emotional identification and options for action.[18] Indeed, let us recall that agency in television can only take the form of action at a distance and there are only two paradigms for conceptualizing public action at a distance in western culture: the agora and the theatre. The first, the action of the agora, is contemplation and depends upon the spectator's objective deliberation and judgement upon suffering. The second, the action of the theatre, is identification and depends upon the spectator's participation in the psychological and emotional states of suffering.[19]

The humane sufferer and the agora: in contemplation, which is the action of the agora, the spectator is expected to watch the sufferer's misfortune without bias and to judge it objectively. But the position of true impartiality is impossible. This is because, as long as there is a hierarchy of places of suffering that divides the world, there will, inevitably, also be a hierarchy of the human lives that inhabit these places. It follows that the spectator is more likely to speak out about the suffering they are watching if the sufferer is construed as somebody like 'us' and, in reverse, they are more likely to switch off if the sufferer fails to appear as one like 'us'. The agency of the spectator to engage in public speech about the suffering then depends upon the humanization of the sufferer.

In the analytics of mediation, humanization is a process of identity construction that endows the sufferer with the power to say or do something about their condition, even if this power is simply the power to evoke and receive the beneficiary action of others. The humane sufferer is the sufferer that acts. The difference, for example, between the September 11th sufferer and the sufferer in the Indian boat accident that I mentioned earlier is a difference in agency. The September 11th sufferer speaks; the Indian does not. The Indian sufferer, who is referred to as a number only, becomes an 'Other', with a capital 'o', in so far as her existence remains purely inactive (Tester 2000; Cohen 2001).

The humanization of the sufferer occurs either through the verbal mode or through the image. Concerning the *verbal mode*, the choice of the narrative type by which the news on suffering is reported plays an important role in the construal of the sufferer's identity as humane. Narration or story-telling proper, for example, includes dramatic elements that may animate the figure of the sufferer as an actor and thus may humanize the sufferer to a greater extent than the factual description of an event.

Concerning the *visual mode*, a key choice is camera position and angle. It makes a difference to film the sufferer from afar and above in a group or to film her frontally gazing at the camera. The gaze, in this context, is appellative action and the camera choice to capture the sufferer's gaze is also a choice to give voice and to humanize the sufferer, whereas the choice to film her through long shots may alienate and dehumanize her. Images of African people filmed en masse in some Darfur safety camp is just one example of how visual 'Othering' contributes to sustaining powerful hierarchies of human life.

The figures of suffering and the theatre: if, in contemplation, the agora model of action at a distance, the what-to-do vis-à-vis the sufferer depends on the representation of the sufferer as properly humane, in the theatrical model of action at a distance the what-to-do takes a different twist. The witnessing of suffering is now mediated by the dynamic of social relationships that are already at play into the scene of suffering, the benefactor or the persecutor. Agency in the theatre depends on the orchestration of these two primary figures of action who connect the reality of distant suffering to the spectator's private feelings vis-à-vis the spectacle they are watching. We should not think of the benefactor and the persecutor only as 'real people' on the television screen, although this is very often the case. Rather, we should think of them as symbolic figures that focalize the affective potential of the spectator towards a particular emotion.

It is only when this private potential for feeling leads the spectator to identify with an ethical value, such as philanthropic care in the case of tender-heartedness or social justice in the case of indignation, that the spectacle of distant suffering is able to constitute a group of spectators into a public – a collectivity with a will to act. Whereas the tender-hearted impulse to protect or comfort the sufferer articulates the moral value of care for the 'other', the indignant impulse to denounce or even to attack the evil-doer articulates the moral demand for civil justice. In this respect, the task of the analytics of mediation is to show how the figures of agency, benefactor and persecutor, literally incorporate the moral value associated with suffering in each particular piece of news and how they make it part of a persuasive theatre of action – of humanitarian activists, political protesters or indulgent voyeurists (see Boltanski 1999: 57–146 for the topics of suffering).

Conclusion

Distant suffering, I argue in this chapter, throws into relief one of the most dramatic cultural conditions of mediation: a de-territorialization of our experience that takes us close to suffering others without giving us the option of acting upon their misfortune. This condition sets the question of ethics and public action today at the top of the agenda for a critical analysis of culture. The key problem here is to conceptualize the link between media text and social action. I argue that, even though social action is not exhausted in media texts, the latter act as a powerful condition of possibility for the formation of media audiences as bodies of agency, insofar as they propose public dispositions for us to feel and act at a distance. Drawing on Aristotle's phronetic research, I outline the 'analytics of mediation', a discourse analytical methodology that enables us to study how the media text is put together in language and image (multimodal analysis) and how, in so doing, it may construe the spacetimes and forms of agency that connect spectator and sufferer in distinct regimes of pity (critical discourse analysis).

Notes

1 See Harrenz (1996); Robertson (1998); Robins (1999); Tomlinson (1999: 184) on de-territotiralization, re-territorialization and the 'closing of moral distance'; Silverstone (1999, 2006) on media, morality and the 'other'.
2 For the distinction see Couldry (2005), who juxtaposes his own approach to the study of media and social action to the Glasgow Media Group's interpretation studies and to CDA-related work.
3 '... for all their virtues, there has been a tension in earlier accounts of how circulated media texts influence social action between (1) emphasizing the moment of individual interpretation and (2) the desire to explain more broadly how interpretation is socially shaped ...' (Couldry 2005: 5).
4 See Chouliaraki (2006: 66) for an account of this pedagogic role of the media in terms of the Foucauldian conception of power as governmentality.
5 Aristotle, *The Nicomachean Ethics*, trans. A.K. Thompson (1976) Harmondsworth: Penguin, 1140a24–1140b12, 1144b33–1145a11.
6 Flyvebjerg (2001: 110–28) for a powerful appropriation of Aristotle's work in post-structuralist epistemology; Ross (1995: 31–49) for Aristotle's inductive methods and analytics.

7 There is also the textual meta-function of semiosis, which looks inwards to the text itself and serves the social purpose of creating meaning that is recognized as coherent and intelligible; in the words of Jewitt and Oyama (2001: 140), the textual meta-function holds together 'the individual bits of representation–interaction' into coherent text wholes. Insofar as it concerns itself with the combination of language and image in coherent texts, the textual meta-function obviously appertains to the multimodal analysis of television that I discussed earlier.

8 In this light, the power asymmetry that is embedded in the social relationships of television viewing may not in itself bring about the economic and political divisions of our world, but it certainly reflects them and consolidates them. Who watches and who suffers reflects the manner in which differences in economic resources, political regimes and in everyday life enter the global landscape of information. Similarly, who acts upon whose suffering reflects patterns of economic and political agency across global zones of influence and their historical divisions, north and south or east and west. For the argument see Tester (2001); Silverstone (1999, 2006); Chouliaraki (2006).

9 I here adapt Chatman's categories of three main text-types in communicative practice: *description, argument* and *narrative* (1991: 9).

10 For the use of Piercean semiotics in visual analysis and in media texts see Hall (1973); Hodge and Kress (1988: 19–20); Jensen (1995); Messaris (1997: x–xxii); van Leeuwen (2001: 92–118); Schroeder (2002: 111–16).

11 See Kress and van Leeuwen (1996; 2001); Jewitt and van Leeuwen (2001) for the grammar of the visual; van Leeuwen and Jaworski (2002); Perlmutter and Wagner (2004: 91–108). The Piercean typology corresponds to other classifications of meaning types, such as Panofsky's (see van Leeuwen 2001: 100–17).

12 'Although there is an obvious analytical value in differentiating among the three narrative types, we should be aware of the fact that news texts often enact more than one narrative function at once. Just like the semiotic modes of language and the visual are multi-functional, narratives, too, co-exist and complement one another. They are intertextual' (Chatman 1991: 30).

13 See Grodal (2002: 67–91) for the terminology of 'perceptual' and 'categorical' realism; Nichols (1995: 165–98) for an insightful but slightly different discussion on realism in documentary.

14 For multi-functionality in language see Halliday (1985/1995); Halliday and Hasan (1989); Hasan (2000); for a Critical Discourse Analysis discussion of the *multi-functional* perspective see Chouliaraki and Fairclough (1999: 139–55).

15 This distinction between representation and orientation is a necessity that enables the analysis of television texts. In practice, representations and orientations are not separate parts of the television text and we must look at once into both meta-functions in order to determine how they are brought together in each news sequence. Halliday (1985/1995: 23).

16 For an elaboration of these categories see Chilton (2004); also Fairclough (2003).

17 Although Bakhtin says that all events have their own chronotopic universe, I reserve the term 'chronotopicity' for those events, which involve more than one spacetime. We can talk, therefore, of the chronotope of a news event as that regime of multiple spaces (danger and safety) and temporalities (present, past or future), through which the event 'moves' back and forth and, in so doing, presents the spectator not with one single reality of suffering but with multiple realities relevant to the suffering. Bakhtin (1981: 84–85 and 243–58) in Holquist, M. (ed.) (1981).

18 Rose (1999), Barnett (2003) for a 'governmentality' perspective on the production of subjectivity through the various proposals of identification embedded in institutional forms of discourse.
19 For a similar treatment of the public spaces of mediation in terms of agora and theatre see Sennett (1998) 'The spaces of democracy', the Raoul Wallenberg Lecture, University of Michigan.

References

Aristotle, *The Nicomachean Ethics*, trans. A.K. Thompson (1976) Harmondsworth: Penguin.

Barnett, C. (2003) *Culture and Democracy: media, space and representation*, London: Edinburgh University Press.

Boltanski, L. (1999) *Distant Suffering: politics, morality and the media*, Cambridge: Cambridge University Press.

Chatman, S. (1990/1) *Coming to Terms: the rhetoric of narrative in fiction and film*, Ithaca, NY and London: Cornell University Press.

Chilton, P. (2004) *Analysing Political Discourse: theory and practice*, London: Routledge.

Chouliaraki, L. (2006) *The Spectatorship of Suffering*, London: Sage.

Chouliaraki, L. and Fairclough, N. (1999) *Discourse in Late Modernity*, Edinburgh: Edinburgh University Press.

Cohen, S. (2001) *States of Denial: knowing about atrocities and suffering*, Cambridge: Polity Press.

Couldry, N. (2005) 'Media discourse and the naturalisation of categories', in R. Wodak and V. Koller (eds) *The Handbook of Applied Linguistics: language and communication in the public sphere*, Berlin: Mouton de Gruyter.

Ellis, J. (2000) *Seeing Things: television in an age of uncertainty*, London: IB Tauris Books.

Fairclough, N. (1995) *Media Discourse*, London: Edward Arnold.

—— (2003) *Analysing Discourse: textual analysis for social research*, London: Routledge.

Flowerdew, J. (2004) 'The discursive construction of a world-class city', *Discourse and Society*, 15(5): 579–605.

Flyvbjerg, B. (2001) *Making Social Science Matter*, Cambridge: Cambridge University Press.

Foucault, M. (1984/2000) 'Confronting governments', in J.D. Fabion, *Essential Works of Foucault 1954–1984*, vol. 3, London: Power Penguin.

—— (1991) 'Governmentality', in G. Burchell, C. Gordon and P. Miller (eds) *The Foucault Effect: studies in governmentality*, London: Harvester Wheatsheaf.

Grodal, T. (2002) 'The experience of realism in audiovisual representation', in A. Jerslev (ed.) *Realism and 'Reality' in Film and Media*, Copenhagen: Museum Tusculanum Press.

Hall, S. (1973) 'Encoding/decoding in television discourse', in S. Hall, D. Hobson, A. Lowe and P. Wills (eds) *Culture, Media, Language*, London: Hutchinson.

Halliday, M.A.K. (1985/1995) *Introduction to Functional Grammar*, London: Edward Arnold.

Harrenz, U. (1996) *Transnational Connections: culture, people, places*, London: Routledge.

Hasan, R. (2000) 'The disempowerment game: Bourdieu and language in literacy', *Linguistics and Education*, 10(1): 25–87 (63).

Hodge, R. and Kress, G. (1988) *Social Semiotics*, Cambridge: Polity.

Holquist, M. (ed.) (1981) *The Dialogic Imagination: four essays by M. Bakhtin*, Austin, TX: University of Texas Press.

Jensen, B.K. (1995) *The Social Semiotics of Mass Communication*, London: Sage.

Jewitt, C. and Oyama, R. (2001) 'Visual meaning: a social semiotic approach', in C. Jewitt and T. van Leeuwen (eds) *The Handbook of Visual Analysis*, London: Sage.

Jewitt, C. and van Leeuwen, T. (2001) *The Handbook of Visual Analysis*, London: Sage.

Kress, G. and van Leeuwen, T. (1996) *Reading Images: the grammar of visual design*, London: Routledge.

—— (2001) *Multimodal Discourse: the modes and media of contemporary communication*, London: Arnold.

Livingstone, S. and Lunt, P. (1994) *Talk on Television*, London: Routledge.

Messaris, P. (1997) *Visual Persuasion*, London: Sage.

Nichols, B. (1991) *Representing Reality*, Bloomington, IN: Indiana University Press.

Perlmutter, D. and Wagner, G. (2004) 'The anatomy of a photojournalistic icon', *Visual Communication*, 3(1): 91–108.

Robertson, R. (1995/1998) 'Globalisation, time-space and homogeneity–heterogeneity', in M. Featherstone, S. Lash and R. Robertson (eds) *Global Modernities*, London: Sage.

Robins, B. (1999) *Feeling Global*, New York: New York University Press.

Rose, N. (1999) *Powers of Freedom: reframing political thought*, London: Routledge.

Ross, D. (1995) *Aristotle*, London: Routledge.

Schroeder, K. (2002) 'Discourses of fact', in K.B. Jensen (ed.) *A Handbook of Media and Communication Research*, London: Routledge.

Scollon, S. (1998) *Mediated Discourse as Social Interaction*, London: Longman.

Sennett, R. (1998) 'The spaces of democracy', the Raoul Wallenberg Lecture, University of Michigan.

Silverstone, R. (1999) *Why Study the Media*, London: Sage.

—— (2004) 'Media literacy and media civics', *Media, Culture and Society*, 23(3): 440–9.

—— (2006) *Media and Morality: on the rise of the mediapolis*, Cambridge: Polity Press.

Tester, K. (2000) *Compassion, Morality and the Media*, Oxford: Oxford University Press.

Tomlinson, J. (1999) *Globalisation and Culture*, London: Sage.

van Dijk, T. (1987) *Communicating Racism*, London: Sage.

van Leeuwen, T. (2001) 'Semiotics and iconography', in C. Jewitt and T. van Leeuwen (eds) *The Handbook of Visual Analysis*, London: Sage.

van Leeuwen, T. and Jaworski, A. (2002) 'The discourses of war photography', *Journal of Language and Politics*, 1(2): 255–76.

Wodak, R. (1996) *Disorders of Discourse*, London: Longman.

—— (1999) 'Critical discourse analysis at the end of the 20th century', *Research on Language and Social Interaction*, 32: 185–94.

Suggestions for further work

1 What is meant when discourse is claimed by CDA to be a form of social action?
2 CDA studies relations between discourse, power, dominance and social inequality. Think of some specific social situations where these elements are crucial and consider their possible relationships.
3 Think of some communicative events which might be amenable to positive discourse analysis, as proposed by Martin (1999).
4 Flowerdew explains how systemic functional linguistics is a preferred method of CDA. Consider (a) the extent to which this model is appropriate for CDA and (b) the extent to which it might be suited to multi-modal analysis, as exemplified by Chouliaraki.
5 Flowerdew exemplifies resistance in discourse through appropriation by members of gay communities. Think of other social situations where appropriation is likely to occur.

Part VII

Mediated discourse analysis

Mediated discourse analysis (MDA) is the newest approach to discourse represented in this book, and, although it has a history of less than a decade, it has developed a myriad of strategies for approaching a variety of social contexts including food and commerce (R. Scollon 2006, this volume), AIDS prevention (Jones 1999, 2001a, 2002; Jones and Candlin 2003), political change (S. Scollon 2003), education (Rowe 2005; Scollon *et al.*.1999), international adoption (McIlvenny and Raudaskoski 2005), disability (Al Zidjaly 2006), and drug abuse (Jones 2005a). MDA has also had an effect on the development of other recent approaches to discourse, including a Geneva school of discourse analysis known as modular discourse analysis (Filliettaz and Roulet 2002) as well as the multimodal interaction analysis of Norris (2004, this volume).

The underlying principle of mediated discourse analysis is that discourse cannot be studied in isolation from the situated social actions that people take with it. This concern for human action gives MDA a unique perspective on discourse: on the one hand, discourse is seen as *consequential* insofar as works to either limit or amplify particular social actions and the social identities that are associated with them. On the other hand, discourse is not automatically privileged as an object of study, but only seen as important insofar as it relates to concrete actions in the world; discourse is simply one of the many 'cultural tools' with which individuals take action and which link them, through these actions, to their socio-cultural environments. This perspective on discourse lends itself to MDA's 'activist' stance. Just as critical discourse analysts attempt to link textual features to larger ideologies at work in society, mediated discourse analysts insist that our ability to take everyday concrete social actions such as preparing a meal, buying a cup of coffee, or putting on a condom is inextricably linked to larger issues of policy and power. All instances of concrete, real-time social actions, says R. Scollon (2001), represent both the production and reproduction of the structures of our social worlds, structures which either enable us or prevent us from taking subsequent social actions. Thus, every action holds within it not just the history of the society in which it is taken, with its structures of domination and power, but also the opportunity to resist these structures of domination and create positive social change.

Recent theoretical concerns of mediated discourse analysis have included how actions are configured in space and time (Scollon 2005), including the 'virtual' spaces and times of computer mediated communication (Al Zidjaly; Jones 2005b, c), how 'agency' is exercised and experienced in mediated actions (Scollon 2005), how discourse 'cycles' through individuals and situations (Scollon and Scollon 2004), and how it is transformed through concrete social actions and into multiple modes and materialities (Jones 2005b; Norris 2005). It is this last concern that R. Scollon focuses on in his chapter. Mediated discourse analysis shares with many other approaches to discourse an interest in *intertextuality*, the ways texts are *dialogically* linked to other texts. It adds to this, however, the realization that texts are not just linked to other texts, but also linked to past actions and to material objects in the world as they cycle through different semiotic systems and their materialities, a process Iedema (2001, 2003) calls *resemiotization*.

Through an analysis of the word 'organic' on a bag of brown rice, Scollon (this volume) maps out what he calls an 'itinerary of transformation', which begins with the action of planting rice, and moves through various processes of resemiotization like narrativization, certification and remodalization before finally being 'technologized' into a labelled object for consumption. MDA should take as its central task, he argues, to map such itineraries in order to understand not just how discourse affects action, but how action affects discourse.

As Scollon points out, intertextuality is by its nature, historical. Intertextual ties link texts and actions to previous texts and actions and anticipate subsequent texts and actions. This temporal nature of intertextuality is what concerns Jones in the chapter that follows Scollon's. From its beginnings the focus of mediated action theory has been on ways mediated actions reflect social structures that have been integrated into the individual's 'habitus' or 'historical body'. Jones seeks to understand the 'historical body' as it is revealed in the stories gay men tell of unsafe sexual encounters. Traditional individualistic theories of health education, he notes, have failed to account for why, even when equipped with adequate knowledge about HIV and how to prevent it, people continue to engage in unsafe sex. MDA, with its focus on the complex inter-relationship between discourse and action, he suggests, provides a useful alternative to this individualistic and linear model. One way of understanding how people *use* safe sex discourse and the effect it might have on subsequent sexual encounters, claims Jones, is through attention to the anticipatory and retrospective discourse contained in their stories about sex. The notions of anticipatory and retrospective discourse were first introduced in MDA by S. Scollon (2001) and later more fully developed by de Saint-Georges (2003) and Al Zidjaly (2006). Anticipatory discourse is about how people anticipate, prepare for or seek to avoid specific outcomes of their actions, and retrospective discourse involves how they make sense of and assign agency and motives to past actions in things like accounts, anecdotes and explanations.

Taken together, anticipatory and retrospective discourse provide a meta-discursive or reflective structure through with which people perform and interpret actions and anticipate future outcomes. In light of his analysis, Jones suggests that rather than prescribing for people what they should do during sex, a more effective approach to HIV/AIDS education might be to help them to reflect on the actions they already take surrounding the sexual act and the ways they assign agency to these actions.

Fruitful additional reading on mediated discourse analysis can be found in R. Scollon (2001), Scollon and Scollon (2004) and Norris and Jones (2005).

References

Al Zidjaly, N. (2006) 'Disability and anticipatory discourse: the interconnectedness of local and global aspects of talk', *Communication and Medicine*, 3(2): 101–12.

de Saint-Georges, I. (2003) 'Anticipatory discourses: producing futures of action in a vocational program for long-term unemployed', PhD dissertation, Georgetown University.

Filliettaz, L. and Roulet, E. (2002) 'The Geneva model of discourse analysis: an interactionist and modular approach to discourse organization', *Discourse Studies*, 4(3): 369–92.

Iedema, R. (2001) 'Resemiotization', *Semiotica*, 137(1–4): 23–39.

—— (2003) 'Multimodality, resemiotization: extending the analysis of discourse as multi-semiotic practice', *Visual Communication*, 2(1): 29–57.

Jones. R. (1999) 'Mediated action and sexual risk: searching for "culture" in the discourses of homosecuality and AIDS prevention in China', *Culture, Health and Sexuality I*, (2): 161–80.

—— (2001) *Mediated Action and Sexual Risk: discourses of AIDS and sexuality in the People's Republic of China*, unpublished PhD dissertation, Macquarie University, Sydney.

—— (2002) 'A walk in the park: frames and positions in AIDS prevention outreach among gay men in China', *Journal of Sociolinguistics*, 6(3): 575–88.

—— (2005a) 'Mediated addiction: the drug discourses of Hong Kong youth', *Health, Risk and Society*, 7(1): 25–45.

—— (2005b) '"You show me yours, I'll show you mine": the negotiation of shifts from textual to visual modes in computer mediated interaction among gay men', *Visual Communication*, 4(1): 69–92.

—— (2005c) 'Sites of engagement as sites of attention: time, space and culture in electronic discourse', in S. Norris and R. Jones (eds) *Discourse in Action: introducing mediated discourse analysis*, London: Routledge, pp. 144–54.

Jones, R. and Candlin, C.N. (2003) 'Constructing risk along timescales and trajectories: gay men's stories of sexual encounters', *Health, Risk and Society*, 5(2): 199–213.

McIlvenny, P. and Raudaskoski, P. (2005) 'Mediating voices of transnational adoption on the internet', in S. Norris and R. Jones (eds) *Discourse in Action: introducing mediated discourse analysis*, London: Routledge, pp. 62–71.

Norris, S. (2004) *Analysing Multimodal Interaction: a methodological framework*, London and New York: Routledge.

Norris, S. and Jones, R. (eds) (2005) *Discourse in Action: introducing mediated discourse analysis*, London: Routledge.

Rowe, S. (2005) 'Using multiple situation definitions to create hybrid activity space', in S. Norris and R. Jones (eds) *Discourse in Action: introducing mediated discourse analysis*, London: Routledge, pp. 123–34.

Scollon, R. (2001) *Mediated Discourse: the nexus of practice*, London: Routledge.

—— (2005) 'The rhythmic integration of action and discourse: work, the body and the earth', in S. Norris and R. Jones (eds) *Discourse in Action: introducing mediated discourse analysis*, London: Routledge, pp. 20–31.

—— (2006) 'Food and behavior: a Burkean motive analysis of a quasi-medical text', *Text & Talk*, 26(11): 107–25.

Scollon, R. and Scollon, S.W. (2004) *Nexus Analysis: discourse and the emerging internet*, London: Routledge.

Scollon, R., Tsang, W.K., Li, D. Yung, V. and Jones, R. (1999) 'Voice, appropriation, and discourse representation in a student writing task, *Linguistics and Education*, 9(3): 227–50.

Scollon, S. (2003) 'Political and somatic alignment: habitus, ideology and social practice', in R. Wodak and G. Weiss (eds) *Critical Discourse Analysis: theory and interdisciplinarity*, Basingstoke: Palgrave Macmillan, pp. 167–98.

—— (2005) 'Agency distributed through time, space and tools: Bentham, Babbage and the census', in S. Norris and R. Jones (eds) *Discourse in Action: introducing mediated discourse analysis*, London: Routledge, pp. 20–31.

15 Discourse itineraries

Nine processes of resemiotization

Ron Scollon

A bag of organic brown rice

'Intertextuality' has been widely used as a term to capture the observation that any use of language ties back into antecedent language at the same time that it anticipates subsequent language. Among discourse analysts this idea is most often associated with Bakhtin's (1981) concept of dialogicality or Becker's (1994) prior text; Kristeva (1986) introduced the term intertextuality itself. Mediated discourse analysis starts with the actions of social actors and uses discourse analysis among other analytical tools to examine these actions. Within this framework language, whether spoken language or written text, is seen as a mediational means by which actions are undertaken, not the action in itself. In this view the relationship of text to text, language to language, is not a direct relationship but is always mediated by the actions of social actors as well as through material objects of the world. Using the example of the word 'organic' this chapter argues that it encapsulates or resemiotizes an extended historical itinerary of action, practice, narrative, authorization, certification, metonymization, objectivization and technologization or reification. My colleague, Suzie Wong and I suggested (Scollon and Scollon 2004) that the phrase 'cycle of discourse' would be an apt characterization of such sequences. Here I propose the word 'itinerary' in its place. Because discourse inherently operates along such itineraries of transformation, mediated discourse analysis takes it as a central task to map such itineraries of relationships among text, action, and the material world through what we call a 'nexus analysis'.

Mediated discourse analysis (MDA) takes the mediated action as its unit of analysis. As a theoretical position this close focus on a moment of action within a site of engagement (R. Scollon 2001) might easily mistakenly fall into what Blommaert (2005) has called synchronization, that is, taking the moment of action to be all that is of interest to be studied. As this theoretical–methodological framework has developed, however, it has become clear that much discourse which is of relevance to a moment of action is, in fact, displaced from that action, often at quite a distance and across a wide variety of times, places, people, media, and objects. As we have expanded the circumference (Burke 1969 [1945]) of our view of the moment of action we have come to consider these complex displacements to work across multiple moments in which the discourse is transformed semiotically. We call the historical path of these resemiotized displacements discourse itineraries. As a way of capturing the kind of analysis that we need in order to trace these discursive displacements from a crucial moment of action we have used the term 'nexus analysis'.

My purpose in this chapter, therefore, is to illustrate how the concept of intertextuality has become elaborated in nexus analysis with a relatively simple problem, the ways in which the word 'organic' in reference to foods, may be used as descriptor to transform a rather complex set of actions, practices, objects and discourse carried out over multiple timescales by multiple social actors. In this case I will identify nine processes of transformation or resemiotization (Iedema 2003) through which the discourse of 'organic' food is transformed: action, practice, narrative, authorization, certification, metonymization, remodalization, materialization and technologization or reification.

I will illustrate by beginning with the action of buying a 25-lb bag of brown rice. My wife and I normally buy our rice by special order in large bags. We also prefer to eat organic foods wherever we are able to do that. This bag of rice is labelled 'Lundberg ORGANIC – CALIFORNIA – SHORT GRAIN BROWN RICE' and my concern is to show that we need considerably more than to just use our common-sense knowledge to understand what the word 'organic' might mean as part of this action of buying this bag of organic rice. We will ultimately need to engage in a rather extended analysis of both discourse and practice to see how we understand this word.

There are the two uses of the word 'organic' in the bag of rice. On the upper portion of the bag in the first instance 'organic' occurs as the modifier of a noun in the noun phrase 'organic rice'. Here the focus is on the object, rice. 'Organic' is linguistically positioned as a property of the object. Here at the outset we see the process which I have called *materialization*. It is the object, rice, which is considered to be organic.

In the lower portion of the bag there is a seal-like image in which 'organic' occurs as an adverbial modifier of a verb in the phrase 'organically grown rice'. What is organic is not the rice itself but the way in which the rice is produced. The focus in this case is on processes of *action* and of *practice*, not the material object.

A mediated discourse analysis focuses on the actions of social actors not on the texts themselves. This is a theoretical shift in focus from the texts on the bag to our actions of buying the bag of rice, bringing it home in the back of the truck, opening it, making a pot of rice, and eating it for dinner. The discourse analytical question is: how has discourse (or text, etc.) worked as a mediational means (along with the bag, the rice, the truck and the rest) in our accomplishing these actions. In this case a relevant question might be: how do I know this is brown rice? Or more to the point, how do I know it is organic? Possibly only a glance at the word 'organic' is sufficient. Perhaps just seeing the brand name 'Lundberg' would be sufficient to tell me this. From a mediated discourse perspective the rest of the text, graphics or images may simply be decoration, colour or design, but not used as mediational means in buying this bag of organic rice.

Time and space

One of the central problems of mediated discourse analysis is dealing with different levels at which an action might be characterized. When I want to focus on the action I am engaged in when I buy this rice, I might just phrase it as that – buying a bag of rice. Or I might phrase it as preparing for dinner. More broadly I could say it is the action of trying to maintain a diet of organic and whole foods and to avoid foods to which we are allergic. Or it might be conceived even more particularistically. I might say it is handing over money in the store, handling the 25-lb bag, driving our pick-up, putting water in the rice pot and so forth. Or very much more broadly I could say it is supporting the economy of California, since the rice was grown there. Any description of one of these levels runs the danger of eclipsing or 'synchronizing' (Blommaert 2005) all of the other possible descriptions at different levels and in different timescales.

As an example of this distribution of action across different timescales and spaces, when I say I eat organic brown rice, these statements cover a timescale that can be measured in years, what elsewhere I have called the solar time cycle (R. Scollon 2005). When I say I handed the clerk my credit card this statement covers a timescale of just moments, what I have called the cardio-pulmonary time cycle. These actions, like all of the other statements I have not considered here can be located in time as having quite different temporal extensions.

Those different temporal extensions entail different spatial distributions as well. When I locate my eating of brown rice across a distribution of years I also locate it across the many places I have lived in those years. And with that distribution come other consequences. To say I eat brown rice is relatively facile when we consider the period of time we lived in Korea where brown rice was abundantly available in the local store just at the bottom of the hill where we lived. To distribute that same statement across the six years we lived in Hong Kong requires a certain degree of exception. We did sometimes eat brown rice there but it was not easy to buy in stores and it was impossible to find in restaurants.

These timescales and spatial distributions bring with them different daily practices. Further clarification is needed: I eat organic brown rice whenever I can do so easily; in Hong Kong that meant rarely, in Korea it meant often, in Alaska it means we have to special-order the rice in large quantities and store it in our pantry, or buy it by the pound as we do in Washington. Time and space have important consequences for practice and so the characterization of an action within a specific timescale entails much in the way of other practices and actions which are tied into the action to which we are directing our attention.

To say nothing more than that I eat organic brown rice air-brushes out the periods of time over the past two decades in which by necessity and even by choice I have not eaten rice which is either brown or organic. The statement about the action synchronizes the ebb and flow of practice and flattens the scope of our view of the present moment, as well as our view of the history flowing into this moment and of the future emanating away from it. A central concern of a nexus analysis, then, is to map these multiple historical trajectories and anticipatory emanations from moments of action in order to keep alive our understanding of the layered simultaneity of human action.

Modal complexity (multimodality)

As soon as we open up the circumference of our analysis (Burke 1969 [1945]; Scollon and Scollon 2004), we become increasingly aware that all of our actions (and discourses) are constructed out of complex interweavings of semiotic materials in multiple modes. This multimodality includes both material representations such as texts, images, designs, and the built environment (Kress and van Leeuwen 1996, 2001) and the many semiotic systems which come together in face-to-face social interactions (Norris 2004). When the clerk comes out of the storeroom with a bag of rice and asks, 'Here, is this it?' she employs language including the pronominal deictics 'here' and 'it', she gives a slight emphatic pulse to the word 'this', but she also hefts the bag a bit to signal the indexable bag which those deictics are indexing. She further focuses her gaze momentarily on the bag as she hefts it to redundantly confirm that it is indeed this bag of rice she is speaking about.

What is important to note here is that this bit of modal density (Norris 2004) (linguistic deixis, phonological emphasis, gaze and bodily hefting the 25-lb bag a bit higher) does not occur independently of the other modes employed on the bag of rice. There is not only the package labelling (this is Lundberg organic brown rice) but also a hand-written note 'S/O' (for 'special order') and the price ($25.88), as these are not otherwise available to either the clerk or to me the customer. All of these modes foreground momentarily this bit of interpersonal transaction with the bag of rice.

What Norris then reminds us to also not forget is that while this foregrounded delivery of the bag is occurring there are at the same time in the background of the multimodal continuum the common activities of Mountain Market all signalled by layout, colour, design and a host of signs forming a semiotic aggregate (Scollon and Scollon 2003) which we recognize as a health food store and contemporary coffee shop. My action in buying this bag of rice is far from a simple matter of paying for a bag of rice; it is a highly symbolic ratification of the circulation of health food discourses throughout the world. This broad level of signification is not carried by any single one of the modes through which this action takes place but is a syncretic, or with further study we may find it is a grammatical outcome of their simultaneous and integrated production.

But what of the design of the bag text in itself? In the upper section are the brand name and product identification forming the 'ideal' semiotic display area (Kress and van Leeuwen 1996). Here in this upper section 'organic' is presented as an attribute of the object 'rice' with a modifier-noun noun-phrase grammatical construction. To put this in the terms I am developing here, the upper (ideal) portion of this text/image emphasizes *metonymization* and *materialization*. That is, the entire historical cycle of practice and action that results my buying this bag of rice is carried on the metonym of rice and is manifested in the material object, the rice.

Within the lower, the real, section, however we have both an extended textual description of Lundberg's way of growing this rice (that is, without pesticides, herbicides, fungicides and the like) and a graphically imposing circular 'seal'. This 'seal' which is not, in fact, a seal at all but just a graphic design presents the meaning of 'organic' as an adverbial in the adverbial phrase 'organically grown'. Here two of the processes can be observed. 'Organic' refers to the *actions* and *practices* of the Lundberg farmers and the seal *certifies* these practices.

We still have some work to do to see what 'organic' means and how can we know if a food is organic.

The Free Dictionary website first gives definitions as the word is used in organic chemistry and only turns to the semantic territory of organic foods in the fifth and sixth definitions:

> 5.**organic** – of or relating to foodstuff grown or raised without synthetic fertilizers or pesticides or hormones; 'organic eggs'; 'organic vegetables'; 'organic chicken'
>
> *health food* – any natural or prepared food popularly believed to promote good health
>
> *wholesome* – conducive to or characteristic of physical or moral well-being; 'wholesome attitude'; 'wholesome appearance'; 'wholesome food'
>
> 6.**organic** – simple and healthful and close to nature; 'an organic lifestyle'
>
> *healthful* – conducive to good health of body or mind; 'a healthful climate'; 'a healthful environment'; 'healthful nutrition'; 'healthful sleep'; 'Dickens's relatively healthful exuberance'.
>
> (http://www.thefreedictionary.com/organic
> accessed 17 July 17 2004, 6:22 a.m. AKT)

These definitions make it clear that, in the first place, 'organic' is largely defined negatively, that is, what is organic is defined by how it was not made, not grown or not raised. In the second place 'organic' in these definitions is a mix of several of the processes we are examining. In Paragraph 5 'organic' is used as a modifier on objects such as eggs, vegetables or chicken, or more generally any form of food (*materialization*). At the same time, however, those foods are said to achieve their 'organic' character as part of a process of farming (*practices*).

Paragraph 6 shifts the focus from *practices* of farming to living *practices* or lifestyle. We could also note that this includes the process of *technologization* or *reification* (Barton and Tusting 2005; Wenger 1998) by inference, at least, because the 'organic lifestyle' is constituted not by farming (or socialization) *practices* carried out *on* the person but by *actions* (eating, etc.) of the person in which organic objects (*materialization*) are used or consumed.

From this point of view it is not surprising that on the reverse side of the bag of rice is a rather extended text which is a discourse on how Lundberg grows their rice from rice seeds to rotation crops.

> We are pleased to offer you this high quality Organic Short Grain Brown Rice. Good food is basic to good health, and at Lundberg Family Farms we treat the food that we produce with great respect and care.
>
> Our organic rice begins with the finest seed. Special agricultural practices are employed which insure organic purity and a healthy growing environment. In the fall, the straw and stubble that remain from the previous organic crop's harvest are tilled into the ground instead of being burned. Purple vetch, a leguminous plant that delivers nitrogen and other vital nutrients to the soil, is used as a rotation crop and winter ground cover.
>
> On this soil the rice seed is planted. The seedlines are irrigated with clear Feather River water from the Sierra Nevada mountains. No chemical fertilizers, fungicides, herbicides, insecticides, or pesticides are used. We allow the rice plants to reach full maturity in the fields, which guarantees maximum flavor and nutrition. After harvest in the fall, the rice is stored in cooled bins and milled only to order.

Lundberg provides this extended *narrative* of their history and practices in support of their claim that the rice is organically grown. This *narrative* begins with a static *materialization* much in the way that on the other side of the bag we see *materialization* ('organic rice') in the upper or ideal section of the text/image: 'Our organic rice begins with the finest seed.' This is followed by a shift to *practices*: 'Special agricultural practices are employed.' This is followed by a *narrative* beginning with tilling in the fall, carried through planting and maturity to harvest and storage the following year. It is a full yearly cycle we are given here and in this we see *narrative* emerge as the key element in making the determination of whether or not a product can be labelled 'organic'.

Dictionary definitions and product advertising blurbs, however, are not the legal substance we need in order to see what this word might mean. The National Organic Standards Board (NOSB) was established by the Organic Foods Production Act of 1990 for the purpose of providing a legal definition of 'organic'.

The national organic standards board definition of 'organic'

The following definition of 'organic' was passed by the NOSB at its April 1995 meeting in Orlando, FL.

> Organic agriculture is an ecological production management system that promotes and enhances biodiversity, biological cycles and soil biological activity. It is based on minimal use of off-farm inputs and on management practices that restore, maintain and enhance ecological harmony.
>
> 'Organic' is a labeling term that denotes products produced under the authority of the Organic Foods Production Act. The principal guidelines for organic production are to use materials and practices that enhance the ecological balance of natural systems and that integrate the parts of the farming system into an ecological whole.
>
> Organic agriculture practices cannot ensure that products are completely free of residues; however, methods are used to minimize pollution from air, soil and water.
>
> Organic food handlers, processors and retailers adhere to standards that maintain the integrity of organic agricultural products. The primary goal of organic agriculture is to optimize the health and productivity of interdependent communities of soil life, plants, animals and people.
>
> (http://www.ota.com/organic/definition.html
> accessed 17 July 2004, 6:20 a.m. AKT)

The NOSB's definition is, not surprisingly, an operational definition: 'Organic' is what the law authorizes. For that the law has established the NOSB (*authorization*). The NOSB says, in effect, 'organic' is whatever they say it is and then proceeds to outline some basic principles. The first principle is based on agricultural *practices*: 'an ecological production management system'. Key to the word 'system' is that it is *not* simply a set of actions but must be perceived (by the NOSB) as *practices* which are regular, consistent and carried out in predictable ways over a period of time – a system.

The second paragraph enters into the issue of *certification*. When the *practices* are *authorized* by the NOSB, this *authorization* will allow the producer to label products (*certification*) as 'organic'. As we shall see below, what is of interest here for us as discourse analysts is how heavily discursive these principles are and how deeply they are based in practice. What we read here is that 'organic' is what people who do 'organic' things produce.

But this right to define through narrative of practice given over to this legal body is not uncontested. Not everyone feels sure that a legally constituted board whose goal is to review the practices of food producers is sufficient to give us confidence in the meaning of the word 'organic'. Pitchford (2002: 17) in his book *Healing with Whole Foods* comments:

> [In some cases] the term 'organic' is used to mask an unwholesome food. When consumers see the word 'organic' on a product, they often believe it is a top-quality whole food. Using the highly regarded 'O' word to lure consumers to buy inferior foods fools nearly everyone and is one of the slickest, most deceptive marketing ploys today.

We can note in this paragraph an example of *technologization* or *reification*. It is now the word 'organic' itself which has become the tool or mediational means by which other actions are carried out. The word is 'used to mask' or used 'to lure consumers'.

Perhaps the most outspoken and most thoroughly discursive in their characterization of what they will accept as organic practices are the producers of the Sanctuaerie website. Sanctuaerie, going beyond negatives, gives the following 'organic definition':

> We feel that the definition of organic that we garden by is important to put forth as 'organic' has become a much-used term with varied meanings. For us, organic is more than not using pesticides, herbicides, chemicals or 'green' substances (i.e. rotenone, diatomaceous earth). Our practice of organic includes:
> * feeding the soil at a rate equal or greater to what we take out of it;
> * using compost, green manure crops and green manure tea to feed plants and enrich soil;
> * using hand tools and non-disruptive or gently disruptive gardening techniques (we warn the earthworms to go deep when we are forking beds);
> * using collected rainwater for watering; using mulch to minimise watering, soil erosion and weeding; using raised beds to minimise soil compaction;
> * tithing 10–20% (often more – we don't have a fully fenced garden) of our garden produce to wildlife that shares the land;
> * using companion planting techniques;
> * saving much of our own seed;
> * communicating with nature so that our gardening co-exists with and is inclusive with all of nature, not solely for our own benefit.
>
> (http://www.sanctuaerie.ca/OrgDef.html
> accessed 17 July 2004, 6:25 a.m. AKT)

Here we see 'organic', again, as a lifestyle that is fully nominalized ('our practice of organic'). Further, organic practice becomes organic plain talk in speaking to the earthworms to 'go deep' when the Sanctuaerie gardeners are forking beds for planting and 'communicating with nature'.

The word 'organic' on my bag of rice encodes the transformation of quite an extended itinerary of actions and discursive descriptions of those actions into a certified, authorized label. The rice is organic because it is organically grown. It is organically grown because the producers have engaged in many years of practice which qualifies them to place this label on their product. Thus we can see that this itinerary of discourse and practice has extended over quite long timescales and is encapsulated in rather opaque linguistic form.

Resemiotization and discourse itineraries

A nexus analysis is just this kind of work of tracing pathways and trajectories of texts, actions, practices, and objects, of people and communications across time and space and multiple modes. Iedema (2003) uses the term 'resemiotization' for these processes of transformation across events, spaces, times, modes and media. Others such as Bernstein (1990), Latour (1996), Silverstein and Urban (1996), Wenger (1998), Lemke (2002), Thibault (2004), and Barton and Tusting (2005) have used a variety of terms (such as 'traversal', 'recontextualization', 'reification', 'entextualization' and 're-envoicement') to capture some aspect of this process. As we have seen in the case of organic rice, foods become organic objects through social and discursive processes of narration about the historical processes involved in growing and through social legitimation by others who are authorized to transmute these narratives of growing processes into the label 'organic'. It is not the rice that is organic; it is the Lundberg family, their entire constellation of agricultural practices, and the spaces and material objects of their farms. It is the Lundberg family's narrative about their organic history which makes their rice organic. The word 'organic' on the rice bag label is a resemiotization of this complex of discourses, people, events, actions, and objects, a discourse itinerary which has been ambling forward 'since 1937'.

Nine processes in the discourse cycle of buying organic rice

Out of this rather sketchy nexus analysis I can now extract nine processes which occur in the array of transformations or resemiotizations that constitute 'organic rice' as a food which I buy, cook, and eat. We can use the narrative on the bag of Lundberg rice to enter into this.

> In the 1930s, Albert and Frances Lundberg left western Nebraska with their four sons, Eldon, Wendell, Harlan and Homer. During the Dust Bowl years, Albert saw huge tracts of land across the midwest erode.

Nutrient-giving organic matter had disappeared from the soil, and fierce winds created enormous dust clouds that made life miserable and farming impossible. Albert decided to take his family to Richvale, and begin a life of farming in northern California.

The four Lundberg brothers, who now run Lundberg Family Farms, were deeply influenced by their late father, Albert. He believed in ecological farming long before it was fashionable. 'He didn't really fit in with the thinking of the time,' Harlan says. Influenced by his Dust Bowl experiences, Albert 'always had the attitude that he wanted to make the soil better.' He wanted to act as nature's caretaker from the ground to the living things residing there. Now, Albert's sons think and farm that way, too.

1   **action** – an individual or group of social actors acting momentaneously in real time. Albert Lundberg plants rice in a certain way in California in 1937.

2   **practice** – a regular, repeated action that is socially recognized as 'doing the same thing'. Eldon, Wendell, Harlan and Homer Lundberg continue to grow their rice in this same careful way for more than 60 years since 1937.

3   **narrative** – a descriptive and historical (i.e. retrospective) characterization of a sequence of actions or practices. This narrative accompanies each of the Lundberg packages, whether it is their organic brown rice or their rice cakes. In this case the narrative is used both as a marketing point to back up their claim to producing organic rice and in registering their claim to be authorized as an organic foods producer.

4   **authorization** – the institutional or social legitimization of a narrative of practice which anticipates predictable and unchanged continuation of practice. The NOSB has been set up by the US Government to receive, monitor and authorize such narrative claims. Other similar authorities by which Lundberg is authorized appear on the company website. It is important to note that rarely are direct inspections made; authorization is based on self-monitoring accounts or narratives of the producers.

5   **certification** – the right gained by authorization to identify through signs or texts one's practices and their outcomes as authorized. With authorization Lundberg Farms can legally print their claim to be an organic producer of food on their packages. This is the first point at which the consumer can enter into this discourse cycle. The certificate allows the buyer to assume that there has been authorization preceded by an acceptable narrative of practice, whether or not the consumer sees that narrative.

6   **metonymization** – the simplification of the action, practice, narrative, authorization, certification sequence through labelling. Out of these 60 or more years of farming practice, including ploughing fields, maintenance of buildings, packaging, marketing and the rest, just the rice is selected

as the metonymic representative. It is the rice that is called 'organic', not the tractor, not the storage silos, not the action of ploughing. The rice itself now stands in for objects, actions, practices and places called Lundberg Farms.

7   **remodalization** – shifting from a mode such as text to a mode such as graphic images. Organic rice is symbolized in the Lundberg brand colour scheme and a graphic looking like an official seal.

8   **materialization** – shifting the focus of attention from history and practice to the object which is the outcome. This shift leads to the idea that the test for 'organic' should be based on testing of the rice for pesticide or genetic modification. 'Organically grown rice' becomes 'organic rice'. The modifier is shifted from the process (growing) to the object (rice).

9   **technologization/reification** – the use of the labelled object as a mediational means in undertaking subsequent action. We buy the rice, we cook it, we eat it. For us it is entirely sufficient that the package says that it is 'organic'. This rice enables us to eat organic rice as an action but also as a practice. It further enables narratives of our practice such as this one. In some cases it has enabled a certain degree of authorization among other consumers of organic foods ('he's one of us').

There are surely many other processes of resemiotization such as have been taken up by Iedema (2003), where a discussion becomes a blueprint which, in turn, becomes a hospital wing and then a social-organization problem for hospital management. What I hope to have made clear in this chapter is that our actions, practices, texts and objects itinerate along over such sequences of transformation, now material, now discursive, now actional. MDA is one approach to understanding both the production of meanings in text and the meanings of actions in the world through the study of neither language alone nor action alone. Mediated discourse analysis seeks to keep the circumference of our analysis open to these lengthy itineraries transformations. Mediated discourse analysis uses the term 'nexus analysis' for such a study.

Bakhtin's very important insight that all texts speak in response to and in anticipation of subsequent texts, dialogicality, has given us the word 'intertextuality'. It has been a useful word, but here I suggest that this word may also obscure the multiple, transformative and interlinked processes of resemiotization that constitute the itineraries which discourses take.

References

Bakhtin, M.M. (1981 [1934–5]) *The Dialogic Imagination*, Austin, TX: University of Texas Press.

Barton, D. and Tusting, K. (2005) *Beyond Communities of Practice: language, power, and social context*, Cambridge: Cambridge University Press.

Becker, A.L. (1994) 'Repetition and otherness: an essay', in B. Johnstone (ed.) *Repetition in Discourse*, vol. 2. Norwood, NJ: Ablex Publishing Corporation, pp. 162–75.

Bernstein, B. (1990) *The Structure of Pedagogic Discourse: class, codes and control*, vol. 6, London: Routledge.

Blommaert, J. (2005) *Discourse: a critical introduction*, New York: Cambridge University Press.

Burke, K. (1969 [1945]) *A Grammar of Motives*, Englewood Cliffs, NJ: Prentice-Hall.

Iedema, R. (2003) 'Multimodality, resemiotisation: extending the analysis of discourse as multi-semiotic practice', *Visual Communication*, 2(1): 29–57.

Kress, G. and van Leeuwen, T. (1996) *Reading Images: the grammar of visual design*, London: Routledge.

Kress, G. and van Leeuwen, T. (2001) *Multimodality*, London: Edward Arnold.

Kristeva, J. (1986) 'Word, dialogue and novel', in T. Moi (ed.) *The Kristeva Reader*, Oxford: Basil Blackwell, pp. 34–61.

Latour, B. (1996) 'On interobjectivity', *Mind, Culture, and Activity*, 3(4): 228–45.

Lemke, J. (2002) 'Travels in hypermodality', *Visual Communication*, 1(3): 299–325.

Norris, S. (2004) *Analysing Multimodal Interaction*, London: Routledge.

Pitchford, P. (2002) *Healing with Whole Foods: Asian traditions and modern nutrition*, Berkeley, CA: North Atlantic Books.

Scollon, R. (2001) *Mediated Discourse: the nexus of practice*, London: Routledge.

—— (2005) 'The rhythmic integration of action and discourse: work, the body, and the earth', in S. Norris and R. Jones (eds) *Discourse and Action: introduction to mediated discourse analysis*, London: Routledge.

Scollon, R. and Scollon, S.W. (2003) *Discourses in Place: language in the material world*, London: Routledge.

—— (2004) *Nexus Analysis: discourse and the emerging internet*, London: Routledge.

Silverstein, M. and Urban, G. (1996) *Natural Histories of Discourse*, Chicago, IL: University of Chicago Press.

Thibault, P.J. (2004) *Agency and Consciousness in Discourse: self-other dynamics as a complex system*, London: Continuum.

Wenger, E. (1998) *Communities of Practice: learning, meaning and identity*, Cambridge: Cambridge University Press.

16 Good sex and bad karma

Discourse and the historical body

Rodney H. Jones

One of the chief concerns of mediated discourse analysis (MDA) is how, through mediated actions, discourse is submerged into the 'historical body' of the individual social actor as social practice, and how this discourse re-emerges from the 'historical body' through subsequent mediated actions. In their description of *nexus analysis*, the Scollons (2004) argue that all social actions take place at a *nexus* of:

1   the 'interaction order' (the social roles and relationships in a situation)
2   the 'discourses in place' (including both discourse in the surroundings like signs and public broadcast announcements and those introduced by participants as speech, writing or other forms of communication)
3   and the 'historical body' (the storehouse of discourse sedimented in the history and memory of the individual and manifested in 'habitual' practices: ways of speaking, of making bodily movements, and of generally living in the world).

The concept of the 'historical body' reminds us that we can only understand action as we see it within the histories of those who are doing it. It gives MDA a unique theoretical tool with which to explore how discourse is transformed into the practised thoughts, words and movements of the individual social actor, and how it is later re-transformed into discourse which reproduces those social practices and the historical bodies of those who engage in them. Studying the 'historical body' also, however, presents challenges, the first being to pin down what we mean by the 'historical body' as an object of analysis in the first place, and the second being to come up with a way to analyse it – a 'way in'.

As discourse analysts of course, our main 'way in' is usually through the discourse. MDA, with its focus on social actions goes about it the other way around, through first trying to understand what kinds of social actions social actors are taking, and then how discourse is being used to take them. Through analysing discourse *in action* (Jones and Norris 2005) we come to understand how and why particular social actions or practices are performed and how discourse comes to be used as a tool for reproducing social actors and social worlds. The primary aim of *nexus analysis*, say Scollon and Scollon (2003), is to study how discourse 'cycles' in what R. Scollon (this volume) calls 'itineraries' through the interaction order, the discourses in place and the historical body.

The aim of this chapter is to explore the relationship between discourse and the historical body and to suggest how, through attention to *retrospective* and *anticipatory* discourse (de Saint-Georges 2003, 2005; S. Scollon 2003), analysts can better understand not just how discourse is transformed into social practice within the historical body, but also how the historical body itself becomes a discursive tool in social interaction, how we 'write' our historical bodies onto situations through our mediated actions, and how people 'read' though our behaviour, our speech and our bodily movements the narratives of our past experiences, our present intentions and our future plans.

I will consider these issues with reference to the discourse of gay men around sex and sexual risk behaviour and the problems of 'unsafe sex' and HIV transmission, a topic I have been studying for a number of years (Jones 2000, 2005a, b; Jones and Candlin 2003; Jones *et al.* 2000). The traditional way health educators have viewed the relationship between discourse and action in HIV/AIDS prevention is based on the underlying assumption that discourse leads (or should lead) rather directly and unproblematically to some kind of desired behavioural outcome (see, for example, Fishbein and Middlestadt 1989, and Wellings 1994 for review). The dominant model of AIDS education in most settings is a refinement of what might be called the 'KAB' (knowledge, attitudes and behaviour model) – a model which posits a linear relationship between discourse and action. Discourse is seen as 'knowledge', and 'knowledge' is assumed to shape attitudes which then determine behaviour (Kippax *et al.* 1993). More recent research on HIV-related risk behaviour, particularly among gay men, however, has begun to question this 'one to one' relationship between discourse and action. Linked with this questioning has been a move away from models of behaviour focusing on individual knowledge and decision making and towards explanations which focus more on the social and cultural context in which risk behaviour takes place (Hurley 2003; Rofes 1998; Turner 1997; Wright 1998).

The concept of the historical body within the framework of mediated discourse analysis, I will argue, provides an alternative way of understanding the relationship between discourse and sexual risk behaviour. Rather than focusing on discourse as 'knowledge', MDA focuses on discourse as a means to take social action. This focus on action allows us to see 'knowledge', 'attitudes' and 'behaviour' not as separate entities in a linear relationship, but rather as integrated with and circulating within the historical body. It allows us to understand how, through mediated actions, individuals write their embodied histories onto social situations, and as they do so, compose new 'selves' to carry into subsequent social situations.

The historical body

The concept of the 'historical body' comes from the Japanese Zen philosopher Kitaro Nishida, but also owes a great deal to Bourdieu's (1977) notion of *habitus* as the repository of an individual's life experiences which manifest psychologically as habits, goals, mental dispositions and schemes of perception, and physically as bodily features, habitual ways of acting (including posture, gait, gestures) and various forms of physical dexterity.

In some ways, however, Bourdieu's vision of *habitus* as the 'system of durable and transposable dispositions', and 'structured propensities to think, feel, and act in determinate ways' (1977: 72) which result when 'society becomes deposited in persons' (Wacquant 2005: 316) jars with Nishida's notion of the 'historical body' as an expression of the instability and ineffability of the self and its relationship with the collective. The historical body is about becoming rather than being. It represents a movement, as Nishida (1959) says, 'from the formed to the forming'. It never really exists because it is always changing.

Perhaps closer to this 'Zen' view is S. Scollon's (2003) organic metaphor for 'the historical body', which sees it as 'a compost heap of social practices' (2003: 193). In this view, *habitus* is not just the storehouse of past social practices but also the ground for the ontogenesis of new social practices. 'What resides in the *habitus* is not hard fossil remains nor abstract rules,' she says, 'but humas and detritus, not buried treasure, but compost that prepares the ground for new growth' (2003: 186).

This approach in some ways better resonates with the Buddhist notion of *karma* which no doubt influenced Nishida. McLeod (n.d.), in fact, insists that, rather than the often used 'cause and effect' metaphor of modern physics, 'growth' is a much better metaphor to use to talk about *karma* – it is about how actions grow into experiences. The Buddha himself spoke of actions as seeds which grow or evolve into our experience of the world. Every action either starts a new growth process or reinforces an old one. Every action has the potential to reinforce or dismantle previous patterns of ripening.

R. Scollon (2001b) also uses an 'organic' metaphor in his description of how discourse is taken into the historical body and then re-emerges as discourse in the social world, much like water vapour forms clouds that lead to precipitation which enters into the soil and gathers in lakes and rivers, and later, through evaporation, is taken back into the atmosphere to form more clouds (see Figure 16.1).

The point the Scollons are trying to make with such metaphors is that the 'historical body' is an 'unstable, dissipative structure in interaction with its environment' (S. Scollon 2003) rather than an objective, regular, or 'durable' set of dispositions. This focus on the *dynamic* aspect of the historical body helps us to understand not just how it reproduces the social world (as does Bourdieu's *habitus*), but how it *transforms* it (S. Scollon 2003). Within the 'lived body' (Merleau-Ponty 1962) of the social actor, discourse ripens into

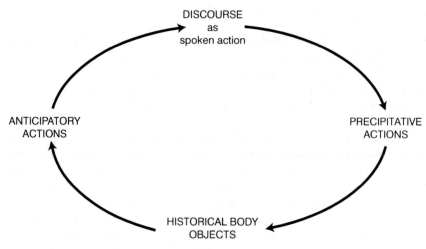

Fgure 16.1   Adapted from Scollon 2001b

social practices as it interacts with other discourses and practices, some commensurate and some incommensurate, already present in the embodied history of the individual, forming what S. Scollon (2003: 177) calls, 'a whole history of hidden dialogicality'.

The key to understating the historical body, I will argue along with the Scollons, lies in understanding its dynamic, dialogical nature, and in understanding the links and fissures produced as commensurate and incommensurate practices 'rub up against' one another.

The historical body and unsafe sex

The past ten years have seen a sharp increase in HIV infections among urban gay men, in North America, Europe and Australia, as well as in Asian cities like Hong Kong (Centers for Disease Control 2000; EuroHIV 2005; Hong Kong Department of Health 2005). The irony of this is that these men are more likely than most other people to be well informed about HIV and safe sex practices (Gold and Skinner 1992; Kippax *et al.* 1993).

Health researchers and other observers have put forth a number of theories for continued unsafe sex, especially among younger men, observing, for example, that young men have not witnessed the suffering of AIDS 'first hand' and so are not scared enough of it, or that new treatments make the consequences seem less severe. Others have noted how, in the context of a history of condom use, unsafe sex can be used to mark the transition to a more serious relationship, in other words, to symbolize 'love' and commitment (Rosenthal *et al.* 1998).

Still others blame the 'historical body', suggesting that there is something about the disposition of many gay men as it has developed over time which predisposes them to unsafe sex. Crossley (2004), for example, sees 'barebacking' (intentionally having unprotected intercourse) as a manifestation of a 'resistance' or 'transgressional' *habitus* that has come to be a consistent feature of gay identity since the early days of gay liberation (see also Pollak 1988).

Faced with such a problem, the theoretical questions I raised above become practical ones. How does a 'practice' like 'using a condom', which is transformed into a piece of discourse (like the phrase 'use a condom every time' in the context of HIV prevention discourse) become submerged into the historical body as a practice? How does it interact there with other discourses and social practices that are already circulating through the individual? And how does it finally re-emerge as discourse used to take subsequent mediated actions in specific circumstances?

The story below, told by a participant in a public forum on unsafe sex (Cotten *et al.* 1999), gives us a clue.

> So it was a weird thing, we're using a condom but we're talking about 'yeah, I'm going to come inside you and I'm gonna fuck you without a condom', that sort of thing. And it was just really hot and very compelling ... and we pull off the condom, and we're doing it.
>
> And you know I'm not high, I'm on no drugs. I am who I am. I know what's going on, and it's really hot, it's really compelling. He comes inside me, it's really brief, he pulls out. I get off and I'm nearly in tears now, it's all hitting me like 'How could I do this, what did I just do, oh my god. I just broke this intense barrier. I went on the other side.'

Stories like this force us to re-evaluate our understanding of the relationship between HIV prevention discourse and sexual behaviour. In this case, for example, the discourse of safe sex has emerged not as part of safe sex but as part of the context in which unsafe sex occurs. We might, with Crossley, chalk it up to a durable disposition in gay men to resist authoritative discourses, but this does not tell us how this disposition developed and why it emerged when it did. After all, the teller of this story is a man who in countless previous encounters (and indeed in the beginning of this encounter) had taken authoritative discourse on board and used a condom. For mediated discourse analysis, the answer lies in how, in the historical body of the storyteller, safe sex discourse interacts with multiple other discourses and practices, and how, when it emerges in an episode of sex, it gets linked to still other discourses and practices, linkages that are carried back into the historical body.

Two places where these linkages can be mapped are in what Scollon (2001b) calls in the chart reproduced above 'anticipatory' actions and 'precipitative' actions. 'Anticipatory' actions are those which anticipate future actions; in this case, actions like the storyteller buying a box of condoms, putting one or several into his bag or pocket or onto a bedside table, opening the package, putting the condom on in a practised way (itself perhaps the product of some earlier written text or oral instructions), all in anticipation of the act of safe sex. In this episode, however, there is another chain of anticipatory actions forming as well, those which lead first to the anticipatory discourse ('I'm gonna fuck you without a condom') and finally to the action of taking off the condom. The answer to how these two seemingly incommensurate chains of anticipatory actions can co-exist is that they cannot exist apart – they are inseparably entwined. The 'safe sex' discourse cannot exist without the possibility of (the *anticipation* of) 'unsafe' sex, and the 'unsafe' sex discourse cannot exist except against the background of 'safe' sex. Putting on the condom is the most important anticipatory action involved in taking it off.

'Precipitative' actions are those that follow from an action, in this case actions involving rationalization, self-rebuke, as well as the actions surrounding telling this story in the context of a public forum. 'Precipitative' actions are retrospective – they make discourse out of past actions in the form of things like accounts and subsequent actions and deposit them back into the historical body. In the 'retrospective' section of this passage, for example, the speaker transforms his action into a series of questions: 'How could I do this, what did I just do, oh my god?' Here again we can see two seemingly incommensurate retrospective discourses forming simultaneously, the 'it was very compelling' discourse, linked to a detailed narration of the sexual act, and the 'how could I do this?' discourse linked to an analysis of the thought process leading to the sexual act.

Further complicating things is the way the speaker himself constructs agency in the anticipatory and retrospective parts of the account, creating essentially two historical bodies: the 'we' body which produces the anticipatory discourse leading to unsafe sex ('we're talking about 'yeah, I'm going to come inside you ...') and performs the act of unsafe sex itself ('we pull off the condom, and we're doing it'), and the 'I' body, which evaluates the incident using the 'individualistic' discourse of 'safe' sex ('I went on the other side').

The historical body that performed this act of unsafe sex, therefore, can best be seen as a *nexus* of multiple trajectories of actions, each at different stages in their ontogenesis as social practices, and each associated with different notions of agency and identity linked to them.

The ontogenesis of safe sex

What I have been arguing here is that the historical body is formed at an intersection between what has happened in the past and what will happen in the future through *concrete actions* which anticipate future actions and bear the history of their relationship with past actions. It is created bit by bit through incremental anticipatory chains of actions that propel an individual towards the future and precipitative chains of actions that link the individual to the past. I further argued that attention to anticipatory and retrospective discourse can help us to discover the interdiscursive links between practices that are formed, reinforced or broken in the historical body's constant process of becoming. Finally, I suggested that through these actions and the discourses we take them with it we actually 'write' our historical bodies onto situations. We might 'write' our bodies in different ways onto different situations, sometimes, for example, as individual, autonomous selves, and sometimes as a part of a 'we' and 'us'. Historical bodies are multiple, because they are processes (chains of actions), not things.

One important part of understanding the impact of HIV prevention discourses, then, is understanding the complex linkages of social practices into which it is introduced. Where and how do these discourses enter into the historical body? What are the practices associated with them in the ontogenesis of their transformation into social practices? What 'histories of hidden dialogicality' are being written when phrases like 'always use a condom' are introduced into this dynamic system?

The following story was related by a 22-year-old man in Hong Kong in the context of a diary study I did of gay men's sexual experiences (Jones and Candlin 2003).

> When I was studying at F3 or 4. I read a magazine article which mentioned about a homosexual got arrested because of his indecent behaviour in the public toilet in Jordan. The article also reported on all the public toilets in Hong Kong which were very popular among gay people. After reading the article I could hardly wait and decided to go to the toilet in Shamshipo on Saturday in the same week. I arrived there at 6pm, it took me quite a while to get there because I was unfamiliar with that area. I felt scared and excited. Scared because there might be bad guys, triad people, cops and I was only a 14–15 young man, you couldn't tell what others might think. Excited because of the unknown situation: I could meet a late teenager or someone at his early 20s, someone athletic with a sexy body, big dick … things which could be very exciting. My heart was bouncing heavily when I came close to the toilet. My dick was solid hard when I got there. I saw some men at the cubicles, some were at the urinal. I walked to the washing basin and started washing my hands and looked at the mirror as the article described about how gay men cruise in the toilet. I saw a man in his 20s, he looked at me in the mirror and signaled us to leave together. I followed him. I was very nervous and also because it was my first time, I didn't really choose. When we were outside, this gay started to me questions about my name, age and my work … I said to myself that he really had lots to say. We walked into a small park where there was a toilet. He went in first to check if there were other people around. He then took us in a cubicle and started to undress me and kissed me. He even used his mouth … I was very excited then that I ejaculated in his mouth. He then cleaned me with Kleenex. I jerked him off after I had come. Before we parted, he talked to me sincerely for a while: 'The gay circle is very complicated and you need

to be careful. Police may come in at any time; play safe and don't get an STD ...' He gave me his telephone number then left. On my way home, I was still recalling what had just happened. I asked myself if he would get AIDS because he had sucked my dick. But I didn't think he would. I kept wishing that I would have more similar experiences in the future. I want the thrill, the excitement. Since then, whenever I have time, I would look and cruise around.

As in the above account, this story portrays the sexual act as part of a series of anticipatory actions that lead up to it and retrospective actions that lead back to it. The primary piece of discourse with which anticipatory actions are taken is not a safe sex pamphlet, but a newspaper article about the arrest of a gay man in a public toilet, and this article provides an overall outline for the narrator's subsequent actions, an 'outline of social practice' to which he refers as the episode unfolds ('(I) looked at the mirror as the article described about how gay men cruise in the toilet'). The important thing to note, of course, is that the purpose of this piece of discourse was clearly not to provide cruising instructions to underage boys, but to perform other actions such as alerting the public to a 'social problem', or asserting the dominant moral standards of the society, or selling newspapers. It should also be noted that the end result of the anticipatory actions described in the article was not pleasure, but arrest. Within the historical body of the social actor, however, with its own narratives of desire, this piece of discourse is resemiotized into a fantasy narrative ('I could meet a late teenager or someone at his early 20s, someone athletic with a sexy body, big dick ... things which could be very exciting.') which the actor also carries into the action as another 'outline of practice'.

Knowledge of how to do something (provided by the journalistic discourse) and a favourable attitude towards doing it (evidenced in the fantasies) is not enough, however, to produce behaviour. The way knowledge and attitudes become behaviour is dependent upon a myriad of other practised behaviours, in the case of this story, practices of riding on buses, practices of using public washrooms, practices of following, all practices which have a long history in the life of the social actor. While the unfolding of this chain of actions is in part driven by the 'master narratives' described above, it is also driven by the momentum of multiple 'mundane' social practices that are sedimented within the historical body of the social actor. Such practices themselves consist of chains of actions which, because they are so 'practised', form what R. Scollon (2001) has referred to as a 'funnel of commitment', a chain in which each action makes it more difficult for the actor to avoid the subsequent actions in the chain. 'Riding the bus to the toilet in Shamshuipo' is an example. Each action in this practice, going to the bus stop, waiting for the bus, getting on the bus, paying the fare, etc., all further commit the actor to arriving at his destination and make it more difficult for him to reverse this procedure. 'Following' is another example of such a practice, one which has its ontogenesis in early childhood. Each step we take when following someone commits us to continue following. The point I'm trying to make here is that what 'drives' unsafe sex (or safe sex for that matter) is not just what we know and what we think and what we do about sex, but also the force of all the other sedimented social practices that surround the sexual act.

It must be remembered that the anticipatory actions portrayed in this account are portrayed within the framework of retrospective discourse – the telling of a story. The ways actions are portrayed serve multiple functions in such a context such as portraying oneself in a certain light as a research subject and creating suspense for the reader. As I argued above, retrospective discourse helps to reveal the links among different social practices in the historical body of the speaker. It reveals how participants make sense of their social practice as embedded in a network of other discourses and social practices and it also constitutes the tools with which participants will interpret and conduct future social actions. As I also argued above, in such discourse people write different versions of the historical body onto past situations, and the way they do this can help to show how previous actions and the discourses used to take them are sedimented within the historical body.

Just as in the first example I gave above, in this excerpt the locus of agency in the chain of anticipatory actions (beginning with the initial encounter in the toilet and ending with the sexual act) is not the narrator. Instead these actions are taken by the other ('He went in first to check if there were other people around. He then took us in a cubicle and started to undress me and kissed me. He even used his mouth') or in cooperation with him ('We walked into a small park where there was a toilet'). And, just as in the above example, the individualistic voice of the 'I' ('I asked myself if he would get AIDS') returns in the retrospective part of the account.

The safe sex discourse in this account is not portrayed as being used to take anticipatory actions, but rather to take precipitative actions after the fact, with the narrator's partner advising him to 'play safe and don't get an STD'. Thus the function of the discourse is not the prevention of the unsafe sex that has already occurred. Instead it functions in other practices like the exchange of phone numbers and the construction community identities of novice and expert.

This is probably not the first time such phrases and the practices they represent had entered the consciousness of the storyteller. Here the phrase is combined with previous knowledge about what 'playing safe' means and why one should do so to construct a retrospective form of discourse, a risk assessment. Interestingly, just as the portrayal of anticipatory actions focuses on the agency of the other, so the retrospective assessment focuses on the risk of the other ('I asked myself if he would get AIDS because he had sucked my dick'). There is no anticipatory discourse regarding future 'safe' practices of the storyteller, but, on the contrary, a resolution to seek our 'similar experiences' by performing practices ('cruising around') which have been transformed from discourse into practice through the actions in this episode.

The emerging social practices around gay sex portrayed in this story remind us that such practices are always linked in their ontogenesis to other social practices circulating through the historical body. The circumstances in which a piece of safe sex discourse is introduced within a chain of actions are as important as the 'message' in that piece of discourse, for these circumstances serve to link it with other social practices within the historical body.

Conclusion

With the examples above I have argued that the historical body is not a durable structure, but rather, as Mead (1934: 26) suggests in the quote Sigrid Norris uses at the beginning of her chapter in this volume, 'an eddy in the social current', a dynamic flow of actions, And, if it is actions that make up the historical body, it is to actions that we should look to study it. I have also suggested that in order to understand the continuity of the historical body as it develops over time one ought to focus on anticipatory actions, actions which make subsequent actions possible, and precipitative actions, actions that arise from other actions and point back to them. It is in these actions that links are established among multiple social practices in the embodied experience of the social actor.

I also have shown how understanding the historical body as action leads naturally into an exploration of agency, the degree of control we perceive ourselves to have over the actions we take. Agency lies at the crux of understanding unsafe sex and how historical bodies are more or less empowered to practise it. In previous debates on *habitus, agency* has been seen as caught between the influence of society and the individual will. MDA's approach to the historical body sees agency as a matter of multiple chains of social action, each with its own 'momentum'. Thus, typically, as these chains of actions converge, actors engage multiple agentive positions at once.

What these observations mean for AIDS prevention is adopting a strategy which, in the words of Connell and his colleagues (Connell *et al.*, 1988: 3, cited in Bartos and Middleton, 1995: 10) 'operates at the intersection between the physical actions through which the virus is transmitted, and the meanings through which the action is apprehended and experienced and through which it can, therefore, be re-shaped'. Such an approach would see learning not as a matter of what goes on in people's heads, but as a matter of fully embodied experiences embedded in concrete situations within a material, social and cultural world (Gee 1996; Lave and Wenger 1991; Rogoff 1990). With the insights of such a perspective, anticipatory and retrospective discourses themselves can be used as tools by counsellors to encourage clients to reflect upon the interconnectedness of their actions and their own shifting sense of agency and self-efficacy (see, for example, Gold and Rosenthal 1998).

What this means for discourse analysis is a greater need for the kind of interdisciplinarity advocated in this volume. In order to understand the historical body in the way I have described, contributions will be necessary from conversation analysis, which can help us better develop our understanding of the sequential chains of actions along which the historical body evolves, and from multimodal discourse analysis, which can broaden the focus of action and discourse to include things like bodily movements, gait, and posture as well as explore the influence of other modes such as architectural layout. It will also benefit from insights from critical discourse analysis, which can help us understand how broader discourses interact with situated actions, and ethnographic approaches to discourse analysis, which can teach us how to design the kinds of in-depth, longitudinal studies of discourse in use though which we can examine the historical body as it develops over time.

References

Bartos, M. and Middleton, H. (1995) 'Gay men's risk reduction in context', *AIDS and Society 1995. Social Science: from theory to practice*, Sydney: National Centre in HIV Social Research, Macquarie University.

Bourdieu, P. (1977) *Outline of a Theory of Practice*, Cambridge: Cambridge University Press.

Centers for Disease Control and Prevention (2000) 'Need for sustained HIV prevention among men who have sex with men'. Online. Available HTTP: http://www.cdc.gov/hiv/pubs/facts/msm.htm (accessed 12 December 2006).

Cotten, P., Lustre, N., Schimel, S., Thomas, R. and Wagner, K. (1999) 'Speaking out about sex in silent spaces', transcription of a public forum entitled *The Rubberless Fuck*, which took place at UC Berkeley on 8 May 1999. Online. Available HTTP: http://hivinsite.ucsf.edu/InSite?page=pr-rr-09 (accessed 12 December 2006).

Crossley, M.L. (2004) 'Making sense of "barebacking": gay men's narratives, unsafe sex and "resistance habitus"', *British Journal of Social Psychology*, 43(2): 225–44.

de Saint-Georges, I. (2003) 'Anticipatory discourse: producing futures of action in a vocational program for long-term unemployed', PhD thesis, Washington, DC: Georgetown University.

—— (2005) 'From anticipation to performance: sites of engagement as process', in S. Norris and R. Jones (eds) *Discourse in Action*, London: Routledge, pp. 155–65.

European Centre for the Epidemiological Monitoring of AIDS (EuroHIV) (2005) *HIV/AIDS Surveillance in Europe: End of year report 2004*, Saint Maurice: Institute de Veille Sanitaire No. 71.

Fishbein, M. and Middlestadt, S.E. (1989) 'Using the theory of reasoned action as a framework for understanding and changing AIDS-related behaviours', in V.M Mays, G.W. Albee and S.F. Schneider (eds) *Primary Prevention of AIDS*, Beverley Hills, CA: Sage.

Gee, J.P. (1996) *Social Linguistics and Literacies*, 2nd edn, London: Taylor & Francis.

Gold, R. and Rosenthal, D.A. (1998) 'Examining self-justifications for unsafe sex as a technique of AIDS education: the importance of personal relevance', *Journal of STD AIDS*, 9(4): 208–13.

Gold, R. and Skinner, M. (1992) 'Situational factors and thought processes associated with unprotected intercourse in young gay men', *AIDS*, 6: 1021–30.

Hong Kong Department of Health (2005) 'Factsheet: HIV Situation in Hong Kong', Hong Kong: Government Information Office.

Hurley, M. (2003) 'Then and now: gay men and HIV', Australian Research Centre in Sex, Health and Society Monograph No. 46, Melbourne: La Trobe University.

Jones, R. (2000) 'Factors contributing to unsafe sex among men who have sex with men in Hong Kong', paper presented at the 2nd AIDS Prevention and Control NGO Working Meeting/4th Hong Kong–China AIDS Joint Planning Meeting, Zhuhai, PRC, 26–30 March.

—— (2005a) '"You show me yours, I'll show you mine": the negotiation of shifts from textual to visual modes in computer mediated interaction among gay men', *Visual Communication*, 4(1): 69–92.

—— (2005b) 'Sexual risk and the Internet', paper presented at the Language and Global Communication Conference, 7–9 July 2005, Cardiff, Wales.

Jones, R. and Candlin, C.N. (2003) 'Constructing risk along timescales and trajectories: gay men's stories of sexual encounters', *Health, Risk and Society*, 5(2): 199–213.

Jones, R. and Norris, S. (2005) 'Discourse as action/discourse in action', in S. Norris and R. Jones (eds) *Discourse in Action: introducing mediated discourse analysis*, London: Routledge, pp. 141–54.

Jones, R., Yu, K.K. and Candlin, C.N. (2000) 'A preliminary study of risk behaviour and HIV Vulnerability of MSM in Hong Kong', report to the Council for the AIDS Trust Fund, Hong Kong: Council for the AIDS Trust Fund, HK Department of Health. Online. Available HTTP: <http://personal.cityu.edu.hk/~enrodney/Research/MSM/MSMindex.html> (accessed 12 December 2006).

Kippax, S., Crawford, J., Davis, M., Rodden, P. and Dowsett, G. (1993) 'Sustaining safer sex: a longitudinal study of homosexual men', *AIDS*, 7: 257–63.

Lave, J. and Wenger, E. (1991) *Situated Learning: legitimate peripheral participation*, Cambridge: Cambridge University Press.

McLeod, K. (n.d.) 'Karma and growth'. Online. Available HTTP: <http://www.unfetteredmind.com/articles/growth.php> (accessed 12 December 2006).

Mead, G.H. (1934) *Mind, Self and Society from the Standpoint of a Social Behaviourist* ed. C.W. Morris, Chicago, IL: University of Chicago Press.

Merleau-Ponty, M. (1962) *Phenomenology of Perception*, trans. C. Smith, New York: Humanities Press.

Nishida, K. (1959) *Intelligibility and the Philosophy of Nothingness*, Tokyo: Maruzen Co. Ltd.

Pollak, M. (1988) *Les homosexuels et le sida: sociologie d'une epidemie* (*Gay Men and AIDS: Sociology of an Epidemic*), Paris: Metailie.

Rofes, E. (1998) 'Context is everything: thoughts on effective HIV prevention and gay men in the United States', in M.T. Wright, B.R.S. Rosser and O. de Zwart (eds) *New International Directions in HIV Prevention for Gay and Bisexual Men*, London: Harrington Park Press, pp. 133–142.

Rogoff, B. (1990) *Apprenticeship in Thinking: cognitive development in social context*, Cambridge: Cambridge University Press.

Rosenthal, D., Gifford, S. and Moore, S. (1998) 'Safe sex or safe love: competing discourses?', *AIDS Care*, 10: 35–47.

Scollon, R. (2001) 'Action and text toward an integrated understanding of the place of text in social (inter)action', in R. Wodak and M. Meyer (eds) *Methods of Critical Discourse Analysis*, London: Sage, pp. 139–82.

Scollon, R. and Scollon, S.W. (2004) *Nexus Analysis: discourse and the emerging internet*, London: Routledge.

Scollon, S.W. (2003) 'Political and somatic alignment: habitus, ideology and social practice', in G. Weiss and R. Wodak (eds) *Critical Discourse Analysis: theory and interdisciplinarity*, New York: Palgrave, pp. 167–98.

Turner, D.C. (1997) *Risky Sex: gay men and AIDS prevention*, New York: Columbia University Press.

Wacquant, L. (2005) 'Habitus', in J. Beckert and M. Zafirofski (eds) *International Encyclopedia of Economic Sociology*, London: Routledge, pp. 315–19.

Wellings, K. (1994) 'Assessing AIDS preventive strategies in Europe: lessons for evaluative research', in M. Boultin (ed.) *Challenge and Innovation: methodological advances in social research on HIV/AIDS*, London: Taylor & Francis, pp. 199–216.

Wright, M.T. (1998) 'Beyond risk factors: trends in European safer sex research', in M.T. Wright, B.R.S. Rosser and O. de Zwart (eds) *New International Directions in HIV Prevention for Gay and Bisexual Men*, London: Harrington Park Press, pp. 7–18.

Suggestions for further work

1 In his chapter, Scollon traces the 'itineraries' associated with a rather 'mundane' piece of discourse, the word 'organic' on a bag of rice, showing how it is linked both to the histories and habits of those who buy and consume the rice and the practices and policies of those who produce it and the government bodies that regulate its production. Choose an everyday piece of discourse such as a product label, an advertisement, a memo or an email and, using Scollon's theoretical framework for resemiotization, trace how the text is linked to multiple social actions, practices and material objects and people, and consider how understanding these linkages can help us to better understand the discourse.

2 One of the central problems of mediated discourse analysis is dealing with what Blommaert (2005) calls the 'layered simultaneity' of human action – the fact that actions are always performed on different levels and in different timescales and that the way we interpret them depends upon which of these levels and timescales we choose to focus on. Consider how our understanding of a particular action and the discourse associated with it might change as we widen or narrow the circumference through which this action is viewed.

3 Collect a series of accounts by various people surrounding a particular social practice and, using the theoretical framework introduced by Jones, examine how the retrospective and anticipatory discourse in the accounts reveals something about the relationship among discourse, action and the 'historical body' of the individual.

4 One of the central concerns of mediated discourse analysis is the issue of agency. Rather than a simple matter of individual 'will' or societal 'conditioning', Jones argues that agency is typically distributed among the multiple chains of social actions that converge in a given moment of time. Consider the different chains of actions that go into a particular event and the various agentive positions social actors might take in these chains.

Index

Lightning Source UK Ltd.
Milton Keynes UK
UKOW05f1835040315

247289UK00003B/191/P